Can't Touch This

Digital Approaches to Materiality in Cultural Heritage

Edited by
Chiara Palladino and Gabriel Bodard

]u[

ubiquity press
London

Published by
Ubiquity Press Ltd.
Unit 3N, 6 Osborn Street
London E1 6TD
www.ubiquitypress.com

First published 2023

This book had a minor update soon after publication, adding funding information to the author biography of Rebecca Kahn. No other content was changed. [Date of revision: March 2024].

Cover design by Tom Grady
Cover image: Piranesi, F. (illustrator and etcher). Niche dans le temple d'Isis, à Pompeia. In: Piranesi F., *Antiquités de la Grande Grèce aujourdhui Royaume de Naples...*, Piranesi frères, 1804–1807, vol. III, Tav. I. Public domain. Source: Wikiart.

Print and digital versions typeset by Siliconchips Services Ltd.

ISBN (Paperback): 978-1-914481-32-1
ISBN (PDF): 978-1-914481-33-8
ISBN (EPUB): 978-1-914481-34-5
ISBN (Mobi): 978-1-914481-35-2

DOI: https://doi.org/10.5334/bcv

The full text of this book has been peer-reviewed to ensure high academic standards. For full review policies, see https://www.ubiquitypress.com/

Suggested citation:
Palladino, C. and Bodard, G. (Eds.). 2023. *Can't Touch This: Digital Approaches to Materiality in Cultural Heritage*. London: Ubiquity Press. DOI: https://doi.org/10.5334/bcv. License: CC BY 4.0

To read the free, open access version of this book online, visit https://doi.org/10.5334/bcv or scan this QR code with your mobile device:

This volume is dedicated to Joyce M. Reynolds (1918–2022), who, while insisting she did not like computers herself, emphatically understood—and contributed to—the value of rigorous documentation, consistent vocabulary, quantitative recording and most importantly accessibility to colleagues worldwide enabled by digital study and publication of heritage objects.

Contents

Acknowledgements

The editors would like to acknowledge funding that supported this volume from the Furman Humanities Center, the Research and Professional Growth Fund at Furman, and the University of London Research Services Open Access Fund.

We are also grateful to Kira Hopkins, Tim Wakeford and all at Ubiquity Press for making the technical process of publishing a multi-author, open-access volume not only painless but a pleasure.

We owe many people an immeasurable debt for feedback, advice or help on the volume as a whole or individual chapters: not least all of the authors who commented on other parts, gave feedback to colleagues, and identified many links between the chapters. We also thank Paula Curtis, Nadia Kanagawa, Yukiko Kawamoto, Thomas Kollatz, Colleen Morgan, Ruth Mostern, Patricia Murrieta-Flores, Jun Ogawa, Chiara Piccoli, Annette Schmiedchen, Rada Varga, Andrea Wallace, Sean Winslow, and the anonymous reviewers of other chapters and the collection as a whole, all of whom contributed to the quality and coherence of the volume.

Contributors

Ceri Ashley
British Museum & Nottingham Trent University

Ceri Ashley has been Head of the Endangered Material Knowledge Programme at the British Museum since it was launched in 2018 (www.emkp.org). Since 2021 she has held a part time position as Professor of Cultural Heritage at Nottingham Trent University. Ceri's background is in archaeology, particularly in eastern and southern Africa, with a long term focus on material culture. She was previously an Associate Professor of Archaeology at the University of Pretoria, South Africa, and has held postdoctoral positions at UCL and UCLA, and led research in Kenya, Uganda, Botswana and South Africa. ORCID: https://orcid.org/0000-0002-1243-3183.

Hajime Baba
Nara National Research Institute for Cultural Properties

Baba Hajime (Doctor of Letters in the field of Japanese History). Born in 1972, Tokyo. Graduated from Faculty of Letters, University of Tokyo in 1995, completed the doctoral program at the University of Tokyo in 2000. He joined the Nara National Research Institute for Cultural Properties in 2000, where he currently resides as Director of the History Section, department of Imperial Palace Sites Investigations. His specialization is in ancient Japanese history and the study of *Mokkan*. He also conducts excavation surveys and comparative research with other inscribed artifacts around the world. Moreover, he has led the digitization of Japanese *Mokkan* with database and Linked Data technologies, establishing a collaboration with the Historiographical Institute of the University of Tokyo, the National Institute of Japanese Literature, the National Institute for Japanese Language and Linguistics, the Institute for Research in the Humanities, the Institute of History and Philology at Kyoto University, and the Academia Sinica.

Francesco Bianchini
University of Cambridge

Francesco Bianchini is a Research Fellow in Silk Roads history at King's College Cambridge. He holds a DPhil from Oxford and has published on Buddhist and Hindu classical texts, as well as epigraphic documents from South and Southeast Asia. Apart from the history of religions, he is also interested in the cultural history of danger, communal safety and wellbeing, which he studies with a transdisciplinary approach. ORCID: https://orcid.org/0000-0002-6482-977X.

Christopher W. Blackwell
Furman University

Christopher Blackwell earned a B.A. in Classics, summa cum laude, from Marlboro College in Vermont, and a Ph.D. in Classics from Duke University. He has written books on ancient Greek history, classical Athenian democracy, and Alexander the Great. With his collaborator Neel Smith he is the developer of the CITE Architecture and Canonical Text Services, technologies for building scholarly digital libraries. With Neel Smith he is Project Architect of the Homer Multitext, a project of the Center for Hellenic Studies of Harvard University. ORCID: https://orcid.org/0000-0003-2933-3493.

Gabriel Bodard
University of London

Gabriel Bodard is the Reader in Digital Classics at the Digital Humanities Research Hub and the Institute of Classical Studies, School of Advanced Study, University of London. He teaches MA-level courses on digital epigraphy, digital classical philology, and digital approaches to cultural heritage, a summer schools and workshops on 3D imaging and modelling in cultural heritage, EpiDoc, and digital editing with TEI XML, and co-directs the international, highly collaborative Sunoikisis Digital Classics programme of online teaching materials. His current research includes the areas of applying digital standards to ancient epigraphic and papyrological texts and objects, Linked Open Data for geographic and prosopographical data, ethical responsibilities in 3D approaches to cultural heritage, the classical heritage of North Africa, and pedagogy and public engagement with digital methodologies and heritage objects and cultures. ORCID: https://orcid.org/0000-0002-8566-6666.

Daria Elagina
University of Hamburg

Daria Elagina received her PhD in Ethiopian Studies in 2019 at the University of Hamburg, Germany. Her research interests with the main focus on the region of Ethiopia and Eritrea include textual criticism, manuscript studies, and sigillography. Since 2018, Elagina has been applying various digital research methods in her studies. She is currently PI of the project 'The Chronicle of John of Nikiu: Text-Critical Edition and Digital Research Platform' funded by the German Research Foundation (DFG Project number 470097824) and a member of the Faculty of Humanities at the University of Hamburg. ORCID: https://orcid.org/0000-0001-9892-6837.

Martina Filosa
University of Cologne

Martina Filosa is a postgraduate fellow in the framework of the project DiBS—"Creating a Sustainable Digital Infrastructure for Research-Based Teaching in Byzantine Studies" funded by the Volkswagen Foundation and PhD candidate in Byzantine Studies at the University of Cologne, where she specializes in Byzantine Sigillography. Her research focuses on the administration of charitable foundations, such as orphanages, hospitals, and homes for the elderly, in the middle-Byzantine period as reflected by lead seals. Her main research interests include Byzantine prosopography, catena-type commentaries to the Psalter, as well as the application of the methodologies offered by the Digital Humanities to Byzantine Sigillography, Epigraphy, and Greek Palaeography, with a focus on data modeling and text encoding. ORCID: https://orcid.org/0000-0003-1900-4231.

Usama Gad
Ain Shams University

Dr. Usama Gad is a tenure-track assistant professor of papyrology and Greco-Roman studies at Ain Shams University, Cairo, Egypt. His PhD titled *Edition of Greek Documentary Papyrus Texts from the Egyptian Museum in Cairo*, was completed at the University of Heidelberg, Germany in 2016. He is the co-founder of *Everyday Orientalism* (https://everydayorientalism.wordpress.com/), a platform that reflects on how history and power shape the way in which human societies define themselves through the "Other," and the founder of *Classics in Arabic: Greco-Roman Legacy in Egypt* (http://classicsinarabic

.blogspot.com/), a blog that aggregates publications and activities related to Arabic scholarship in the field of Greco-Roman studies. His current research interests include the reception of classical studies and ancient history in post-colonial Egypt. ORCID: https://orcid.org/0000-0003-4370-4588.

Paula Loreto Granados García
British Museum

Dr. Paula Granados García is the Digital Curator of the Endangered Material Knowledge Programme (EMKP) at the British Museum, where she leads the digital vision of the programme, including repository management, metadata research and safeguarding and all aspects of digital asset ingest and publication. Paula's work focuses on the representation and dissemination of indigenous and traditional cultural heritage via digital technologies, looking at issues of access, sustainability, data ownership and digital ethics. Her doctoral research focused on the possibilities that the Semantic Web and Linked Open Data technologies bring to the representation and mediation of knowledge, especially from the point of view of digital cultural heritage and museum databases. Paula is Digital Repository Advisor for the Imagining Futures through un/Archived Pasts Project at the University of Exeter and is a member of the board for the InDIGenius (Indigenous Languages + Technology) sharing initiative. ORCID: https://orcid.org/0000-0001-8029-7286.

Rebecca Kahn
University of Vienna

Rebecca Kahn is a post-doctoral researcher in Digital Humanities at the University of Vienna, funded through the European Union's Horizon 2020 Marie Sklodowska-Curie/REWIRE programme (Grant Agreement No 847639). Her work focuses on museum digitisation and how cultural heritage institutions leverage linked data models for managing their collections data. ORCID: https://orcid.org/0000-0002-8837-5813.

Rita Lucarelli
University of California, Berkeley

Rita Lucarelli is an Associate Professor of Egyptology at UC Berkeley and Faculty Curator of Egyptology at the Phoebe A. Hearst Museum of Anthropology of the University of California, Berkeley. She is presently working on a project aiming at realizing 3D models of ancient Egyptian coffins (http://3dcoffins.berkeley.edu/), and she is completing a monograph on demonology in ancient Egypt. Her specialty is the study of the ancient Egyptian religion and its reception in modern and contemporary times. She is also an instructor for courses on ancient Egyptian and comparative religion at the Mount Tamalpais

College program of higher education at San Quentin State Prison. ORCID: https://orcid.org/0000-0003-3117-7688.

Jerome A. Offner
Houston Museum of Natural Science

Jerome A. Offner works with the Houston Museum of Natural Science as Associate Curator for Northern Mesoamerica. Since 1975, he has investigated the materiality and cultural content of the celebrated non-alphabetic graphic manuscripts ("codices") of the Aztec second city, Texcoco, to the east and across the now dry lakebed from the former Aztec capital, Tenochtitlan, now Mexico City. He also works with the community of Cuaxicala in Puebla state, Mexico which has held its own graphic manuscript, recently recognized by UNESCO Mexico as a Memoria del Mundo, for more than four-and one-half centuries. He is developing accessible, on the ground methods of digital collaboration with Indigenous people in the Sierra de Puebla. He is also working towards a replicable online collaborative presentation and annotation module for any Aztec graphic manuscript. ORCID: https://orcid.org/0000-0001-6929-9002.

Chijioke Okorie
University of Pretoria

Dr. Chijioke Okorie is a Lecturer in the Department of Private Law at the University of Pretoria, South Africa, where she leads the Data Science Law Lab, a research group that deploys research in law and produces evidence and policy advice to support the growth of all aspects of data science research and application across Africa. A Nigerian-qualified barrister (since 2006), Chijioke is also the Lead Advisor at Penguide Advisory, a firm that provides research, educational, legal and regulatory advisory services in various fields including intellectual property (IP) and technologies. Chijioke is 'Africa Correspondent' at IP law blog, *The IPKat*, an Associate Editor of *South African Intellectual Property Law Journal* and the author of several articles on IP issues in Africa. Her monograph, *Multi-sided Music Platforms and the Law: Copyright, Law and Policy in Africa* was published by Routledge in 2020. More information about Chijioke can be found at chijiokeo.com. ORCID: https://orcid.org/0000-0002-1794-4396.

Chiara Palladino
Furman University

Chiara Palladino is Assistant Professor of Classics at Furman University. She has a background in Classical Philology and Digital Classics and has worked in several institutions, including the University of Bonn, University of Cologne, the Alexander von Humboldt Chair of Digital Humanities at the University of Leipzig, UNESP Brazil, and Tufts University. Her research focuses on the digital modeling of spatial information in premodern documents and the development of NLP pipelines for the study of ancient languages. She is involved in several DH projects, including the Open Greek and Latin Project, the Pelagios Network, the Digital Tolkien project (https://digitaltolkien.com/), and the Ugarit Translation Alignment Editor (https://ugarit.ialigner.com/). ORCID: https://orcid.org/0000-0002-1811-5602.

Rainer Simon
Rainersimon.io

Rainer Simon is a senior research software engineer and freelance IT consultant. He specializes in the development of tools that help people explore, analyze and manage data more easily, and has been working in the field of information management, knowledge engineering and user interface design for more than 20 years. He has a passion for the Digital Humanities and Digital Library fields, and has been collaborating with major GLAM (Galleries, Libraries, Archives, Museums) and academic partners worldwide. In many of his projects, he has dealt with spatial or cartographic data, and has published extensively on technological issues of digital representation, data modeling and systems design in this domain. In the past, he served as the Technical Director of Pelagios, an international Digital Humanities linked open geo-data initiative. He is also the lead developer of the award-winning Recogito and Peripleo open source tools for geospatial annotation and visualization. ORCID: https://orcid.org/0000-0002-4116-9684.

Valeria Vitale
University of Sheffield

Valeria Vitale is a Lecturer in Digital Humanities at the Digital Humanities Institute (University of Sheffield). She specialises in the representation and reception of historical places. Prior to joining the DHI, she was based at The Alan Turing Institute, working on the use of computer vision and semantic technologies for the enrichment of large digitised map collections for the *Machines Reading Maps* project. From 2020 to 2021 she worked as Research Curator at the British Library, researching ways to improve place-based cross-collection connections for the *Locating a National Collection* project. From 2017 to 2020 she was based at the Institute of Classical Studies in London (School of Advanced Study) where she taught Digital Approaches to Cultural Heritage. While at the ICS, Valeria was Director of Education and co-Investigator for the *Pelagios* project, exploring research and teaching applications of Linked Open GeoData tools and methods. ORCID: https://orcid.org/0000-0002-9695-0240.

Hayley Woodward
Purdue University

Dr. Hayley Woodward is Assistant Professor of Art History at Auburn University. Her research centers on Pre-Columbian and colonial visual communication, placemaking, history-writing, and artistic practices, specifically in sixteenth century Central Mexico. She completed her Ph.D. in Art History and Latin American Studies at Tulane University, and her research has been supported by fellowships at the Getty Research Institute, Dumbarton Oaks Research Library and Collection, and the Newberry Library.

Competing interests

The authors and editors declare that they have no competing interests in publishing this book.

Introduction

Chiara Palladino and Gabriel Bodard

Cultural Heritage is a term that embraces an extremely large and diverse set of knowledge and culture manifestations. In this book, we adopt the official UNESCO definition of Cultural Heritage:

> Artifacts, monuments, a group of buildings and sites, museums that have a diversity of values including symbolic, historic, artistic, aesthetic, ethnological or anthropological, scientific and social significance. It includes tangible heritage (movable, immobile and underwater), intangible cultural heritage (ICH) embedded into cultural, and natural heritage artifacts, sites or monuments. (UNESCO definition of Cultural Heritage: https://uis.unesco.org/en/glossary-term/cultural-heritage)

The idea of a Digital Cultural Heritage is as broad as Cultural Heritage itself (Cameron & Kenderdine 2010), with an increasing diversity of tools and practices in all areas: from preservation and conservation, to new types of archive and museum management (Giannini & Bowen 2019), virtual and augmented reality experiences (Champion 2021), gaming (Reinhard 2018), landscape study (Reinhard & Zaia 2023; Douglas & Harrower 2013; Lake 2020), interpretation of sites and cultural dynamics (Fredrick & Vennarucci 2021), and so on.

How to cite this book chapter:
Palladino, C. and Bodard, G. 2023. Introduction. In: Palladino, C. and Bodard, G. (Eds.), *Can't Touch This: Digital Approaches to Materiality in Cultural Heritage*. Pp. 1–7. London: Ubiquity Press. DOI: https://doi.org/10.5334/bcv.a.

The application of digital techniques has certainly provided new insights into the study of material artifacts and practices: for example, by allowing the digital reconstruction of fragmentary objects or monuments (Koller & Levoy 2006), providing new opportunities for the accessibility and preservation of damaged or endangered heritage (Vafadari, Philip & Jennings 2019), and tremendously improving access to sites and museum collections (Noehrer & Yehudi 2021; Balbi & Marasco 2021). It does not, however, come without issues: these include problems of digital obsolescence and long-term preservation (UNESCO 2003a), algorithmic and technological bias (Hacıgüzeller, Taylor & Perry 2021), quality of digital reproductions, data and standards heterogeneity (de Almeida & Wefers 2017). The errors and limitations, and sometimes even destructiveness, of technology in the management and study of material heritage collections have also been highlighted by scholars (Bentkowska-Kafel & MacDonald 2017).

The key question relates to the impact of digitization, digital analysis and electronic dissemination on the study of material and immaterial aspects of the past. This book starts from the idea that we can use the multifaceted dialogue between concepts of "material" and "immaterial" to explore some of the ethical and epistemological aspects of this debate. This duality of materiality and immateriality provides a conceptual starting point that can transcend the boundaries of disciplines, practices, and geographical areas.

It is no mystery that the materiality of cultural heritage collections (both in terms of artifacts and in terms of space where they are or were located) is an important component and potential limitation to the application of computational techniques (Ciolfi 2021). However, the relationship between material and immaterial is more complex than this simple dichotomy.

First of all, the idea of cultural heritage embraces both tangible and intangible manifestations and practices, including material expressions of culture, such as objects and sites, but also the immaterial systems of knowledge developed by communities, or Intangible Cultural Heritage (UNESCO 2003b). On the other hand, digital techniques are usually associated with the idea of immaterial, but are also dependent upon a very concrete set of material circumstances and infrastructures (Geismar 2018). Furthermore, some of the issues connected with the "immateriality" of digital technologies have very "material" repercussions: for example, on matters of intellectual property and ownership, or on the inequality of access to the necessary resources to implement or benefit from digital practices.

While it is, of course, impossible exhaustively to cover the very broad range of techniques currently applied in the field, we aim to give a representative range of responses to these questions, from scholars and practitioners of different backgrounds.

We have aimed for as diverse as possible a selection of contributions, along several axes. On the one hand, authors of chapters in this volume are from a range of academic disciplines and backgrounds, including working specialists, cultural heritage practitioners, legal experts, established academics, precarious project staff and early-career researchers. Disciplines represented include archaeology, philology, history, classics, anthropology, museum studies, social science, law and development, digital humanities and library science, not to mention the majority of authors with interdisciplinary and multidisciplinary interests. There is also a variety of linguistic origins, geographical areas and cultures represented (both within the content and among the authors): a great many chapters were written with multilingual concerns and experience of cultural translation and sensitivities.[1] Alongside and cutting across this variation in background are several different scholarly methodologies to the digital study of the historical world and its cultures, ranging from 3D modeling and spatial analysis, through text encoding, transcription of inscriptions, to intellectual property and heritage sovereignty.

On the other hand, and perhaps more central in reflecting a diversity of content, chapters in this volume bring different formats and academic approaches to the broader discussion. There are several theoretically oriented chapters (including those of Vitale, Filosa, Palladino, Granados[2]), which explore the impact of digital representation and analysis to particular areas of historical heritage and scholarly inquiry. Without limiting themselves to a single project, these chapters consider the impact on research, ethics, culture and conservation of a range of digital methods in the study of material and immaterial heritage. Others work from specific case studies involving digital reproduction, restoration or curation (and often, but not always, involving their own work) to discuss the wider issues of the volume, whether intellectual property from a legal perspective (Okorie), ethically responsible digital collections (Kahn), or the scholarly use of digital models and immersive environments (Lucarelli).

Some chapters survey their field as part of the framing of exploring digital methods in heritage, while others pull out key examples of good practice, or even make provocative proposals for more rigorous or ethical behavior needed by the discipline. Some actively raise research questions in the area of digital heritage, or engage with critical issues drawing on previous work, or indeed address the disciplinary agendas from such a high altitude perspective that individual examples are less significant. As we shall argue shortly, the volume as a whole makes this wide variation into a coherent argument—with the obvious caveat that there is no single or exclusive answer to most of the questions addressed.

---

1 We have made no attempt to restrict contributions to this volume to "own voices" authors, although the desirability of collaboration with and leadership by local practitioners is a recurring theme.

2 As a shorthand, in this introduction we will refer to chapters by the surname of the first-listed author only.

With such a variety of authors and concerns, the challenge is not only to reconcile scholarly practices, but also to translate frames of reference, to ensure exchange and communication across the boundaries imposed by discipline and occupation. The different concerns of legal specialists, archivists, or cultural heritage practitioners, the effects of cultural background and expected audience, even styles of communication and audience expectation substantively impact both writing style and content.

Cutting across this diversity of backgrounds and concerns requires a particular kind of work to ensure that content is accessible across the board of possible readers, but also that the specific nature of each contribution is meaningfully communicated without banalization. This process of translation also brings a certain amount of exploration and discovery, in domains and fields that usually do not communicate with one another.

Thanks to this process, we discover strong underlying themes, more or less obvious, that are shared across the chapters of this volume: the order of reading we propose, approximately based on types of technology and of objects of study, reflects only one of the many ways in which the content could be read.

More or less overt threads, including some of the most pressing issues in the field of cultural heritage, recur throughout many or all chapters in the volume, although they may be approached in very different ways. Several chapters address digital encoding of texts found on inscribed objects (Baba, Filosa, Bianchini) and manuscripts (Elagina, Woodward); others present digital reconstruction, from 3D modeling of architecture and other archaeological elements 3D (Vitale, Lucarelli), to immersive environments and virtual representations of ritual space and landscape (Palladino, Lucarelli).

Along another axis of commonality, several chapters deal with the development, adoption and adaptation of digital standards and community practices (Baba, Filosa, Bianchini, Elagina, Woodward, Granados); several likewise focus on issues around intellectual property, sovereignty and stewardship of heritage data (Baba, Filosa, Granados, Kahn; especially of course Okorie). Other recurring themes include cultural heritage management, especially via archives and digital libraries (Granados, Kahn, Okorie), and the importance of documentation, metadata and paradata relating to research materials and outputs (Vitale, Filosa).

Other threads that can be discerned throughout this volume may be less obvious, but reveal common concerns and preoccupations that recur across different fields, materials and geographical areas. Several chapters concern themselves with epistemological questions regarding representations of heritage information, especially with regard to the digital technologies that impact on, improve or hinder such representations and models (Vitale, Palladino, Kahn).

Others take a range of approaches to questions of access and community building, including both the involvement of local bodies of knowledge and practice to improve standards and workflows, and the epistemology of digital methods themselves (Woodward, Palladino, Granados, Okorie). Equally, several chapters address the related accessibility issues with intellectual property

(Okorie); decolonization and restitution (Kahn); protection of and sovereignty around local heritage (Granados). Throughout the volume there is an awareness of the importance of open access in making research available, but also the reasonable limitations of this commitment (*passim* but especially Baba, Filosa, Woodward).

The commonalities, threads and patterns in the approaches and concerns that we trace throughout this volume cannot obscure the fact that we have eleven chapters by seventeen authors from different academic, heritage, professional and other backgrounds, across four continents, and with as many different approaches even to sometimes closely related questions or issues. The themes addressed by this volume are of sufficient complexity and ethical ramifications, not to mention sometimes subjective or highly contextually contingent, that we should expect to find differences in approach, tensions and even disagreements. Neither this volume, nor arguably any single chapter, presents a monolithic or monotonous view of the issues, and even less of the solutions to them.

The diversity of responses to heritage restitution and other decolonization practices and approaches signals one of the most complex and environmentally contingent questions under consideration. Some of our authors deal with centralized repositories such as Papyri.info, that are full of material overwhelmingly taken from North Africa and the Middle East, many of which now reside (justifiably or otherwise) in Western institutions (Filosa). In other cases we see manuscripts that belong to localized traditions now spanning modern borders (Elagina). While recognising the care and nuance such questions deserve, it is fair to say that we overwhelmingly reject a facile "world's heritage" argument often put forward to support the status quo and existing/historical power relationships (*e.g.* Cuno 2008; Jenkins 2018).

Power and privilege also impact on the way we research and record heritage and history. The majority of digital infrastructures and standards adopted today are Western in provenance and epistemology. Projects that adopt Western-born and promulgated digital standards as opposed to locally generated systems have made decisions that affect the way digitization itself is conceived (Bianchini, Elagina, Woodward). In contrast we see a Japanese digitization project that originated locally, but whose data was later converted into broadly adopted Western digital technologies like Linked Open Data (Baba). Elsewhere our authors discuss how current Western standards can be adapted to and given additional nuance by local knowledge (Palladino, Granados).

Large-scale projects that deal with collections including localized heritage, inevitably impose some centralization of methodology, modeling and standards (Filosa, Bianchini, Elagina, Woodward, but also almost *passim*). It is not news that all modeling—digital or otherwise—is interpretive and therefore lossy, as most have observed. Availability of funding, implied authority, stable employment, and many other axes of privilege profoundly affect the development of digital projects worldwide; even where the selection bias toward Western heritage is avoided, infrastructure, research agendas and prestige accrued follows many of the same lines.

The very opportunity to write about the scientific and ethical concerns around the study of heritage is contingent on a spectrum of privileges. For salaried (leave aside tenured!) academics, publication of research is a valued part of the job description and career advancement pathway. Heritage professionals do not always have writing and publication as a core part of their contracted responsibilities, and are not rewarded for it in the same way. Further, freelance researchers in many relevant fields depend on receiving remuneration for their written output, whether in the press or for professional bodies, whereas academic publications are not modeled around this way of funding authors. These inequalities will not always or necessarily be superable, but we ought not neglect the fact that they exist.

Sometimes overriding, and often inseparable from, these sorts of issues, the inevitable individual sensitivities, interests, passions, biases, expertise and research agendas also contribute to the diversity of approach and attitudes in this volume. This mélange may on occasion lead to clashes, but more often it leads to a complementarity of approaches, a useful corrective to missed perspectives, and reminder of the subtlety and complexity of our own fields.

References

Balbi, B., & Marasco, A. (2021). Co-Designing Cultural Heritage Experiences for All with Virtual Reality: A Scenario-Based Design Approach. *Umanistica Digitale 11*, 71–98. DOI: https://doi.org/10.6092/issn.2532-8816/13686.

Bentkowska-Kafel, A., & MacDonald, L. (Eds.) (2017). *Digital Techniques for Documenting and Preserving Cultural Heritage.* Kalamazoo & Bradford: ARC Humanities Press.

Boast, R., Bravo, M., & Srinivasan, R. (2017). Return to Babel: Emergent diversity, digital resources, and local knowledge. *The Information Society 23*(5), 395–403.

Cameron, F., & Kenderdine, S. (Eds.) (2010). *Theorizing Digital Cultural Heritage: A Critical Discourse.* Cambridge, MA: MIT Press.

Champion, E. M. (Ed.) (2021). *Virtual Heritage. A Guide.* London: Ubiquity Press. DOI: https://doi.org/10.5334/bck.

Ciolfi, L. (2021). Hybrid interactions in museums: why materiality still matters, in E. M. Champion, *Virtual Heritage. A Guide* (pp. 67–79). London: Ubiquity Press. DOI: https://doi.org/10.5334/bck.g.

Comer, D. C., & Harrower, M. J. (Eds.) (2013). *Mapping Archaeological Landscapes from Space.* Springer Briefs in Archaeology 5. New York: Springer. DOI: https://doi.org/10.1007/978-1-4614-6074-9.

Cuno, J. (2008). *Who Owns Antiquity?: Museums and the Battle Over Our Ancient Heritage.* Princeton University Press.

Fredrick, D., & Vennarucci, R. G. (2021). Putting Space Syntax to the Test: Digital Embodiment and Phenomenology in the Roman House. *Studies in Digital Heritage* 4(2), 185–224. DOI: https://doi.org/10.14434/sdh.v4i2.31521.

Geismar, H. (2018). *Museum Object Lessons for the Digital Age.* London: UCL Press.

Giannini, T., & Bowen, J. P. (Eds.) (2019). *Museums and Digital Culture. New Perspectives and Research.* London, UK: Springer.

Hacıgüzeller, P., Taylor, J. S., & Perry, S. (2021). On the Emerging Supremacy of Structured Digital Data in Archaeology: A Preliminary Assessment of Information, Knowledge and Wisdom Left Behind. *Open Archaeology* 7(1), 1709–30. DOI: https://doi.org/10.1515/opar-2020-0220.

Jenkin, T. (2018). *Keeping Their Marbles: How the Treasures of the Past Ended Up in Museums—And Why They Should Stay There.* Oxford University Press.

Koller, D., & Levoy, M. (2006). Computer-Aided Reconstruction and New Matches in The Forma Urbis Romae. *Bollettino della Commissione Archeologica Comunale di Roma: Supplementi 15.* Roma: L'Erma di Brentschneider, 103–25.

Lake, M. (2020). Spatial Agent-Based Modelling. In M. Gillings, P. Hacıgüzeller & G. Lock (Eds.), *Archaeological Spatial Analysis: A Methodological Guide* (pp. 247–72). London: Routledge.

Moitinho de Almeida, V., Wefers, S., & Murphy, O. (2017). An interdisciplinary discussion of the terminology used in cultural heritage research. In A. Bentkowska-Kafel & L. MacDonald (Eds.), *Digital Techniques for Documenting and Preserving Cultural Heritage* (pp. 3–16). Kalamazoo & Bradford: ARC Humanities Press.

Noehrer, L., Gilmore, A., Jay, C., & Yehudi, Y. (2021). The impact of COVID-19 on digital data practices in museums and art galleries in the UK and the US. *Humanities and Social Sciences Communications* 8, 236. DOI: https://doi.org/10.1057/s41599-021-00921-8.

Reinhard, A. (2018). *Archaeogaming: An Introduction to Archaeology in and of Video Games.* New York: Berghahn.

Reinhard, A., & Zaia, S. (2023). Photogrammetry and GIS in Human-Occupied Digital Landscapes. *Advances in Archaeological Practice*, January, 1–13. DOI: https://doi.org/10.1017/aap.2022.30.

UNESCO. (2003a). *Charter on the Preservation of Digital Heritage.* 15 October. Paris. https://www.unesco.org/en/legal-affairs/charter-preservation-digital-heritage.

UNESCO. (2003b). *Convention for the Safeguarding of the Intangible Cultural Heritage.* Art. 2. https://ich.unesco.org/en/convention#art2. Paris.

Vafadari, A., Philip, G., & Jennings, R. (2019). A Tool and Methodology for Rapid Assessment and Monitoring of Heritage Places in a Disaster and Post-Disaster Context: Syria as a Case Study. In M. Dawson, E. James & M. Nevell (Eds.), *Heritage under Pressure—Threats and Solutions: Studies of Agency and Soft Power in the Historic Environment* (pp. 87–100). Oxford: Oxbow Books. Retrieved from https://dro.dur.ac.uk/29183/.

CHAPTER 1

Ceci n'est pas un temple. Visual secondary sources between representation and documentation

Valeria Vitale
University of Sheffield

Abstract

As 3D models appear more and more often in scholarly and scientific contexts, the need to document the study of the numerous and diverse sources that supports these digital research outputs has become more apparent.

The quest for fragments of information disseminated in various kinds of secondary sources, from travel memoirs to sketches to historical photographs, is of a peculiar nature, though. In many cases these documents become invaluable first-hand accounts of something that may not exist anymore. On the other hand, anyone who has ever worked with secondary sources will be familiar with their inaccuracies, poetic licences and even outright fabrications.

Combining tools from digital humanities, art history and semiotics, and looking at examples from the most represented—and misrepresented—archaeological site in modern history, the buried city of Pompeii, this chapter invites the reader to look at secondary sources describing ancient buildings not simply as resources to be mined to extract nuggets of more or less reliable information, but as representations in their own right that deserve to be investigated beyond their literal value. The challenge then becomes to contextualise these

How to cite this book chapter:

Vitale, V. 2023. *Ceci n'est pas un temple.* Visual secondary sources between representation and documentation. In: Palladino, C. and Bodard, G. (Eds.), *Can't Touch This: Digital Approaches to Materiality in Cultural Heritage*. Pp. 9–28. London: Ubiquity Press. DOI: https://doi.org/10.5334/bcv.b. License: CC BY 4.0

historical representations, and to try to retro-engineer the semiotic processes that went into their creation. We claim that researchers applying 3D modelling to the study of ancient buildings find themselves in the privileged position of analysing these earlier representations through the lens of the act of making, thus untapping further layers of meaning.

Finally, we will show how this approach helps to unravel the rich relationship between disappeared artefacts and their past and present representations, ultimately promoting a view of documentation as a dialogue between the artists and scholars of the past and present, as well as those of the future.

Abstract (Italiano)

L'uso sempre più frequente di modelli 3D in contesti accademici e scientifici sta rendendo evidente la necessità di documentare lo studio delle numerose e diverse fonti che supportano questi prodotti della ricerca digitale.

La ricerca di frammenti di informazioni racchiuse in vari tipi di fonti secondarie, dalle memorie di viaggio agli schizzi alle fotografie storiche, è però di natura peculiare. In molti casi questi documenti diventano preziosi resoconti di prima mano che descrivono qualcosa che non esiste più nella sua forma originaria. D'altra parte, chiunque abbia lavorato con fonti secondarie conosce le loro inesattezze, licenze poetiche e persino vere e proprie falsificazioni.

Combinando gli strumenti delle digital humanities, della storia dell'arte e della semiotica, e utilizzando esempi provenienti dal sito archeologico più rappresentato—e travisato—nella storia moderna, la città sepolta di Pompei, questo capitolo invita il lettore a guardare alle fonti secondarie che descrivono edifici antichi non semplicemente come miniere di dettagli storici più o meno attendibili, ma come rappresentazioni a sé stanti che meritano di essere indagate al di là del loro valore letterale. La sfida diventa quindi contestualizzare queste rappresentazioni e provare a ricostruire, a posteriori, i processi semiotici che hanno contribuito alla loro creazione. I ricercatori che applicano la modellazione 3D allo studio di edifici antichi si troverebbero, dunque, nella posizione privilegiata di analizzare queste rappresentazioni precedenti attraverso la lente del making, accedendo così a ulteriori strati di significato.

Infine, il capitolo propone che questo approccio aiuti a svelare la complessa relazione tra i monumenti scomparsi e le loro rappresentazioni passate e presenti, promuovendo in ultima analisi una visione della documentazione come dialogo tra gli artisti e gli studiosi del passato e del presente, così come quelli del futuro.

Introduction

This chapter advocates for a different approach to the documentation of 3D visualisations in academia; an approach that records the research process behind the digital model but also investigates the secondary sources used as references and their fallacies, instead of including them uncritically in the model. We will show how this process helps to unravel the rich relationship between disappeared buildings and their past and present representations, ultimately promoting a view of documentation as a dialogue between the artists and scholars of the past and present, as well as those of the future. Finally, we will argue that we should not think of the referent of a 3D visualisation as the ancient building per se, but as our collective knowledge of it: an idea of the building that has been shaped by numerous representations in different media, all biased and all imperfect, but nonetheless part of the building's unique history and identity.

1. Models as signs, ancient buildings as referents

The first section of the chapter discusses some of the communicative processes that are set in motion during the production and consumption of three-dimensional (3D) visualisations, and introduces some of the terms that will be used throughout the text. First, when talking about 3D modelling, we will refer to the process of creating a 3D digital object, as opposed to the process of digitising existing 3D artefacts (3D imaging). Although there are several 3D modelling technologies widely used by archaeologists and historians, this text will focus on one particular approach, Computer Aided Design (CAD) software, and one specific application, ancient buildings.

3D models are generally understood as representations that reproduce some of the qualities of an object (in most of our examples, a building). This object, called "referent" in semiotic terms, can be real or imaginary, material or immaterial (Eco 1975). Like the word "model" suggests, 3D representations are not full and identical copies of their referents, but simplifications for the purpose of study or experimentation that focus on selected characteristics (McCarthy 2004). What these characteristics are depends on many variables such as the scope of the visualisation itself, the research questions of its author, and the intended audience for the final outcome.

To frame the argument developed in this chapter, I will also introduce two concepts, one borrowed from art history and one from literary criticism, to highlight the richness and complexity of the relationship between an ancient building (or object) and its digital 3D representation.

1.1 Optical illusions

When creating a 3D model of a historical building, it is likely that the three-dimensionality of the built structure is one of the key qualities of the place that the author wants to reproduce. The fact that 3D technologies enable us to perceive a model as a representation of a three-dimensional space sometimes obfuscates the awareness that, in most cases, we are experiencing it through a 2D screen (on a personal computer, a larger monitor in an exhibition). Although perception becomes more complex in the case of immersive 3D environments, it is usually a combination of 2D views that simulates the third dimension. It is a very reliable illusion, created algorithmically by the software, to the point that we can even accurately measure the space in scale. But this space, although quantifiable, is entirely virtual, or, actually, almost *phantasmatic*: it is a 3D space that only exists as a combination of 2D views generated on the fly by the software. In this perspective, a CAD model might have more in common with a painted trompe l'oeil than a three-dimensional scale model.

1.2 Ekphrasis

Looking at 3D models in light of their relationship with two-dimensional visual representations may elicit a comparison with the concept of *ekphrasis*. "Ekphrasis" is a rhetorical figure that identifies vivid literary descriptions of visual artworks. The most famous example is, perhaps, the description of the shield of Achilles in the *Iliad*, but the practice has remained popular through the centuries, and its study has crossed the boundaries of classics and of ancient texts (Webb 2012). Although the term is still mainly associated with an artistic relationship between words and images, in more recent years scholars and authors have started realising that the "evocation" of an artwork through another artistic language is a very powerful, and partly transferable, concept. Notably, Bruhn (2001) has explored the idea of musical ekphrasis to analyse musical compositions that explicitly describe other forms of art. Digital media, with their intrinsic focus on reproducibility, have also become key components in the current reflection around a broadened concept of ekphrasis (Jansson 2018).

Representing objects (referents) in their present state, has never been the most common, nor the most sensible, use of CAD modelling. Several 3D technologies, including photogrammetry, laser scanning or structure from motion, would be better choices in these contexts. The elective aim of CAD modelling is the visualisation, or recreation, of something (a referent) that is not extant anymore, or to represent a previous (or future) state of something that is still visible. The journey from the invisible (or no longer visible) referent to the visible representation is where the research of a 3D author lies.

To produce accurate and reliable visualisations, researchers must sift through a variety of primary sources, but they also have to look for any previous representation of the same referent in other visualisations, in any media. This is where the broadened concept of ekphrasis becomes useful to unpack the semiotic layers that we can see multiplying. Producing a 3D visualisation of an architectural building would be an ekphrastic representation as we would be recreating the outcome of an art form (architecture) in another (3D software) that relies on a different language. In many cases, though, being 3D modelling devoted to representing the invisible, the destroyed, and the lost, the visualisations are not based on the direct observation of the original referent, but on previous representations that were produced by other authors. Several of these representations—watercolour, sketches, travel notebooks and so on—are also ekphrasis, as they use, with different degrees of accomplishment and different purposes, another art form (painting, drawing, photography, sometimes written word) to recreate or describe a piece of architecture. We could say that academic 3D models of historical buildings are, in a way, double ekphrasis, relying on existing ekphrasis (secondary sources) to conjure a new visualisation of the original architectural object.

1.3 Documentation of 3D models for cultural heritage and academic research

Re-thinking 3D visualisation as ekphrasis (or even double ones) seems to imply that we ought to consider 3D modelling strictly a form of art. However, in the case of research-driven 3D models, it may be more appropriate to talk about the use of a visual language, or a visual medium more than the act of artistic creativity. The line between scholarly 3D visualisation and works of art lies more in their purposes than in their aesthetic qualities. Another substantial difference is that artists usually don't explain their creative process and do not want their work to be replicated. For researchers applying 3D modelling, on the other hand, reproducibility is key to academic transparency. A 3D model can only be considered compliant to the scientific method if it is accompanied by a discussion of the rationale guiding the different modelling choices, and a description of the sources that have been used as references and comparanda (Vitale 2016).

Documentation is a very broad term that is used with slightly different meanings in different disciplines. In computer science, documentation often means making the code more comprehensible and reproducible (and, therefore, more sustainable) adding inline comments. For archaeologists, documentation is made of maps, reports, photographs and matrixes. For a librarian, a good documentation may lie in the production of accurate and detailed metadata accompanying a digital collection. This variety explains why there is not still an agreement on what documentation of academic 3D modelling actually involves. In this chapter, when talking about documentation of 3D architectural models, we will refer to the concept of "paradata", introduced by the London Charter for 3D visualisation of cultural heritage (Denard 2009, revised 2012) and reinforced in the Sevilla Charter (Lopez-Menchero & Grande 2011; Carrillo Gea et al. 2013). A 3D model's paradata are not merely references to author, date of creation, or version of software used (all relevant information that we could ascribe to "metadata"), but they offer a record of the researcher's thinking, and should have the same methodological rigour of a traditional academic publication (Baker 2016).

Since its introduction to the consumer market in the 1990s, CAD software has immediately shown its potential to archaeologists and experts in historical architecture as a way to explore the (hypothetical) former looks of buildings, supporting restoration and conservation efforts, scholarly investigation, as well as the creation of communicative outputs targeting the general public (Earle 2013). But already in the early 2000 it became clear that without documentation 3D models remained opaque, and not replicable, making the model indistinguishable from a purely aesthetic product (Hermon 2008). The issue has been discussed at length by experts in the past years, along with other criticisms that include the use of realism (and hyper-realism) (Favro 2012) and the absence of human actors in the visualisations (then addressed by Favro and Johanson 2010). Thorough documentation is instrumental in making a 3D model re-usable, enabling future researchers to build on top of (documented) work, in the same way as all scholars start their research from literature reviews, and corroborate their arguments with citations and cross-references.

Discussing different strategies for documenting scholarly 3D visualisations goes beyond the scope of this chapter. Here we want to bring the attention to one category of documents that features prominently in most documentations of academic 3D models: secondary sources, and, in particular, those of a visual nature, like drawings, paintings, etchings or photographs.

For the scholar researching historical buildings, secondary sources are invaluable. Not only because, it is often only in these documents that information about buildings that have disappeared or being transformed survives, but also for the role they play (or have played) in generating knowledge about the past (Moser 2015). However, the enthusiasm around these sources, and the time-travelling feeling they elicit, can lead to the temptation of translating them uncritically to the 3D visualisations, forgetting that, like all cultural products (including 3D models themselves) these images are biased, and influenced by a number of variables including the artist's training, the available printing technologies, cultural trends, or even political agendas.

Using previous representations of a historical building (or artefact) just as a resource to be mined for, more or less reliable, nuggets of information about measurements and chromatic records is not only potentially misleading but also reductive. The more visual secondary sources get analysed in their own right, the more they appear as means to learn about the referent, its later reception, and, maybe more important for this argument, the processes and codes involved in the representation of a building in another medium. As Moser (2015) suggests, all the gaps, inconsistencies, and even the "artistic licences" that these images show may tell more complex stories than we had assumed, and have more interesting origins than mere human error or incompetence.

2. Sketchbooks from the Vesuvius

In the second part of this chapter, I will discuss three examples of valuable, although unreliable, visual sources, and how their shortcomings proved to be, at a deeper analysis, clues about the cultural context in which they were produced, and about the ways in which the ancient artworks were perceived, represented, and received by the contemporary public. All the examples that I am about to discuss are related to the archaeological site of Pompeii. The choice has been led by two factors: a) my own experience with the 3D modelling of Pompeian houses, and the related research on secondary visual sources, and b) Pompeii's own popularity. With excavations starting as early as the first half of the 18th century, and a status of sensation and tourist attraction for the cultural elite first and for a larger audience later (Lazer 2009, Blix 2013), the antiquities from Pompeii and Herculaneum have been reproduced countless times, by people with different backgrounds, and during a long span of time, making it an ideal case study per critical visualisation.

2.1 Unforgettable art

Anyone who has worked with visual secondary sources from Pompeii and Herculaneum, and has then confronted them with the original referents they were meant to reproduce, has probably noticed how often these drawings and paintings look heavily distorted. Although cultural products can never be considered objective copies, the grade of unreliability found in early depictions of Pompeii and Herculaneum feels somehow above average. This oddity can be explained with the long and complex history of the sites, and their being, for a certain time, a unique phenomenon in Europe. It is especially interesting, though, to notice how some of the same historical and cultural variables generated two almost opposite trends of distortions, each one with its intertwining motivations.

One kind of recurring distortion is what we could call the *prettification* of Pompeian frescoes in the early records of artists visiting the Vesuvian sites and reproducing those wall decorations in their drawings or paintings. Among the several instances of this trend, we could cite the work of 19th century German painter Wilhelm Ternite. Browsing his rendition of Pompeian frescoes (published ca. 1839), it is easy to notice how the human figures, in particular, look almost statuary, and, perhaps, more Neoclassical in both spirit and appearance than actually Roman. Readers familiar with Pompeian frescoes might be surprised by Ternite's choice, as the vast majority of wall decorations in Pompeii and Herculaneum tend to appear unrefined when compared with modern aesthetics (regardless of their historical and archaeological value). The unrealistic pose of the famous fresco of the Venus in a Shell, for example, contrasts quite strikingly with the harmonious and "regularised" female portraits produced by Ternite (Figure 1.1).

If the aim was to "document" a piece of ancient art, why would artists and antiquarians want to embellish the original? This trend was probably fueled by a combination of factors. One of them might be psychological, if not emotional. There was an incredible hype around Pompeii and Herculaneum in the late 18th and beginning of the 19th centuries (see, among others, Roberts 2015 and Andrews 2010). The mystery surrounding the antiquities, that could be seen only by invitation, and the ban on reproducing them, made it even higher. The

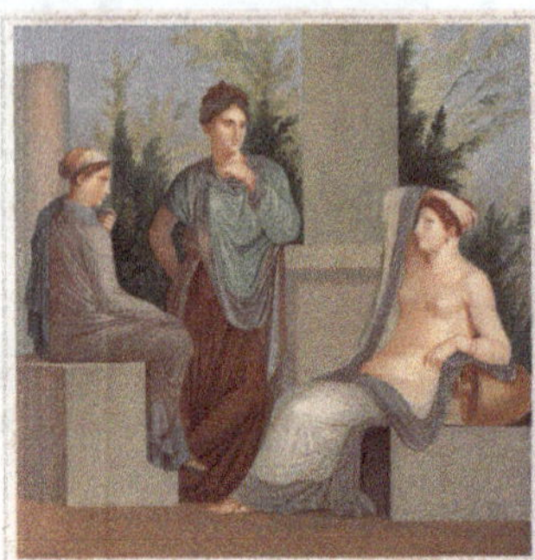
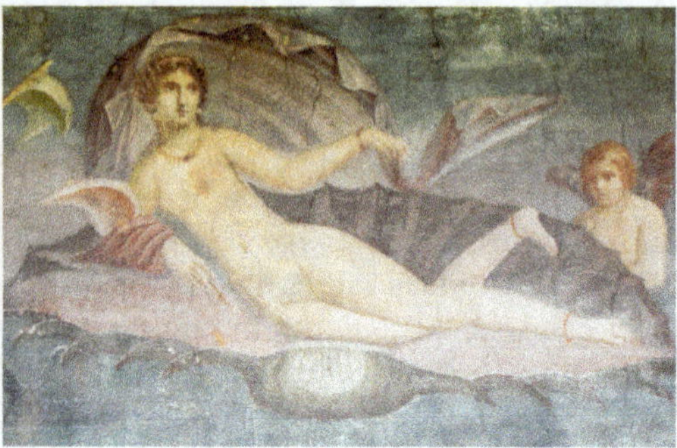

Figure 1.1: On the left: Quellorakel. Wandgemälde aus Pompeji und Herculanum nach den Zeichnungen und Nachbildungen in Farben: von W. Ternite; mit einem erläuternden Text von C. O. Müller. Berlin. Public domain. Source: Arachne. On the right: detail of the wall decorations in the House of the Venus in the Shell in Pompeii. Photo by Matthias Kabel. Source: Wikimedia Commons.

two cities were talked about, and imagined, as proxies of the glory of imperial Rome, relics of a past of order, beauty and wealth (Leppman 1968). The artists surely felt the weight of anticipation and, maybe, some of them did not want to deal with the disappointing sight of just a regular small provincial city. Status may have also played a role. As it was such a privilege to be admitted in Pompeii in those years, it was rewarding for the artists to propagate the idea that everything in Pompeii was stunning, and the artist's experience was well worth other people's envy. There may have, of course, also been more pragmatic thoughts at play, like the desire to please the public and/or the publisher, giving them what they were already expecting to see, as well as the desire to flatter a powerful king who was incredibly proud, and fiercely protective, of this unique trove.

Ternite wasn't an exception, and this approach to antique painted images was actually very common among his contemporaries, to the point that a bitter sense of disappointment and crushed expectations transpires from several accounts of the first visitors. The practice was becoming so apparent and bold, that some experts started being uncomfortable with it, and seeing it as shameful and misleading. As we read from a source cited in Mattush (2011:13):

> "The king is now employing a person to take drawings of all the statues and principal paintings [...]. [T]he writer imagines the world will be vastly deceived with regard to the paintings. For the man is a very nice drawer; and has also managed the colouring to advantage; so that he has made exceedingly pretty things, from originals, which are miserable daubing. The company having seen the drawing first, were extremely disappointed, when they afterwards came to view the originals."

These policies around Pompeii and Herculaneum generated, at the same time, an almost opposite trend in the distortion of representations of pictorial scenes. Because of the strict management of the sites by the Bourbon King, not only was it a rare privilege to be admitted to the excavations as well as the exhibited artefacts in the Portici Museum, but, once there, it was forbidden to reproduce the antiquities in any way (Allroggen-Bedel 1993). Coming from entitlement, political strategy (Roberts 2015) or from a surprising understanding of what we would call today marketing strategies, the rules dictated by the King of Naples were incredibly hard on the enthusiastic artists who managed to get admitted to the sites. Unsurprisingly, despite the restrictions and their enforcement, a number of unauthorised copies of frescoes and statues from the two ancient cities started circulating outside Naples, and soon were reproduced and reprinted all over Europe.

It was a dangerous trade, and, as Gordon (2007) discloses, it even generated an underground network of smugglers and spies. But the temptation must have been impossible to resist for the artists in these early years, and the reward potentially very high. The items exhibited in the Portici museum were always guarded, and it was impossible for the eager artists to simply sit in front of the originals and copy them. They had to start sketching as soon as they exited the museum, and could probably only re-enter a handful of times before raising suspicions. Even with the strongest motivations—pure love for art, economic gain or spite for the King of Naples—there is only so much information that anyone, even a trained artist, can retain in their memory and then transfer hastily in a notebook. These quick, smuggled drawings that ended up being reproduced dozens of times more or less legitimately, often appear simplified, and, on several occasions, they ended up leaving out (or even adding) details from (or to) the original scenes.

The most popular example of this practice is probably the publication assembled, illegally, by French artist Jérôme Charles Bellicard. Once he obtained permission to see the museum, he used it to commit to memory as many surviving frescoes as he could and reproduce them in his notebook, which is now preserved at The Metropolitan Museum of Art, in New York. Overall, the drawings appear faithful enough to make Ramage (2013) suspect that Bellicard was able to bribe one or more guardians and actually was given some time in the museum to produce a few of the sketches. Predictably, though, his reproductions are devoid of details and, as Ramage (2013) points out, in some cases they present variations from the originals (like the drawing of the centaur that, in Bellicard's reproduction, has a different orientation and several inconsistent details).

These two trends that develop around Pompeian artefacts and especially frescoes during the years in which access to the site was tightly controlled remind us of the importance of analysing secondary sources, such as those produced by Ternite or Bellicard, in their historical and cultural context. Perhaps even more important, these two trends highlight how reproductions are only partly about their explicit referent, i.e. the depicted ancient wall, and how much more they tell about the historical, cultural and even idiosyncratic elements that have contributed to the production of each particular document.

2.2 Ghost scenes in the Iseum

The king of Naples' policy about reproducing the antiquities was not mere obscurantism. He wanted people to talk about his astounding antiquities, but he also wanted to control what information about them was circulating and who had access to it. To produce and disseminate the official documentation of Herculaneum and Pompeii, he hired about fifteen of the most talented artists from the Academia in Naples (Risser & Saunders 2013). Professionals such as Giuseppe Chiantarelli, Aniello Cattaneo, Giovanni Elia Morghen, Giovanni Casanova and Carlo Nolli, all contributed to the monumental official publication on the sites: *Le Antichità di Ercolano Esposte* (from now on *Le Antichità*). Although *Le Antichità* was never completed, and its official circulation was limited to a relatively small number of European nobility and celebrities, it became highly influential, and was a crucial document for later reconstructions and restorations.

Despite being commissioned by the King himself in 1755, the reproductions included in *Le Antichità* seem to be less embellished than others that we discussed before. Although influenced by 18th century taste, the cleaness of the lines, the use of a more realistic style, the addition of scales and, perhaps above all, the aura of "officialness" contributed to make these images perceived as highly reliable. Unlike other unauthorised documents, illustrations in *Le Antichità* did not show only de-contextualised decorative scenes, but had documented entire walls, preserving key information about patterns, and their role in how the building was seen and experienced. This choice makes the illustrations in *Le Antichità* not only an invaluable information for a 3D visualisation, but even an ideal source of informative textures for the CAD model.

Among the several buildings in Pompeii that have been studied and reproduced from the 18th century onward, one stands out as the most thoroughly documented, since the early days of the excavations: the complex of the Iseum, better known simply as the Temple of Isis (De Caro 1992). There are several reasons that explain the popularity of this place and its unbroken appeal to the public and the experts alike. Many publications already delve into the story of the reception of this unique place. In this context, it suffices to say that the amount and quality of visual secondary sources of the Iseum makes it a perfect candidate for a 3D visualisation, both analogue and virtual. The first one has been carried out by the experts at the Naples museum and it is part of their permanent collection, the second has been attempted by a number of researchers, including myself.

In my 3D visualisation of the Iseum, I had planned to use the etchings printed in *Le Antichità* as textures for the architectural model. After discovering discrepancies in three different blueprints produced by three different architects in the 18th century—Saint-Non, Piranesi and Soane—I had decided to take manual measurements on site, and to compare them with modern-times surveys such as the ones published by De Caro in 1992. Surprisingly, when measuring the surface of the Iseum's walls in the illustrations in *Le Antichità* according to their own scale, the numbers did not quite add up: the reproduced frescoed walls always seem to be smaller than the recent site measurements. The divergence was not dramatic, but it was big enough to be noticeable and not a simple rounding up the numbers. Prompted by the research of Baker and Blazeby around decorative patterns in Campanian villas (unpublished), I tried to understand what had happened to those missing centimetres. In this quest, I came across the work of academics such as D'Alconzo (2002) who reconstructed the practice of detaching frescoes from walls in Pompeii in the 18th century. As her research points out, in those days the excision was performed leaving a certain margin (on both sides and at the bottom) still attached to the original work. This explanation would reasonably account for the consistent gaps between the scaled drawings and the measurement of the full walls, and it would also suggest that the official copies (and measurements) were not carried out on site, but after the excision. To reflect this awareness, in my 3D model the images used as textures did not cover the entire surface of the related walls, acknowledging the existence of missing areas on the borders that were not included in the secondary sources.

In my 3D visualisation of the Pompeian Iseum, the historical black and white illustrations used as textures were to be superimposed with the photographic images of the surviving fresco fragments, now exhibited in the Museo Archeologico Nazionale di Napoli (MANN). When working specifically with an area of the Iseum known as the ekklesiasterion, a large ceremonial room at the back of the temple, this process led to the discovery of further discrepancies. The walls of the ekklesiasterion depict scenes from the story of Io and her journey to Egypt, alternated with sacred landscapes inspired by the cult of Isis. When comparing the larger scenes in the frescoes with their documentation, the reproductions seem faithful enough, with good attention to details. However, when superimposing the photographs of the fragments on the wall pattern printed in *Le Antichità*, it is easy to notice that there is something wrong. Although the individual scenes appear quite well reproduced, their placement on the walls is arbitrary. In particular, the scenes featured on the walls north and south of the ekklesiasterion have been inverted. The issue had already been noticed and described in detail by Elia in the 1930s, and Sanpaolo in 1992. But the most apparent discrepancy in the documentation can perhaps be found in the central (west) wall. The MANN holds a fragment recorded as "from the temple of Isis" that is catalogued as fragment 1.67, and titled *landscape with sacred door and velum*. As both Elia and Sanpaolo state, there is little room for doubt: that fragment does belong to the ekklesiasterion, and, more precisely, to the right side of the west wall. Not only the records support this knowledge, but the fragment's style, topic, and pattern confirm it. However, this fragment does not appear in Morghen and Casanova's reproduction of the west wall. Even more surprisingly, there is another landscape in its place, that looks so consistent with the original ones that it blends in without drawing any attention. Evidence suggests that this variant sacred landscape is a fabrication at the hands of the Neapolitan artists (Figure 1.2). A fake Roman landscape has probably little room in a 3D visualisation of an ancient building, especially if its goal is to give shape to what we know about its former look. But it is an interesting piece of evidence that sparks a number of research questions. What is the story behind this imaginary landscape? Was part of these documentation efforts also relying on the artists' memory? Are there further cases that have been spotted in the 18th century documentation? Was there an established practice of producing "filler" images as some sort of *passepartout*?

A critical approach to secondary sources enables us to evaluate their contribution to our knowledge of historical buildings, contextualising these documents in the cultural and historical moment in which they were produced. Such an approach also helps us to look at inconsistencies in the secondary sources not simply as limitations or even inconveniences in our research process but, on the contrary, as flags that alert us of some forgotten practice of knowledge that we have the chance to rediscover and investigate.

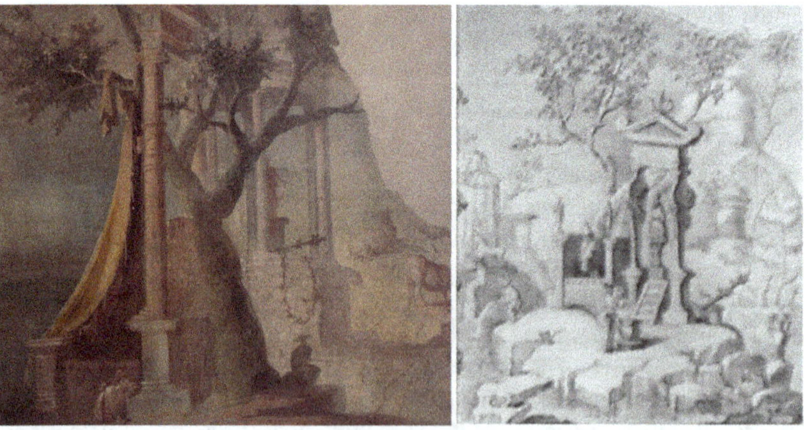

Figure 1.2: On the left: Detail of fragment 1.67, Landscape with sacred door and velum. Museo Archaeologico Nazionale di Napoli. Photo by the author, with permission. On the right: detail of Chiantarelli, G. (illustrator) & A. Cattaneo (etcher) West wall of the ekklesiasterion in the Temple of Isis in Pompeii. Published in Elia, O. 1941. Le pitture del Tempio di Iside. Roma. Low resolution digital copy of the published book.

2.3 Contracting walls

The next example relates to another building in Pompeii, now known as the House of Orpheus, after a large fresco of Orpheus and the animals. The house was a relatively popular destination in the early years, when it was still called House of Vesonius Primus, and it is featured in a number of early, illustrated guides to Pompeii and other publications, due to the richness, in number and variety, of its surviving decorations (see, among others, Neville Rolfe 1888, Mau 1902, Mackenzie 1910).

Before mass tourism came into place, artists and antiquarians who managed to visit Pompeii, Herculaneum, and the Naples museum were quite enthusiastic about communicating to a wider public what they had seen on site, and I believe that, in many cases, these artists and academics approached their work scientifically and methodically. However, even when accompanied by the highest level of dedication, those artists could not rely on an established and clear tradition about systematic documentation of ancient frescoes. Or, if they did, their references may be lost to our modern understanding.

One of the scholars and artists in the 19th century who authored detailed reproductions of Pompeian walls and floors, including those of the House of Orpheus, was German archaeologist Emil Presuhn in his *Die Pompejanischen Wand Dekorationen*. In his book, Presuhn describes some of the most notable houses; the reports are accompanied by a number of full-page plates dedicated to the frescoed walls. At first, I assumed he had chosen the most richly ornate wall for each of the rooms discussed in his work, usually the one in front of the entrance door, as representative of the decorated space. However, when I tried to use one of his illustrations as texture in a 3D visualisation of the House of Orpheus, I found myself, once again, confused by secondary sources I had naively expected to use as "historical wallpaper".

In the case of the yellow, small room at the back of the house, just overlooking the garden, Presuhn's illustration turned out not to be the depiction of a single wall. Instead, it seemed to reproduce the shorter (north) wall and half of the long one (west), seamlessly together (Figure 1.3).

But the illustration proved much less straightforward than I had anticipated. In the actual room, the north wall is marked by a frescoed lunette above the door, decorated with a dainty bird picking at cherries. However, in Presuhn's illustration, there are no doors beneath the reproduction on the lunette. Instead of the door frame, Presuhun depicts a small putto that, in the real building, can be admired on the decorative pattern on the opposite wall, the south one. The south wall doesn't have a door, and, although it was probably originally decorated by a symmetrical lunette, had now lost it. Only after comparing Presuhun's illustration with the actual space in Pompeii, I understood that the image in *Die Pompejanischen Wand Dekorationen* was never meant to be a realistic documentation of how the walls in the room, or part of them, look like. It was, instead, a sort of synthetic, almost coded, documentation that made the most

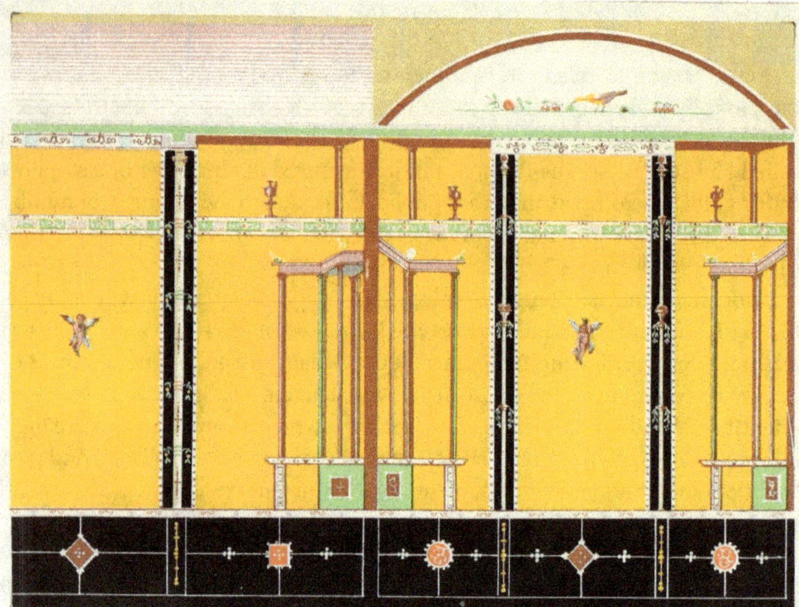

Figure 1.3: Presuhn E., 1878. Pompeji: Die Neuesten Ausgrabungen von 1874 bis 1878. Leipzig: Weigel. (III, Plate VII). Source: archive.org.

efficient use of the available page-space to convey the maximum amount of information about the walls-space: the decoration visible in both short walls (north and south) and only half of the repeating pattern in the long wall (west). After understanding the code, it becomes easy for the 3D modeller to unpack the information and appreciate its clever and functional arrangement that enabled Presuhn to document three walls in a single image.

2.4 Travelling mistakes

When working on a 3D visualisation of an historic building, a key component of the preliminary research is to gather all the relevant sources, primary and secondary, that are still available, and assess how and if they can be included in the new visualisation. It was during this research process around the Iseum in Pompeii that I came across the reproduction of a decorated niche in the temple of Isis. The etcher is Francesco Piranesi, possibly after a drawing of his more famous father, the architect and antiquarian Gian Battista Piranesi. Despite the reliability of the source, I was fairly sure that the niche depicted by the younger Piranesi in that illustration was not originally in the Pompeian Iseum. I subsequently discovered that the niche was actually located in another Pompeian building, the Praedia of Julia Felix, from which it had been moved by excision. The mistake, perhaps surprising coming from Piranesi, is quite understandable given the Isiac theme of the niche. However, before the information was challenged and corrected, it kept being replicated in other publications. In other words, Piranesi's illustration was plagiarised and republished without any acknowledgements, mistakes included. Of all the publications where Piranesi's original image was re-used and illegally reprinted, one of the most interesting for me was Donaldson's guide to Pompeii (1827). To appeal to the public, the illustrations that accompanied the guide were presented as copies "dal vero", and the author of the "original drawing" is proudly credited with his full military title, lieutenant colonel Cockburn, to add reliability to his "witnessing" of the antiquities. Not only is it very unlikely that Cockburn had made the same accidental misattribution as Francesco Piranesi, but his "original" drawing is just too close to Piranesi's, including the exact same light and shading, to be other than an undeclared copy. The misleading image kept travelling to subsequent publications, becoming more reliable the more it was reprinted, regardless of its actual accuracy. We find it again, more than seventy years later, in Gusman (1924), who, curiously, even attempts a more precise location of it in the Iseum, placing it in the main temple dedicated to the goddess. With scholarly practices changing, though, Gusman finally acknowledges the provenance of the image (that is attributed to Cockburne and not Piranesi), saving himself the embarrassment of pretending to have seen the phantomatic niche with his own eyes (Figure 1.4).

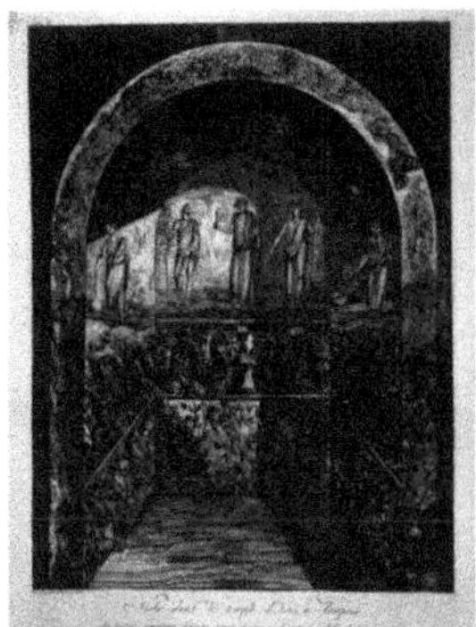
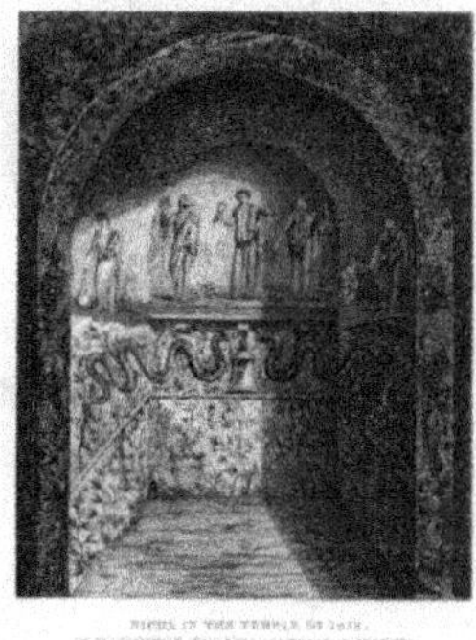
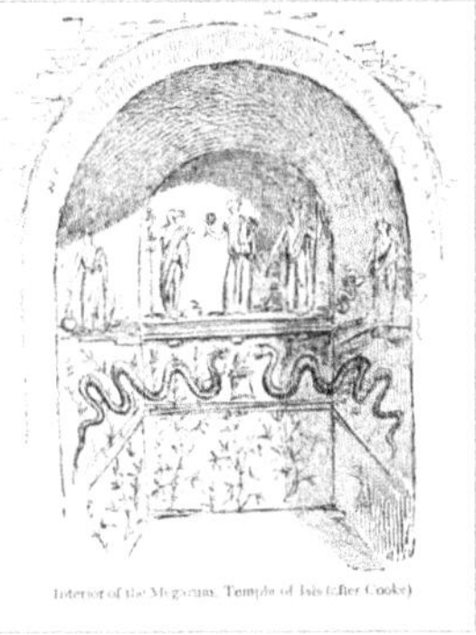

Figure 1.4: From left to right.

i) Piranesi, F. (illustrator and etcher). Niche dans le temple d'Isis, à Pompeia. In: Piranesi F., *Antiquités de la Grande Grèce aujourdhui Royaume de Naples ...*, Piranesi frères, 1804–1807, vol. III, Tav. I. Public domain. Source: Wikiart.
ii) Cockburn (Illustrator) & Cooke, W.B. (Etcher). Niche in the Temple of Isis (1827). In: Cooke, W. B., *Pompeii, illustrated with picturesque views, engraved by W. B. Cooke, from the original drawings of lieut. col. Cockburn ... and with plans and details of the public and domestic edifices, including the recent excavations, and a descriptive letterpress to each plate, by T. L. Donaldson, architect ... in two volumes*. Vol. 1. London, 1827. Public domain. Source: Arachne.
iii) Gusman, P. Interior of the Megarum, Temple of Isis. (1900) In Gusman, P., *Pompei, the city, its life & art*. London 1900. Public domain. Source: archive .org.

A blatant error like the one here discussed can turn into a means to investigate editorial and academic practices of the time, as well as ideas about authorship and attribution, deconstructing the popular narrative of the traveller recounting their "first hand" experience in Pompeii.

3. Conclusions

In this chapter, we discussed the semiotic relationship between 3D visualisations, the secondary sources that are often used as reference, and the original object of representation, but we have also highlighted how the material aspects of the visualisation practices, in 2 or 3D, influence such relationships. I used small, and perhaps anecdotal, case studies to support the following arguments:

3.1 Documentation is necessary

Documentation is an essential component of any research-based visual representation of historical cultural heritage. An accurate and complete documentation enables a 3D visualisation to be replicated and assessed, and to meet the standards of scientific publications. Documentation is also what allows the work of 3D authors today to be still used and understood in the future, detailing not only the technological specifications but also methodological choices and assumptions. In other words, documentation is a communication channel with the scholars of the future, and we should endeavour to keep this channel as open and clear as possible.

3.2 Secondary sources must be contextualised

Secondary sources are invaluable documents about the past, especially, but not only, when they depict buildings or other objects that have disappeared or changed substantially. Researching these sources has always been a key step in scholarly 3D visualisation, and they are often one of the most relevant components of accurate documentation. These documents, however, cannot be taken simply at their "literal" value, and need to be included in their larger historical and cultural context. This process not only enhances the philological accuracy of the 3D visualisation, helping to avoid mistakes and misinterpretations, but should also be considered as a crucial part of the research workflow, as it often leads to new research questions and a better and deeper understanding of the reception of the historical building that is reproduced.

3.3 Making (and re-making) is understanding

Creating a scholarly 3D visualisation of a historical building is a very complex process that blends traditional academic research with practical skills.

This very unusual act of "informed making" generates a deep understanding of the represented object and, even though the reproduction is entirely virtual, it forces the 3D author to think about the materiality of the building, its geometry, its spaces, its ways of being accessed and experienced. Secondary sources become an important component of the re-making of the building, as they are not only used as inspiration but are measured, cut, mirrored, duplicated, superimposed and wrapped around. Under this "making" perspective, it is easier for a 3D scholar to retro-engineer the ways in which these documents were produced in their times, and to re-discover and decode those practices that, maybe common at the time the documents were produced, are mostly lost to us today. Thinking of documentation in these terms makes it a bridge not only with our future collaborators but also with the authors of the past, rediscovering their methodologies and building on top of their work in a more aware and rewarding way.

3.4 What are we representing?

Last, after discussing signs, codes, referents and even ekphrasis, I think it is now reasonable to ask ourselves what is that a scholarly 3D visualisation is *actually* representing? I am convinced that seeing the original building (or object) as the true referent of a 3D visualisation is not only reductive and short sighted but also very likely to be wrong, at least from a semiotic point of view. Especially in the case of ancient and disappeared buildings, it is arguably impossible to represent the original building in all its aspects, as our only knowledge of it is heavily mediated by what others before us have seen, and recorded.

As scholars like Favro (1999 and 2006), Johanson (2009) and more recently Piccoli (2018) have argued, we should think of the referent of a 3D model not as the building itself but *our knowledge of* the building; a palimpsest of layers and layers of interpretations that have accumulated in time and enriched each other and fed the *aura* of the building. What we represent is the history of the building and its reception through time or, as it is called sometimes, its biography.

Our 3D visualisations can be summaries of the previous interpretations and, at the same time, they are just one further layer, one further take on the artistic, historical, and cultural universe to which the building we are representing belongs. Documentation is the best compass to explore such a universe.

4. References

Acton, H. (1956). *The Bourbons of Naples (1734–1825).* London: Methuen.

Allroggen-Bedel, A. (1993). Gli scavi di Ercolano nella politica culturale dei Borboni. *Ercolano, 1738–1988*. Roma: "L'Erma" di Bretschneider.

Andrews, N. (2010). Volcanic Rhythms: Sir William Hamilton's Love Affair with Vesuvius. *AA Files 60*, 9–15.

Baker, D. (2016). Defining Paradata in Heritage Visualization. In A. Bentkowska-Kafel, D. Baker & H. Denard (Eds.), *Paradata and Transparency in Virtual Heritage* (pp. 163–176). Farnham: Ashgate.

Bruhn, S. (2001). A concert of paintings:"Musical ekphrasis" in the twentieth century. *Poetics Today 22*(3), 551–605.

Blix, G. (2013). From Paris to Pompeii. In *From Paris to Pompeii*. University of Pennsylvania Press.

Carrillo Gea, J. M., Toval, A., Fernández Alemán, J. L., Nicolás, J., & Flores, M. (2013). The London Charter and the Seville Principles as sources of requirements for e-archaeology systems development purposes. *Virtual Archaeology Review 4*(9), 205–211.

Chard, C. (1999). *Pleasure and Guilt on the Grand Tour: Travel writing and imaginative geography, 1600–1830*. Manchester University Press.

D'Alconzo, P. (2002). *Picturae excisae: conservazione e restauro dei dipinti ercolanesi e pompeiani tra il 18 e 19 secolo*. Rome: L'Erma di Bretschneider.

Denard, H. (2012). A New Introduction to the London Charter. In A. Bentkowska-Kafel, D. Baker & H. Denard (Eds.), *Paradata and Transparency in Virtual Heritage* (pp. 57–71). Farnham: Ashgate. Retrieved from: http://www.londoncharter.org/introduction.html.

Donaldson, T. L. (1827). *Pompeii, illustrated with picturesque views, engraved by W. B. Cooke, from the original drawings of lieut. col. Cockburn ... and with plans and details of the public and domestic edifices, including the recent excavations, and a descriptive letterpress to each plate, by T. L. Donaldson, architect ... in two volumes*. London: W. B. Cooke.

Eco, U. (1975). *Trattato di Semiotica Generale*. Milan: Bompiani.

Elia, O. (1932). *Pitture murali e mosaici nel Museo Nazionale di Napoli*. La Libreria dello stato.

Earl, G. (2013). Modeling in archaeology: computer graphic and other digital pasts. *Perspectives on Science, 21*(2), 226–244.

Favro, D. (1999). Meaning and experience: Urban history from antiquity to the early modern period. *Journal of the Society of Architectural Historians, 58*(3), 364–373.

Favro, D. (2006). In the eyes of the beholder: Virtual Reality re-creations and academia. In L. Haselberger & J. Humphrey (Eds.), *Imaging Ancient Rome* (pp. 321–334). Portsmouth, RI: Journal of Roman Archaeology.

Favro, D. (2012). Se non è vero, è ben trovato (If Not True, It Is Well Conceived): Digital Immersive Reconstructions of Historical Environments. *Journal of the Society of Architectural Historians 71*(3), 273–77.

Favro, D., & Johanson, C. (2010). Death in motion: Funeral processions in the Roman Forum. *Journal of the Society of Architectural Historians 69*(1), 12–37.

Gordon, A. R. (2007). Subverting the secret of Herculaneum: archaeological espionage in the Kingdom of Naples. In V. Gardner Coates & J. Seydl (Eds.),

Antiquity Recovered: The Legacy of Pompeii and Herculaneum (pp. 37–57). Los Angeles, J. Paul Getty Museum.

Gusman, P. (1924). *Mural Decorations of Pompeii.* William Helburn, Incorporated.

Hermon, S. (2008). Reasoning in 3D: a Critical appraisal of the role of 3D modelling and virtual reconstructions in archaeology. In B. Frischer & A. Dakouri-Hild (Eds.), *Beyond Illustration: 2D and 3D Digital Technologies as Tools for Discovery in Archaeology*, Oxford: BAR International Series 1805.

Jansson, M. (2018). Ekphrasis and digital media. *Poetics Today 39*(2), 299–318.

Johanson, C. (2009). Visualizing history: modeling in the eternal city. *Visual Resources 25*(4), 403–418.

Lazer, E. (2009). *Resurrecting Pompeii.* London: Routledge.

Leppmann, F. (1968). *Pompeii in Fact and Fiction.* London: Elek.

Lopez-Menchero, V. M., & Grande, A. (2011, September). The principles of the Seville Charter. In *CIPA symposium proceedings* Vol. 2011, 2–6.

Mackenzie, W. M. (1910). *Pompeii.* London: A&C Black.

Mau, A. (1902). *Pompeii, Its Life and Art.* London: Macmillan.

McCarty, W. (2004). Modeling: a study in words and meanings. In S. Schreibman, R. Siemens & J. Unsworth (Eds.), *A Companion to Digital Humanities* (pp. 254–270). Oxford: Blackwell.

Moser, S. (2015). Reconstructing ancient worlds: reception studies, archaeological representation and the interpretation of ancient Egypt. *Journal of Archaeological Method and Theory, 22*, 1263–1308.

Mattusch, C. C. (2011). *Johann Joachim Winckelmann: Letter and Report on the Discoveries at Herculaneum.* Los Angeles: The J. Paul Getty Museum.

Neville Rolfe, E. (1888). *Pompeii: Popular and Practical.* Naples: Emil Prass 59–60 Piazza dei Martiri, Palazzo Partanna.

Piccoli, C. (2018). Reconstructing past cityscapes before the digital age: A view on Greek and Roman towns. In *Visualizing cityscapes of Classical antiquity: from early modern reconstruction drawings to digital 3D models* (pp. 6–49). Oxford: Archaeopress.

Presuhn, E. (1878). *Pompeji: Die Neuesten Ausgrabungen von 1874 bis 1878*. Leipzig: Weigel.

Ramage, N. H. (2013). Flying maenads and cupids: Pompeii, Herculaneum, and eighteenth-century decorative arts. In C.C. Mattusch (Ed.), *Rediscovering the Ancient World on the Bay of Naples, 1710–1890* (pp. 161–176). Washington, DC: National Gallery of Art.

Risser, E., & Saunders, D. (Eds.) (2013). *The restoration of ancient bronzes: Naples and beyond.* Los Angeles: J. Paul Getty Publications.

Roberts, C. (2015). Living with the ancient Romans: past and present in eighteenth-century encounters with Herculaneum and Pompeii. *Huntington library quarterly 78*(1), 61–85.

De Caro, S. (Ed.) (1992). *Alla ricerca di Iside. Analisi, studi e restauri dell'Iseo Pompeiano nel Museo di Napoli.* Roma: ARTI.

Ternite, W. (ca. 1839–1858). *Wandgemälde aus Pompeji und Herculanum nach den Zeichnungen und Nachbildungen in Farben : von W. Ternite ; mit einem erläuternden Text von C. O. Müller.* Berlin: Reimer.

Vitale, V. (2016). Transparent, Multivocal, Cross-disciplinary: The Use of Linked Open Data and a Community-developed RDF Ontology to Document and Enrich 3D Visualisation for Cultural Heritage. In: Bodard, G., & Romanello, M. (Eds.), *Digital Classics Outside the Echo-Chamber: Teaching, Knowledge Exchange & Public Engagement* (pp. 147–168). London: Ubiquity Press.

Walsh, K. (2002). *The representation of the past: museums and heritage in the post-modern world.* London: Routledge.

Webb, R. (1999). Ekphrasis ancient and modern: the invention of a genre. *Word & Image 15*(1), 7–18.

CHAPTER 2

Research resources of Japanese Mokkan: Turning information on ancient wooden tablets into research data

Hajime Baba
Nara National Institute

Abstract

This paper focuses on ancient Japanese *Mokkan* (woodcuts) to discuss the background, current status and issues in the digitisation of cultural heritage, including matters of research, protection, and legal rights. As valuable primary sources, *Mokkan* are important in a wide range of academic fields, including history and linguistics. On the other hand, they are extremely fragile and fragmented. Digital technologies can support an improvement in access and study of this material. In this paper, we illustrate the current efforts to improve digitisation workflows and strengthen research capacity: we discuss open data and open access, equal and transparent inter-institutional collaboration, the application of the IIIF standard, the construction of a character database search system, and the application of Deep Learning technology.

The issue of open data and open access is particularly challenging in Japan, where there is still a gap between the legal principles and the actual situation

How to cite this book chapter:
Baba, H. 2023. Research resources of Japanese Mokkan: Turning information on ancient wooden tablets into research data. In: Palladino, C. and Bodard, G. (Eds.), *Can't Touch This: Digital Approaches to Materiality in Cultural Heritage*. Pp. 29–49. London: Ubiquity Press. DOI: https://doi.org/10.5334/bcv.c. License: CC BY 4.0

of cultural heritage institutions. In addition, information needs to be standardized and aggregated, but at the same time the specificity and historical characteristics of the different materials need to be addressed. In this paper, we strongly advocate for the establishment of methods for sharing cultural heritage data. In humanities research, the linkage, open access and standardization of information has become essential, not only to foster data-driven research but also to ensure wide access and dissemination of cultural heritage in Japan. For this reason, we encourage equal and open collaboration not just across cultural heritage stakeholders, but across society as a whole.

チャプターの概要

本稿では、木簡を中心に、デジタル化による文化財の調査・研究、保護・法的権利等について、経緯・現状と課題を説明する。

木簡は、貴重な一次資料として、歴史学・言語学等幅広い学問分野で重要である。一方、木簡は非常に脆弱で断片化が著しい。そのため公開が困難であり、研究には情報の集約が必須である。ここに情報技術への渇望が存在する。

現在は、デジタル化・オープンデータおよびオープンアクセスの強化、平等・継続・透明な機関間連携の実現、デジタル化ワークフローの改善や研究力強化に取り組んでおり、これらを IIIF（International Image Interoperability Framework）規格の利用や、「歴史的漢字データベース検索システム」の枠組構築、Deep Learning 技術の応用などで実現しようとしている。

オープンデータ化の現状を見ると、まだまだ法制度の理念と、実態は乖離している。また、情報は集約・標準化される必要があるが、同時に資料の特異性や歴史的特性にも対応する必要がある。これらの課題を克服し、文化遺産データを共有する方法の確立が必要である。

人文科学研究では、データ駆動型研究の進展など、情報の連携、オープンアクセス、標準化が不可欠となっている。研究機関間だけでなく、社会全体との対等でオープンな連携を求めていきたいと考えている。

1. Introduction

A few decades ago, digital methods and tools were considered just one of many approaches to conducting research and preserving material records, and the only concern about their design was to make them convenient to use.[1] Today,

[1] The present contribution includes research findings pertaining to the JSPS-funded "Development of Integrated knowledge through Establishment of an Interactive Research Scheme based on the Open-Data of Research Resources for Mokkan and Related Topics" (18H05221). The author would

they are the backbone of institutional and research practices, and thinking about digital technologies simply as "tools" is no longer appropriate. Digitization now provides an opportunity to fundamentally review and rebuild traditional workflows, reassess the very objectives of academic research, and rediscover the essential ideas and needs at the origin of traditional analog methods. This reaffirmation extends even more widely to the objectives in handling and managing cultural heritage, from discovery and preservation workflows to the management of legal rights and access (Yamada, Nakamura, Shibuya, Ohmukai & Inoue 2021).

This paper deals with the current project of the digitization of ancient Japanese *Mokkan* at the Nara National Research Institute for Cultural Properties.[2] It will illustrate how the process of digitizing a very specific category of premodern artifact has become, over the years, an opportunity to fundamentally rethink an entire workflow of research, information management, and dissemination to a public audience. This case study is used to further advocate the need for the Japanese government and research institutions to actively pursue open-access policies and practices in the digital publication of cultural heritage material, and to reaffirm some important principles in the translation of analog practices in the realm of digital technologies.

2. The history of Japanese *Mokkan*

In Japanese history and related fields, wooden man-made objects with India ink inscriptions are referred to as *Mokkan*, or "wooden documents." *Mokkan* belongs to the category of excavated artifacts since most of them are recovered from archaeological sites; further, *Mokkan* is classified based on the material of the writing medium, wood, one of the most widely used writing surfaces in Japan after paper (Figure 2.1).

Similar categories of artifacts exist in other areas. There are inscriptions on metal, stone, or earthenware. Similar to wooden documents, bamboo slips with ink inscriptions from China are collectively referred to as *jiǎndú*. Other examples of writing media made of plant materials include the white birch documents of Novgorod or the palm-leaf documents of Southeast Asia. Roman wooden tablets include writing tablets with a wax coating, widely seen on Roman frescos such as the wall painting of Terentius Neo and his wife in

like to express his gratitude for help and advice to Taizo Yamada, University of Tokyo, and Janase Pater, Nara National Research Institute for Cultural Properties. The editors and reviewers, especially Jun Ogawa, are also thanked for their invaluable understanding and assistance.

[2] Nara National Research Institute for Cultural Properties: https://www.nabunken.go.jp/english/.

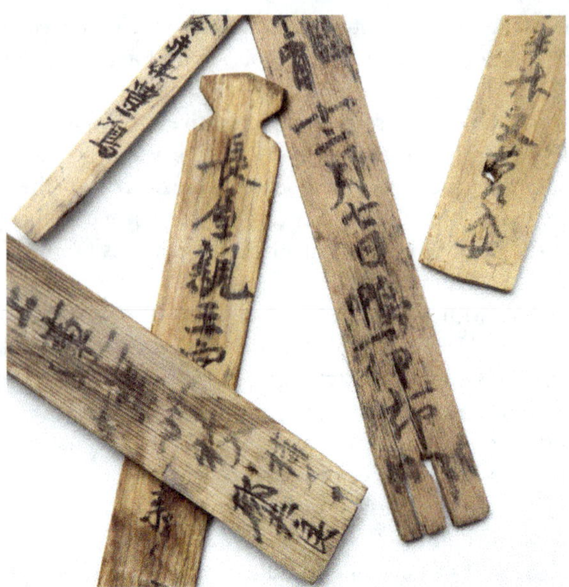

Figure 2.1: An example of *Mokkan*. Credits: https://colbase.nich.go.jp/?locale=en. Reproduced with permission.

Pompeii, or rougher ones where the writing is performed directly on the tablet with ink, such as the Vindolanda tablets of England.[3]

There are four types of environments in which *Mokkan* are commonly found: arid areas, permafrost, wetlands, and water. In all these environments, the activities of wood-rotting fungi are restricted. Japanese *Mokkan* is mainly excavated from wetlands: in this environment, the supply of oxygen is cut off by moisture; however, the decay of the wood is progressive, albeit slow. *Mokkan* is, therefore, usually decayed and deteriorated considerably at the moment of their finding, which makes them extremely fragile. In addition, damage, breakage, and the fading of the inscriptions can also occur depending on the characteristics of the soil. The influence of metal ions in the groundwater or the presence of wood grain can also make deciphering the inscriptions difficult. In addition, information is usually fragmentary because the writing medium itself is small, and there is a high percentage of shavings generated during the reuse of the wood (up to 80% in the case of the Nara Palace Site). Because of their fragility, it is difficult to put *Mokkan* on public display, or even to conduct regular observations on the artifacts themselves (Figure 2.2).

When referring to "ancient Japanese *Mokkan*" in this paper, we refer to *Mokkan* attested from the end of the seventh century to the end of the eighth century, when *Mokkan* were most widely used in the Japanese archipelago.

[3] Vindolanda Tablets Online: http://vindolanda.csad.ox.ac.uk/.

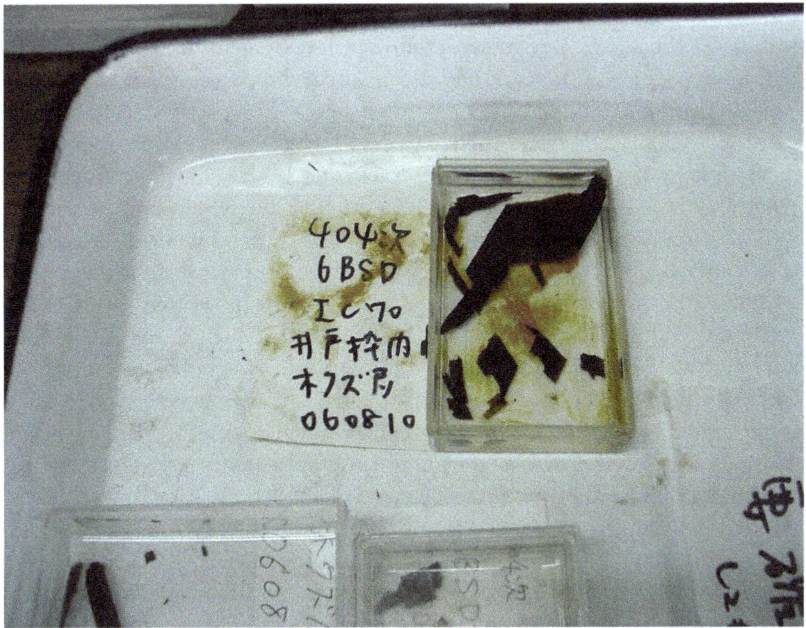

Figure 2.2: The state of wooden shavings from *Mokkan* immediately after excavation. Credits: https://www.nabunken.go.jp/. Reproduced with permission.

This period overlaps with the formative years of the Japanese state and makes *Mokkan* especially important documents to reconstruct aspects of Japanese premodern history that are not documented otherwise.

The number of *Mokkan* excavated throughout Japan is approximately 470,000: 310,000 exemplars are hosted by the Nara Institute alone. The Nara Institute was established in the mid-1950s with the main purpose of performing comprehensive research on Japanese ancient cultural heritage, with a special focus on the ancient city of Nara and the Nara and Fujiwara Palace site. Before *Mokkan* were recovered from the Nara Palace site in the late 1960s, information about eighth-century Japan was primarily provided by legal documents, such as the Ritsuryo legal code or the Rikkokushi, a historical chronicle compiled by the court. These were official court documents, and as such, they did not provide a complete picture of life in that period. A further complication is that they only exist in copies, and there are no extant originals.

The *Mokkan* found at the Nara Palace site, on the other hand, are primary and original sources about the daily life of the court. They are also free of any intentional editing, like in the case of the *Nihon Shoki*. *Mokkan* represent first-hand accounts: there is less risk of forgery or falsification because they were discovered through archaeological excavations, and they were discarded on the same site where they were produced and used. Moreover, as their number increases with new excavations, we can expect further developments in the future.

The importance of *Mokkan* lies also in their ability to document the process of creation and establishment of a Japanese writing system from Chinese writing: the kana script and the kanji-kana mixed text. *Mokkan* is located at the periphery of the so-called "Chinese character sphere," the pre-modern East Asian cultural sphere where ideas, religion, administration, and technology were communicated through the use of Chinese characters. Most of the characters inscribed on *Mokkan* are of Chinese origin, and many of the documents written here could be better described as Japanese texts written with Chinese characters. While official documents and chronicles, such as the Rikkokushi, were considered formal documents, and therefore were only written in plain Chinese (the most formal typology of writing), *Mokkan* were considered less formal and therefore could use less formal writing. In everyday writing, various methods were developed to adapt Chinese characters to the Japanese language: while most of the focus was on the shape of the letters, sometimes Chinese characters were given Japanese readings, or the Chinese pronunciation of a character was used to represent something unrelated with a similar sound. This mix-and-match approach to Chinese characters laid the foundation for the current Japanese writing system, and *Mokkan* documented the process through which the Japanese people learned to express their language in writing through the adaptation of Chinese writing (Baba 2022).[4]

Other scripts in the vicinity of the Sinographic cultural sphere, include the Chữ Nôm of Vietnam, which are local adaptations of Chinese characters. We believe that the Sinographic cultural sphere can be seen both as a single coherent entity or a collection of smaller cultural spheres based on local variations of the Chinese writing system. Recent years have seen a rise in interest in approaches to East-Asian tablets that try to analyze several of these local cultural spheres as a whole rather than as isolated entities. Therefore, the characters inscribed on Japanese *Mokkan* are not only important to elucidate the early establishment of the Japanese state, but can also provide hints to reconstruct the broader development of Japanese civilization.

Mokkan are fragile, fragmentary, raw materials, fascinating, and incredibly troublesome. Their peculiarities, due to their status of preservation, their fragility, and the recording of information about them, constitute an interesting case study about current digitization practices of archaeological findings. We believe that the discussion developed around the digitization of *Mokkan* may provide clues to solve problems that are common not only to various inscribed artifacts, especially those made of plant materials but in general to the application of digital technologies to the preservation and management of material cultural heritage in Japan (Yamada, Inoue & Yamaga 2019).

---

[4] Wooden Tablet Database: https://mokkanko.nabunken.go.jp/en/.

3. Early status of research on ancient Japanese *Mokkan*

As mentioned above, *Mokkan* is incredibly fragile and highly fragmented in both form and content. Because of this characteristic, research on them is conducted necessarily in a comparative fashion: typically, researchers of *Mokkan* have to supplement fragmented information, attempting to combine as many artifacts as possible, cross-referencing fragments, as well as comprehensively examining related materials (such as legislative documents) and conditions of finding (such as the aspect of the site, type of soil, etc.). In other words, to obtain the latent information from *Mokkan*, we have to take a comprehensive and comparative approach. This is made difficult by the very material condition of *Mokkan*, which prohibits extensive analysis.

Extensive digitization and virtual preservation are extremely effective ways to overcome these problems. This was the main driver behind the effort of the Nara National Research Institute for Cultural Properties, in establishing a database of *Mokkan* in the late 1990s, which was later released in 1999 as the Wooden Tablet Database (Baba 2019).

Initially, the database was simply designed to allow researchers to search for inscriptions, including fragmentary ones. The information hosted in the database consisted of data taken from print catalogs and publications, which were more or less systematically turned into metadata. This information included the basic records of print publications from archaeological excavations and the recovery of the materials, as it had been consolidated through practice at the Nara Institute during the excavation of the palace site in the 1960s–1980s: these included the information usually recorded on site, such as the name of the excavation, survey order, excavation grid, excavated remains, stratigraphy and date, and provisional names and identification for the artifacts; later, at the restoration stage, official identification through an R number (a unique number assigned to the wooden batts for storage), storage number, photographs with records, and other information, such as observations on the wood, letters, and handwriting, tree species and woodcutting. This information was transcribed and turned into metadata, and accompanied by tags, such as ancient places and personal names, to assist the exegesis of the material.

This bookkeeping system had been developed gradually, during various stages of the excavation, and it was fundamentally conceived for dissemination through analog methods. Therefore, it did not always have enough structure to be readily digitized. For example, there was a lack of a clear distinction between provenance and artifact information, and interpretive information (such as people or place names) was at the same hierarchical level as material information, such as the legal quantity and storage location. Certain aspects, however, were retained: the combination of excavation grid data and R-number was used as ID for the wooden tablet.

Although at a relatively rudimentary stage of development, the database marked a turning point because it allowed the comprehensive study of fragmented information and its publication on the Internet. Although it was not recognized at the time, the accumulation of digitized metadata on *Mokkan* provided the foundation for all further developments.

A second stage of development was the addition of images, which were connected to the database records. The earlier images consisted of scanned versions of the black-and-white photographs attached to the archaeological inventories. These images were only regarded as supplementary materials, and their quality was low. However, the linking of textual and visual information about each artifact and their publication online as a single entry made it possible to perform cross-searches on fragments, and integrate the photographs of the *Mokkan* with information about their text.

In 2005, we also developed and released an online character dictionary, which was originally designed to allow searches on the characters inscribed on *Mokkan*. This was designed to meet the demand of users who wanted to search for images of specific characters. The database connected a search input based on character codes with images of the characters as they appeared on *Mokkan*: the design was based on how researchers looked up samples of characters when deciphering documents, and therefore it simply translated a traditional paper-based work procedure into the digital world. In essence, it allowed users to upload a small image of a piece of a wood document with an ambiguous character, and show similar characters from the database (Watanabe, Baba & Kurushima 2016; *cf.* Onitsuka, Oyama, Yamada, Inoue & Uchida 2018; Nakamura, Liu, Miyazaki, Inoue, Daisen & Yamada 2022).

The idea that a character search would start from an image, and not from a text, was a very important conceptual and processual innovation. Normally, it is very hard to look up characters that are difficult to decipher, and dictionaries are often ineffective in recognizing hand drawings or require cumbersome scrolling through every character with the same radical or number of strokes (Ly, Nguyen, Nguyen & Nakagawa 2019). The establishment of the images as the foundation for the research work meant that they were no longer regarded as supplementary material to the text and metadata, but they represented effectively an information layer at the same level of importance (Nakamura, Liu & Yamada 2022). The process of digitization offered the opportunity to pile layers of information on top of each other, going from a text-based workflow to one that managed multiple data types. This marked a point in the development where the older black-and-white images were supplemented with additional layers, which included color photographs, infrared photographs, and hand-drawn illustrations, to support the decipherment of the characters as they appeared on the inscriptions.

Another important result of this process was the realization that the database could serve a much wider audience than just researchers of *Mokkan*, and that its generalization could provide the opportunity for full-scale inter-institutional cooperation (see below).

This project has been gradually developed to go beyond the dimension of the character database. In parallel with the image database, other important information about *Mokkan* has been digitized: for example, the information on names of places and people, and literature references, has been made available in a machine-readable format. Location information of *Mokkan* and other artifacts is currently available in a WebGIS interface, where users can search by geographical area, but also object type, name, and prefecture (https://heritagemap.nabunken.go.jp/main).

Moreover, images of *Mokkan* have been updated to versions taken with digital cameras, which allow the automatic conversion of the photographs into data. We also developed a method to acquire multispectral images, which is fundamental when observing wooden tablets, whose ink marks are often obscured.

Today, it is possible to have a system where a single computer connected to the Internet is sufficient for deciphering inscriptions on *Mokkan*. As we move forward, the effort in the digitization of Japanese wooden tablets is increasingly moving in the direction of applying internationally recognized standards for information aggregation, data management, interoperability, and collaboration.

After more than thirty years of collaboration, we are promoting the following fundamental points of development for the current phase of work:

1. Standardization of information and image management through IIIF (International Image Interoperability Framework) standards and Linked Open Data practices; and applications of Deep Learning technologies to improve digitization workflows and to strengthen research capabilities (Clanuwat, Bober-Irizar, Kitamoto, Lamb, Yamamoto & Ha 2018).
2. Implementation of an explicit research and development agenda for Japanese cultural heritage, to empower Open Data and Open Access practices through digitization.
3. Implementation of equal, continuous, and transparent inter-institutional cooperation, within the framework of the Multi-database Search System for Historical Chinese Characters.

4. Current status in the digitization of ancient Japanese *Mokkan*

4.1 Application of IIIF Data Standards

IIIF is becoming a global standard in the field of humanities research, and it enables the creation and publication of high-definition, high-quality metadata, and annotations, at the same time ensuring high versatility and open access (Takada, Fukuyama, Tsutsumi & Kosukegawa 2018).

The IIIF standard includes an Image API, Presentation API, Authentication API, and Content Search API (Liu, Nakamura & Yamada 2022; Baba, Takada & Kuwata 2019). The Image API and Authentication API are standards used for describing image status and rights, and information is organized accordingly. The Image API is used to display specific data about the image (e.g. area, color, format), but also information such as size and ownership of the material object. The Authentication API typically supports various measures of access restriction for images protected by copyright, and it manages permissions to view comments, annotations, and other types of content.

The Mirador Annotation tool is used to associate various categories of information directly with the images of the artifacts as Web Annotations. The workflow adopted by the Nara Institute is based on the *Mokkan* image, and it reproduces a process already adopted by the Academia Sinica in Taiwan. The character images are annotated, and character codes are superimposed on these annotations. This information is stored as JSON files, but we are also aiming at the creation of a CSV output format. Therefore, after searching for one character, it is possible to cross-reference the entire *Mokkan* where that character appears. Other workflows adopted by other institutes are slightly different: for example, the National Institute of Japanese Literature uses individual character images as the basis, and superimposes metadata, including character codes, as annotation on the images. However, even if the data can be prepared in different ways, as long as it complies with IIIF it can be exchanged across institutions. This will be achieved by improving and applying the 'Repair System' developed and operated by the Historiographical Institute of the University of Tokyo, which consolidates various records of repairs of old documents and observation findings as annotations on historical images. Once this system is in operation, almost all of the information acquired during the process of management of *Mokkan* will be digitized, and it will allow the direct conversion of information originally appearing in print.

The Presentation API enables aggregation of various types of information as cross-referenced annotations based on standardized descriptions, and it is typically used for displaying graphic objects. It is used to describe and display Web Annotations and other metadata related to the *Mokkan* images in the database. This allows storing text images associated with metadata (e.g. character codes, holding institution, etc.) as aggregated information, which can be structured and exported as individual layers as needed. The process of metadata encoding is currently being restructured according to the CIDOC-CRM standard for the best compatibility with Linked Open Data systems.[5] Work is also underway to switch to a system based on ISO 14721 (OAIS reference model) for the creation of information and research resources.

The conventional Content Search API, which is generally used to search within a single manifest, was judged unsuitable because the system needs to search across a large number of manifests, although on a small scale. There-

[5] The CIDOC Conceptual Reference Model (https://www.cidoc-crm.org/) is the most important data model for information integration in the field of cultural heritage.

fore, further implementation is experimented to improve the performance of this API.

The standardization of historical information is a complex process, which requires balancing the recording of detailed individual observations with the requirements of the standard. Sometimes, this means discriminating between types of information regarded as fundamental, and others that end up being ignored, and considered rather as interpretive observations (Unsworth 2000; Shibayama, Morimoto, Tashiro, Kameda, Yamada & Hara 2018). In other words, this process may happen at the expense of certain descriptive aspects of the data for the benefit of exchange and interoperability. This is particularly important in the context of inter-institutional cooperation, where each institution manages different kinds of materials, periods, and records.

A practical example is the process of character decipherment. With traditional analog methods, several types of information are recorded about the characteristics of individual occurrences in context: not just the character code, but also a description of how it appears, writing habits, stroke styles, etc. This information is suppressed when the character is associated with a specific code in a digital database: character codes, most notably Unicode, are a highly versatile way of describing written information, as they ensure seamless exchange of data across different platforms and unique identification. Modern digital research simply cannot do without the association or creation of Unicode characters. However, the external information associated with the specific occurrence of a character in context, such as calligraphic style, writing style, personal habits of calligraphers, or stroke styles, could not be reproduced in Unicode and is therefore suppressed when individual occurrences get associated with a standardized instance.[6]

For this reason, it is also essential to associate object records with high-quality reproductions that can be considered "copies" of the originals. Furthermore, it is essential to allow users to access this material so that they can also record their observations in the form of annotations, and freely accumulate descriptive information. The joint availability of digital copies and standardized metadata is the way to achieve interoperability through versatility. The release of information that is as close as possible to being a "copy" of the original, such as high-resolution images, is fundamental. These reproductions can be used for detailed observation and research, alongside standardized metadata. For this reason, we are preparing born-digital data of visible light and infrared images,

6 For this point, in Japan, the Center for Open Data in the Humanities (CODH) has recently been promoting the 'curation API' (http://codh.rois.ac.jp/iiif/curation/index.html.en) and made it possible to have a character, its images and other external information together in the common format of IIIF standard. See also Filosa, Gad & Bodard (Chapter 3 in this volume), section 2.2 on the relationship between text transcription, image and explicit encoding.

and in the future, we are considering producing 3D reproductions. Moreover, it is important to release image data in a type and size that is easy to use, even if institutions manage higher-quality and resolution images.

One of the fundamental needs is to strengthen the connection between annotations and related information, and the material object that they describe. Therefore, we are re-building our databases by integrating a production workflow that allows the generation of data (including pre-existing metadata and unstructured observations) in the form of annotations linked to the digital copy of the object.

The annotation workflow, while it allowed user annotation for characters and strokes, was not feasible to generate information about stroke order at a database level. The plan is to combine it with a system of information acquisition about stroke order, developed in the context of the Web App Nazorkun, a citizen science project for acquiring brush stroke order information from general users (Hatano & Baba 2022). Furthermore, a prototype of a wood grain eraser AI system has been completed as an auxiliary tool to sharpen wood grain images and make strokes easier to detect (Terras 2006). The system uses deep learning to extract the outline of the woodblock and ink marks from the woodblock images. The main goal is to facilitate the observation of the materials (e.g. with automatic retrieval of character images) and deepen character observations on them, using the generated output as a starting point to implement the range of information available, especially in the stroke order estimation system (Ohyama, Hatano & Baba 2020).

As a part of this development, we also designed a learning application for children. This application was initially developed as a citizen science project to accumulate records on the stroke order of characters seen on *Mokkan*, to broaden social participation in research. Later, it was developed into a learning platform for elementary and junior high school students, to encourage familiarization and learning with the Japanese culture of writing. This project was well-received by the public and it became a tool for both social participation in research and dissemination for educational use.

Finally, it is important to enable cross-references across different data types, so we are building a Linked Open Data system to appropriately link our data with other institutional repositories.[7] On the one hand, this will lead to a clear distinction and acknowledgment of the role of each piece of information (and managing institution) in the digital ecosystem on *Mokkan* research, while at the same time allowing seamless data aggregation and discovery (Baba 2021).

[7] Japan Search (https://jpsearch.go.jp/) is a good example of Linked Open Data resources about Japanese Cultural Heritage.

4.2 Open Data and Open Access

Open Data needs to be the foundation for this process. The publication and sharing of research data is a method of promoting research in the new era, where large amounts of data can be easily produced, and it is also the responsibility of those involved in research.

While Japan's law for the Protection of Cultural Property clearly states that "cultural properties are the common property of the people", the reality is that the concrete operation of promoting and preserving it is the "burden of the beneficiaries" who are tasked with its curation. In the practical application of Open Data technologies and standards, Japan is considerably lagging behind, especially outside of the research sector. While the government is taking the lead in promoting digitisation and open access,[8] there is still a long way to go to better position the country within a global context.

Globally, Open Data is being promoted at an accelerated pace, with the G8 2013 Summit concluding an agreement on an Open Data Charter. In 2016, the G7 Science and Technology Ministerial Meeting "Tsukuba Communiqué" (Tsukuba, Ibaraki) issued a joint statement that, among other things, emphasized the need of Open Data and sharing policies for Japan.[9] In 2020, the official Japanese translation of the FAIR Data Principles (Wilkinson et al. 2016) was published.[10]

The Law for the Protection of Cultural Properties is the central cultural heritage law in Japan. The chief aim of the law is to "preserve and utilize cultural properties, thereby contributing to the cultural improvement of the people and to the advancement of world culture" (Art. 1). The broad principle is an official acknowledgment that "cultural property is indispensable for a correct understanding of the country's history and culture, and that it forms the basis for cultural improvement and development" (Art. 3). The law also makes various provisions with the direct involvement of the general public, governmental institutions, and individual owners, in the preservation and promotion of Japanese cultural heritage. More specifically, Article 4 stipulates that "the general public shall sincerely cooperate with the measures taken by the Government and the Authorities" in the application of the Law, and that "owners and other persons concerned with cultural property [...] shall preserve it carefully for the public good, and shall endeavor to make cultural use of it,

8 See, for example, the open data portal of the Japanese public administration (https://data.e-gov.go.jp/info/en) and the current discussion on the application of Open Data standards between the USA and Japan (https://liquitous.com/lisearch/journal/2020/09/30/317/).

9 Tsukuba Communiqué: https://www8.cao.go.jp/cstp/english/others/20160517communique.pdf.

10 The Fair Data Principles: https://biosciencedbc.jp/about-us/report/fair-data-principle/.

including, as far as possible, *making it available to the public*" (Art. 4.2). At the same time, however, the same article clearly states the preservation of ownership and property rights (Art. 4.3).

In 2016, the Basic Law for the Promotion of the Use of Public and Private Data was enacted to oblige the State and local governments to the use of Open Data. Although this law mainly covers administrative data, its spirit, and direction are considered to expand onto cultural heritage management as well.

In the case of cultural property managed by the government and public institutions, the spirit of this legislation has been actively pursued, and the dissemination of knowledge about the Japanese cultural heritage is actively encouraged. For example, archaeological sites and artifacts and the so-called rescue archaeology are being surveyed and published as part of cultural property protection management. On the other hand, however, the specific application of Open Data and Open Access practices is more complex at various levels.

In terms of the spirit of the law, it seems that the open digitization of cultural heritage is precisely the type of practice that should be promoted and encouraged because it pursues at the same time the goals of preservation and protection through the creation of digital reproductions and the goals of dissemination and promotion through open access publications.

However, on the one hand, the burden of planning and creating digitized resources is entirely placed locally, on the institutions that host cultural heritage collections (see also Takata & Yanase 2021). On the other hand, there is the question of the protection of property rights, which intersects with several other complex legislative questions.

Property rights in the area of cultural heritage include, in addition to ownership of the property, usufruct rights of artifacts, or of the site of excavation, of the surrounding areas, material infrastructures involved, and copyright. These aspects are only minimally covered by the Law on the Protection of Cultural Property, and it is necessary to refer to laws that guarantee separate rights for each area. For example, the ownership of excavated cultural heritage is also governed by the Lost and Found Property Act, but a full explanation of this legislative body would be too extensive for the space of this article.

In other words, it is very difficult to navigate through the various legal implications of digitally publishing cultural heritage data in Japan, partly because there is little direct legal precedent in this area. So, the National Institute for Cultural Heritage, the umbrella organization of the Nara National Research Institute, is taking careful measures and holding study groups with lawyers and lecturers to better understand the implications of copyright legislation.

The current status of *Mokkan* digital data is as follows. First of all, we have to do with artifacts that were created in the 7th century, so there is no author's copyright. Flat photographs of the wood tablets are mainly overhead photographs, and they are regarded as "reproductions" and do not accrue fresh copyright under the current legislation. Therefore, the main aspect to be considered is the ownership rights of the institutions that host and preserve

Mokkan collections. Public institutions in Japan can pursue public data disclosure only after legal consultations and official agreements: for example, the Nara Institute is pursuing this effort with various other entities that host *Mokkan* collections, including the Kyushu Historical Museum, the Kunitachi City Board of Education, Hamamatsu City Board of Education, Higashihiroshima City and the Tohoku Museum of History.[11]

However, the fact that institutions claim ownership rights on cultural heritage collections is a serious hindrance to institutional collaboration in Japan. Research institutions are among the major stakeholders and managers of Japanese cultural heritage: they play a central role not only in the creation of research data, but also in managing rights, ensuring the preservation, and promoting access. Furthermore, they are chiefly responsible for the privately owned materials that they manage and must ensure that the owners' rights are adequately protected according to the law. On the other hand, this exclusivity encouraged a tendency to build extremely specialized resources that emphasized the particularity of individual collections: this approach was seen as a way to provide the public only with the highest quality of information while ensuring that the institution responsible for the management of the collection would retain rights and authority on it. This mechanism created the conditions to seriously hinder cooperation and accessibility of Japanese cultural heritage data: on the one hand, there was the concern that data published openly could be affected by lack of quality control, and on the other, there is still a lack of infrastructure and legislative clarity on ownership and copyright.

For these reasons, efforts in inter-institutional cooperation are exceptional in Japan, and institutions must operate under very specific conditions to ensure a good outcome.

[11] A related project is the online publication of the *Journal of Mokkan Studies* (*Mokkan Kenkyu*). This is a research journal published annually by the *Mokkan* Gakkai (Society of *Mokkan* Studies), an academic society that aims to conduct comprehensive research on *Mokkan* and that has strong institutional connections with the Nara institute. It publishes information on the excavation of tablets from all over Japan, as well as articles and book reviews. The journal is already at issue 45, and a vast amount of information has been disseminated through it. The digital publication of the issues was preceded by the obtainment of the consent to publication by the various authors, and for the drawings and photographs the consent of the institution holding the material was obtained (even for drawings, which are normally considered public domain, since they are copies of excavated artifacts, we preferred to err on the side of caution and ask for permission). As a result, the rights to the data published in PDF format are centrally owned by the *Mokkan* Gakkai, but are not currently considered open data.

4.3 Inter-institutional cooperation

The database established by the Nara Institute alone would be sufficient if its only focus were on *Mokkan* themselves. However, when we move towards the digitization of historical characters, we have to acknowledge that images of historical characters are not limited to *Mokkan*, but include many other artifacts—especially documents written on paper. Researchers of *Mokkan* often look up samples of characters used on paper documents. Therefore, it is desirable to have a digitized database that allows comparison and cross-reference of such diverse and rich sources of character images. Therefore, in 2008, we developed and released a term-linked search system in cooperation with the University of Tokyo's Historiographical Institute, which hosts a database of paper-based character images from the thirteenth to sixteenth centuries (Yamada & Inoue 2018).[12]

This project marked the first official collaboration between research institutes in the humanities in Japan, and it was unprecedented in the history of Japanese cultural heritage management: to break the barriers and realize this collaboration, it was necessary to build a shared understanding of the core ideas and goals to pursue, from the conceptualization stage to the concrete implementation, while respecting the uniqueness and particularity of each institution. The engagement in this deeper discourse provided the conditions for an inter-institutional research initiative that went beyond the mere creation of a joint database, and it also led to other organizations taking an interest in the project, placing the conditions for the exploration of multi-organizational collaboration.

On the one hand, it was necessary to manage the concrete differences that marked the creation of very different resources: the *Mokkan* at the Nara Institute on one side, and the paper documents of Tokyo on the other side. These artifacts were very different in material, history, origin, and even period (*Mokkan* being 6th–7th century and paper documents ranging from the 13th to the 17th century): consequently, they had been handled very differently in research and preservation, and the data was created in very different ways. These differences need to be reconciled. An indispensable condition for inter-institutional cooperation was a common commitment in the direction of a more substantial disclosure of the data, through practices of standardization and increased accessibility of the information.

Looking forward, it is desirable to establish a system where all kinds of research resources can be mutually shared, and a relationship of mutual trust among institutions is essential. In 2020, the Nara Institute and various research parties, including the University of Tokyo, the National Institute of Japanese Literature, the National Institute for Japanese Language and Linguistics, the Academia Sinica, and the Kyoto University Research Center for Cultural

[12] Multi-database Search System for Historical Chinese Characters: https://mojiportal.nabunken.go.jp/en/.

Sciences, co-signed and released a Declaration of Cooperation with the common goal of creating common specifications for the digitization and open dissemination of their cultural heritage data (Nara National Research Institute for Cultural Properties, University of Tokyo, Historiographical Literature, National Institute of Japanese Literature, National Institute for Japanese Language and Linguistics, Kyoto University Research Centre for the Cultural Sciences and Institute of History and Philology, Academia Sinica 2020a). This declaration was followed by an Open Data Specification, currently in its first edition, which establishes guidelines for the creation of open data standards, with the explicit intent of following IIIF specifications (Nara National Research Institute for Cultural Properties, University of Tokyo, Historiographical Literature, National Institute of Japanese Literature, National Institute for Japanese Language and Linguistics, Kyoto University Research Centre for the Cultural Sciences and Institute of History and Philology, Academia Sinica 2020b).

The spirit of the declaration and the directions outlined in the guidelines aim at achieving much more openness than in the past, both in terms of collaboration and data exchange. We believe that it is essential in the age of digitization to free the source material from individual stakeholders. Based on this declaration and guidelines, it will be possible to expand and share data through broader collaboration among overseas institutions, domestic institutions, and common citizens, and at the same time maintain the centrality of cultural heritage in society, overcoming the many limitations currently imposed by budget and administration.

5. Conclusions

In conclusion, this examination of the digitization practices for ancient *Mokkan* allows us to expand our considerations into more general issues in the tension between digital technology and the management of material cultural property in Japan.

We want to reaffirm the core ideas and objectives concerning cultural property, in light of the changes initiated by the digital revolution:

1. Cultural property is the common property of the people (of Japan, and even of the world). Therefore, adequate conservation and active public disclosure of the findings are necessary. Institutions and people dealing with cultural heritage should be equal and cooperate. More specifically, open data can support a wide operation of dissemination for a large number of people.
2. Information should be aggregated, standardized, and organized rigorously and according to the specificities of the material. On the one hand, this reaffirms the importance of the practice of cataloging, a method that has a long tradition in Japan since the Heian period. On the other hand,

> digital technology requires that information about artifacts is organized systematically according to specific standards. We need to take care when designing and using standardized models, that the research needs of the project are not sacrificed to the technology and methods of digitization, but that the historical approach is privileged.

The current recommendation is to promote the provision of high-quality and diverse digital resources by first prioritizing cultural heritage that can be easily handled in terms of legal rights, and then to make the significance and benefits of this openness widely known to society so that this becomes accepted as a fact. This will make it easier to expand the benefits of digitization and wide open access in the future, and eventually to address their impact in the area of legislative regulations on the dissemination of cultural heritage data.

Digital technology has made it easier than ever to access cultural properties and to keep costs low. It is now possible, and necessary, to establish a new way of sharing cultural heritage data, overcoming the large concrete discrepancy between the ideal stated by the law and the actual conditions of heritage institutions. Moreover, open access to cultural heritage information will produce richer and better research.

We believe that the role of informatics will only increase in the humanities. Data-driven research will become increasingly important in humanities research, and it is essential to pursue the goals of cooperation, open access, and standardization of information (Yamada & Inoue 2021; Nakamura & Yamada 2021). The attitude of seeking equal and open collaboration, not only across institutions, but also with society at large, will lead to new and important developments in the dissemination of new knowledge, and be beneficial for the community as a whole (*cf.* Yamada 2018).

6. References

馬場　基. Baba, H. (2019). 奈良文化財研究所のICTへの取り組み. Nara National Research Institute for Cultural Properties' ICT Efforts. *Japanese Historical Society 848*(9–13).

馬場　基・高田　祐一・桑田　訓也. Baba, H., Takada, Y., & Kuwata, K. (2019). IIIFの導入による木簡画像データベースの連携強化. Enhancement of linkage of wooden tablet image database by introduction of IIIF. 奈良文化財研究所紀要2019. *Bulletin of the Nara National Research Institute for Cultural Properties* 2019. 18–19.

馬場　基. Baba, H. (2021). 史的文字データベース連携検索システムの理念と未来. Philosophy and future of historical character database linked search system. ふみ *Fumi 16*, 6–7.

馬場 基 Baba, H. (2022). 日本古代漢字漢字運用規範を木簡から探す. Searching for ancient Japanese kanji usage rules from wooden tablets. 日本文学研究ジャーナル. *Journal of Japanese Literature 24*, 25–36.

Clanuwat, T., Bober-Irizar, M., Kitamoto, A., Lamb, A., Yamamoto, K., & Ha, D. (2018). Deep Learning for Classical Japanese Literature. *Neural Information Processing Systems 2018 Workshop on Machine Learning for Creativity and Design*. Retrieved from: arxiv:1812.01718. DOI: https://doi.org/10.20676/00000341.

畑野吉則・馬場基. Hatano, Y., & Baba, M. (2022). 市民参加型筆順情報取得アプリケーション「ナゾルクン」. Nazoru-kun: a Web App for acquiring brush stroke order information. 『奈良文化財研究所紀要. *Bulletin of the Nara National Research Institute for Cultural Properties* 2022, 56–57. DOI: http://doi.org/10.24484/sitereports.129169-119461.

劉冠偉・中村覚・山田太造. Liu, G., Nakamura, S., & Yamada, T. (2022). 研究資源としてのWEB　APIの利用：歴史資料・古典籍の字形を横断的に検索するアプリケーションの開発. The Utilization of WEB API as a Research Resource: Development of an Application for Cross-sectional Search of Glyphs in Historical Materials and Classical Books. じんもんこん2022論文集. *Jinmonkon Proceedings 2022*, 165–170.

Ly, N. T., Nguyen, K. C., Nguyen, C. T., & Nakagawa, M. (2019). Recognition of Anomalously Deformed Kana Sequences in Japanese Historical Documents. *IEICE Transactions on Information and Systems*, Vol. E102-D, No. 8, 1554–1564. DOI: https://doi.org/10.1587/TRANSINF.2018EDP7361.

Nara National Research Institute for Cultural Properties, University of Tokyo, Historiographical Literature, National Institute of Japanese Literature, National Institute for Japanese Language and Linguistics, Kyoto University Research Centre for the Cultural Sciences and Institute of History and Philology, Academia Sinica. (2020a). *Declaration of Cooperation*. Retrieved from https://mojiportal.nabunken.go.jp/files/declaration1en.pdf.

Nara National Research Institute for Cultural Properties, University of Tokyo, Historiographical Literature, National Institute of Japanese Literature, National Institute for Japanese Language and Linguistics, Kyoto University Research Centre for the Cultural Sciences and Institute of History and Philology, Academia Sinica. (2020b). *Open Data Specifications*. First Edition. Retrieved from https://mojiportal.nabunken.go.jp/files/declaration2en.pdf.

Nakamura, S., & Yamada, T. (2021). Development of data-driven historical information research infrastructure at the Historiographical Institute in the University of Tokyo. *Proceedings of JADH2021*, 148–151.

中村覚・劉冠偉・山田太造. Nakamura, S., Liu, G., & Yamada, T. (2022). NDLOCRを用いた東京大学史料編纂所史料集版面画像に対する検索システムの開発. Development of a Retrieval System for Historiographical Edition Images Using NDLOCR. 研究報告人文科学とコンピュータ（CH) 1月8日. *Research Report Humanities and Computers (CH), 1*(8).

中村覚・劉冠偉・宮崎・肇・井上聡・大山航・山田太造.Nakamura,S., Liu, G., Miyazaki, H., Inoue, S., Daisen, S., & Yamada, T. (2022). 花押を対象としたデータ駆動型歴史情報学研究の実践. Implementation of data-driven historical informatics research on Kao Signature. じんもんこん2022論文集. *Jinmonkon Proceedings 2022*, 171–178.

大山 航・畑野 吉則・馬場 基. Ohyama, W., Hatano,Y., & Baba, H. (2020, December). 深層学習による木簡実測図の自動作成. Automatic generation of measured drawings for Mokkan using Deep Learning.「人文科学とコンピュータシンポジウム」2020年12月. *Humanities and Computer Symposium*, December 2020, 235–240.

鬼塚 洋輔・大山 航・山田 太造・井上 聡・内田 誠一 Onitsuka, Y., Oyama, W., Yamada, T., Inoue, S., & Uchida, S. (2018). 花押類似検索のための畳み込みオートエンコーダによる画像特徴抽出. Convolutional Feature Extraction for Kaou Image Retrieval. じんもんこん2018論文集. 252–262.

Shibayama, M., Morimoto, S., Tashiro, A., Kameda, A., Yamada, T., & Hara, S. (2018). Building an Ontology-Oriented Archaeological Knowledge-Base "ArcOnBase" in Mainland Southeast Asia. *2018 Pacific Neighborhood Consortium Annual Conference and Joint Meetings (PNC)*, San Francisco, CA, 1–6. DOI: https://doi.org/10.23919/PNC.2018.8579462.

高田智和・福山雅深・堤智昭・小助川貞次. Takada, T., Fukuyama, M., Tsutsumi, T., & Kosukegawa, S. (2018). 資料画像公開・利用の国際化と高度化の取り組み—「日本語史研究資料［国立国語研究所蔵］の事例—. Implementation of Image Disclosure System Using IIIF. 国立国語研究所論集 第15号. *NINJAL 15*, 10–31. DOI: http://doi.org/10.15084/00001601.

Takata, Y., & Yanase, P. (2021). The Production, Preservation and Dissemination of Archaeological Data in Japan. *Internet Archaeology 58*. DOI: 10.11141/ia.58.11.

Terras, M. (2006). *Image to Interpretation: An Intelligent System to Aid Historians in Reading the Vindolanda Texts*. Oxford: University Press. DOI: https://doi.org/10.1093/acprof:oso/9780199204557.001.0001.

Unsworth, J. (2000, October). *What is Humanities Computing and What is Not?* Paper presented at the Distinguished Speakers Series of the Maryland Institute for Technology in the Humanities at the University of Maryland, College Park MD.

Watanabe, A., Baba, H., & Kurushima, N. (2016). *Mojizo: Image matching search for Mokkan or cursive characters*. Nara National Research Institute for Cultural Properties. Retrieved from https://mojizo.nabunken.go.jp/.

Wilkinson, M. D., Dumontier, M., Aalbersberg, IJ. J., Appleton, G., Axton, M., Baak, A., Blomberg, N., Boiten, J.-W., Bonino da Silva Santos, L. O., Bourne, P. E., Bouwman, J., Brookes, A. J., Clark, T., Crosas, M., Dillo, I., Dumon, O., Edmunds, S., Evelo, C. T., Finkers, R., Gonzalez-Beltran, A., Gray, A. J. G., Groth, P., Goble, C., Grethe, J. S., Heringa, J., 't Hoen, P. A. C., Hooft, R., Kuhn, T., Kok, R., Kok, J., et al. (2016). The FAIR Guiding Principles for scientific data management and stewardship. Scientific Data 3, 160018. Retrieved from: https://www.nature.com/articles/sdata201618.

山田　太造. Yamada, T. (2018). 収集史料の体系化と永続的な利用に向けた管理. Organization of Collected Historical Materials and Management for Permanent Utilization. 研究報告人文科学とコンピュータ（CH）. *IPSJ SIG Technical Report*, Vol. 2018-CH-118 1.

Yamada, T., & Inoue, S. (2018). A Common Base of Knowledge for Japanese Historical Materials and its Application. *2018 Pacific Neighborhood Consortium Annual Conference and Joint Meetings (PNC)*, San Francisco, CA, 1–6, doi: 10.23919/PNC.2018.8579468.

山田 太造・井上 聡・山家 浩樹, Yamada, T. Inoue, S., & Yamaga, H. (2019). 日本史史料データ流通基盤に向けた歴史データリポジトリの整備. Developing a historical data repository for a data distribution platform for Japanese historical materials. じんもんこん2019論文集. *Jinmonkon 2019 Proceedings*, 3–10.

Yamada, T., & Inoue, S. (2021). Personal Name Authority Data Repository for Advancement Data-driven Research in Japanese History. *2021 Pacific Neighborhood Consortium Annual Conference and Joint Meetings (PNC)*, 13–17. DOI: https://doi.org/10.23919/PNC53575.2021.9672287.

山田太造・中村覚・渋谷綾子・大向一輝・井上聡. Yamada, T., Nakamura, S., Shibuya, A., Ohmukai, I., & Inoue, S. (2021). 日本史史料を対象とした研究データ基盤整備における課題. Issues in developing a research data infrastructure for Japanese historical materials. じんもんこん2021論文集. *Jinmonkon 2021 Proceedings*, 80–87.

CHAPTER 3

Description, translation and process: Making the implicit explicit in digital editions of ancient text-bearing objects

Martina Filosa
Universität zu Köln
Usama Gad
Ain Shams University
Gabriel Bodard
University of London

Abstract

Digital editions of ancient texts and objects follow the nineteenth–twentieth century tradition of academic editing, but are able to be more explicit and accessible than their print analogues. The use of digital standards such as EpiDoc and Linked Open Data, that emphasise interoperability, linking and sharing, enables—we shall argue, obliges—the scholarly editor to make the digital publication open, accessible, transparent and explicit.

We discuss three axes of openness: 1. The edition encodes dimensions and physical condition of the inscribed object, as well as photographs and other imagery,

How to cite this book chapter:
Filosa, M., Gad, U. and Bodard, G. 2023. Description, translation and process: Making the implicit explicit in digital editions of ancient text-bearing objects. In: Palladino, C. and Bodard, G. (Eds.), *Can't Touch This: Digital Approaches to Materiality in Cultural Heritage*. Pp. 51–75. London: Ubiquity Press. DOI: https://doi.org/10.5334/bcv.d.

and should include translations to modern languages, rather than assuming fluency. 2. Contextual and procedural metadata include the origins of scholarly work, permissions, funding, influences on academic decision-making, material and intellectual property, trafficking, ethics, authenticity and archaeological context. 3. The digital standards and code implementing them, enabling interoperability among editions and projects, and depend on consistency and accessible documentation of practices, guidelines and customisations. Standards benefit from training in scholarly and digital methods, and the nurturing of a community to preserve and encourage the sustainable re-use of standards and editions.

Ancient text-bearing objects need to be treated as material artefacts as well as the bearers of (sometimes abstract or immaterial) strings of historical text. All elements of the publication of both object and text are interpretive constructs. It is essential that we not neglect any of the material or immaterial information in all of these components, in our scholarly quest to make them explicit, interoperable and machine actionable.

الملخص

الإصدارات الرقمية للنصوص والآثار تتسق مع تقاليد القرن التاسع عشر والعشرين في النشر الأكاديمي إلا أنها أكثر وضوحًا وسهلة الوصول إليها أكثر من نظائرها المطبوعة. نحاول أن نوضح فى هذه الورقة أن إستخدام المعايير الرقمية مثل لغة (EpiDoc) والبيانات المفتوحة المرتبطة (Linked Open Data) ، والتي تؤكد على قابلية التشغيل البيني والربط والمشاركة عبر أشغلة التنظيم المختلفة ، تسمح -إن لم تكن تجبر- المحرر على جعل المنشور الرقمي مفتوح المصدر وعلى قدر كبير من الشفافية والوضوح أكثر من نظيره الورقي.

وبناءاً عليه نحاول أن نناقش في هذه المقالة ثلاثة محاور متعلقة بفكرة المصدر المفتوح في النشر العلمي: (1) وهنا نقول أن النشر العلمى الرقمى يجب أن يحتوي على المقاسات والحالة المادية للمادة (بمعنى الأثر) المكتوبة عليها النص المنشور ؛ بالإضافة إلى صورة فوتوغرافية لهذا الأثر أو غيرها من المجسمات ثلاثية الأبعاد. ويجب أن يتضمن أيضاً ترجمة للنص القديم إلى لغة حديثة ، بدلاً من افتراض أن الباحثين ملمين بهذه اللغات القديمة. (2) يجب عليه أيضاً أن يتضمن على بيانات وصفية وإجرائية لسياقات العمل الأكاديمي ، بما في ذلك تصريح النشر، والتمويل ، وغيرها من المؤثرات الخارجية على محرر النص (الناشر) بالإضافة أي بيانات أخرى متعلقة بالملكية المادية والأدبية والفكرية لوعاء النص (سواء كان أثر أو غيره من الأوعية) وكذلك غيرها من المعلومات المرتبطة بعملية الحصول على الأثر والاتجار في الوثائق ، وأخلاقيات العمل ، والأصالة ، و غيرها من السياقات الأثرية. (3) ثم أنه يجب أن يتطرق إلى المعايير الرقمية والتعليمات البرمجية التي تم تنفيذها و قابلية التشغيل البيني بين الإصدارات والمشاريع الرقمية بشكل متناسق و توثيقى بحيث يسهل عملية الوصول إلى الإرشادات التوجيهية (guidelines) والتخصيصات (customisation). كما أن التدريب على الأساليب العلمية والرقمية يساعد فى هذا المجال بحيث يرعى المجتمع الرقمي ويحافظ على هذا المنتج الرقمي ويعزز ويشجع فرص إعادة الاستخدام المستدام للمعايير والإصدارات الرقمية.

وخلاصة القول نريد أن نؤكد على فكرة أن الآثار التي تحمل نصوصاً تاريخية ليست مجرد آثار صماء بل هى فى نفس الوقت أيضاً حمّالة معاني وأن جميع عناصر النشر سواء الأثر أو النص تخضع للتفسير وإن شئت قلت تفسيرات متبايينة. من الضروري ألا نهمل أى معلومة سواء مادية أو معنوية إذا ما أردنا أن نجعل هذه النصوص وتلك الآثار واضحة المعاني (explicit) وقابلة للتشغيل الرقمي البيني (interoperable) وقابلة للتنفيذ الآلي (machine actionable).

1. Introduction

Formal openness and transparency of digital editions of material, text-bearing objects, along several axes, serves social and ethical ends as well as academic communication and accessibility.[1] Producing electronic editions is an advanced academic discipline in its own right—not purely technical or secretarial work as some hidebound professors would have us believe—requiring scholarly expertise in digital encoding, philology, history and archaeology. A digital publication needs to record the traditional information about text, object description, scholarly history, attribution and metadata, and also detailed processual details and explicit links between data and interpretation that are machine actionable and robustly sustainable. The standards that enable this machine-assisted scholarly work themselves need to be transparently documented and communicated to the reader.

The authors of this chapter are experts in philological and archaeological methods, sigillography, papyrology and epigraphy, and in digital humanities methods for reading, encoding, imaging, disseminating and critiquing ancient texts.[2] As we are scholars of the ancient and mediaeval Mediterranean, our explicit focus is on antiquity; this is not to say that most (if perhaps not all) of the questions we raise are equally applicable to other periods of history and cultural areas. We are concerned with the interplay between the linguae francae of scholarship and the spoken languages of people's lives and countries of origin—in particular the disjunct between publications of Mediterranean antiquities and the ability of people whose national cultural heritage they are to read them—and the colonial legacy of these scholarly practices.

While all information that can be expressed in print publications (and much more) will generally be captured in digital editions, as digital humanists we are aware that all modelling is simplification, and digital modelling is no exception. Reducing complex records to the bits of digital data leads to occasional loss of analogue information, but our goal, by being explicit and transparent, and licensing open content for reuse, is to keep such simplification to a minimum, and empower the reader to reconstruct the processes and decisions along with as much open original data as possible.

---

[1] The authors would like to thank several colleagues for comments or other work that have contributed to our thinking about the topic of this chapter, including: Paula Granados García, Thomas Kollatz, Chijioke Okorie and Andrea Wallace.

[2] We shall at times use "epigraphy" in its more general sense of "text written on material objects" to encompass all of the subdisciplines represented in this chapter.

2. Transparency of the edition itself

This first axis may feature information that also customarily occurs in print editions of such texts, but that digital encoding and processing make more explicit. For instance, machine-actionable encoding of numerical or quantifiable data, such as date or dimensions, can both be displayed to readers in an accessible, human-readable form, and be rendered or transformed so as to sort, filter, index, visualise, or otherwise process the editions according to multiple criteria, including some not foreseen or designed by the original project.

Transparency, explicitness and even redundancy enhance the accessibility of the publication—to both a disciplinarily broad audience, readers from different national and linguistic backgrounds, those with different accommodations or needs, and with interests in different parts of the publication or edition.[3] The digital medium permits the presentation of multiple views of material, while avoiding repetition and duplication of effort.

We shall consider here six elements of an edition that might be made more explicit: 1. Machine-actionable encoding; 2. Full object description; 3. Presentation of the text edition; 4. Transparency of vocabularies and language; 5. Translation to modern languages; 6. Provision of or linking to supporting materials.

2.1 Machine-actionable encoding

"Machine-actionable" encoding embeds in a digital edition standardised, digital codes (whether XML or database fields) that make explicit to a processing environment information implicit to a human reader. Where a print edition may give dimensions of an object—commonly without even the abbreviations 'w', 'h' and 'd' for dimensions:

w: 0.55 x h: 0.87 x d: 0.54

The underlying XML in the EpiDoc edition of the same publication might include the code:

```
<dimensions unit="metre">
      <width>0.55</width>
      <height>0.87</height>
      <depth>0.54</depth>
</dimensions>
```

[3] We are inspired by and support the arguments (in a different discipline) of Vitale 2016; see Vitale (Chapter 1 in this volume).

This more verbose record is not necessarily entered by hand by human editors, nor read on the page, but has several benefits for the processing, interoperability and sustainability of the data behind any one publication. TEI XML is a common standard that promotes compatibility between humanities datasets (including ancient texts), and gives editors and users the opportunity to share a large body of code and software for the publication, processing and querying of these digital materials. Digital encoding, at least with a well-understood and documented language like TEI, is also a more explicit record of each dimension, especially when abbreviations may differ between languages, or not all objects may have the same dimensions given (not all objects have a recordable "depth"—letters cut on a building or a rock face, say—; circular objects may be better described with a diameter). Digitally encoding this information may also enable further computational processing of this information beyond display, perhaps including: searching for objects of certain dimensions; indexing or sorting objects of a certain size; filtering a search interface for "tiny," "large" or "huge" artefacts. Some projects might find it valuable to create an artificial visualisation of an object, for example in an automated 3D modelling library, as a wireframe onto which to project a photograph or other surrogate of the text.[4] This sort of information could be used in a process that proposes compatible fragments for a machine-assisted resolution of broken texts or objects (e.g. Koller & Levoy 2006; Lewis 2015; Toler-Franklin et al. 2010; Reggiani 2017: 152–54; Brusuelas 2016).

Some of these suggestions may seem highly specialist or unlikely, but as with much digital work, the point of openly sharing data and encoded texts is that the reuse others make of it will be unpredictable to the creators of the original data, and what may seem overkill for the purposes of a Web publication immeasurably enhances the value and therefore sustainability of the dataset for future users.

2.2 Full object description

Epigraphy and the cognate disciplines have always involved a complex relationship between philology and object archaeology, and such interplay of skills requires interdisciplinarity or collaboration, each of which brings its own challenges.

The seeming redundancy of including a description of an object alongside a photograph (or, indeed, palaeographical description of text alongside photograph, squeeze or drawing) may be outweighed by different purposes, audiences and processes served by each representation. Multiple views and descriptions of an object may involve time and expense to produce, deliver

[4] See e.g. the Python library Mayavi: https://docs.enthought.com/mayavi/mayavi.

and maintain, so involves a cost-benefit decision, but where the question is whether to publish available data in redundant formats or views, as with digitally transformed data, the value of different views may prevail.

An archaeological photograph with scale and colour palette may be the most efficient, accurate and compelling way to communicate the shape, texture and decoration of an inscribed object to (some) human readers of an edition. Just as Web accessibility guidelines mandate the use of an `@alt` attribute to describe (or functionally explain) an image for visually impaired readers or low-bandwidth network connections or text-only browsers, both digital and print publishers should think of different consumers of their editions. As well as accessibility issues for disabled readers, we might consider that a description can be encoded and processed (as discussed above), searched as plain text or read by a screen reader, unlike images, and can be used to categorise editions by various criteria. A written description and explanation of an object is also an act of interpretation and commentary by the editor, and therefore communicates valuable expertise to a reader—and for which the photograph serves as the "raw data" against which to assess this description.

2.3 Presentations of the text edition

Analogous to parallel human-readable and machine-readable versions, and redundant image and text relating to an inscribed object, digital encoding makes it possible to publish multiple, explicitly aligned renditions of the text itself. The essential views of a text might include:

I. **Photograph** or other surrogate of the text-bearing face—this could include photographs, drawings, facsimiles, epigraphic squeezes or rubbings, 3D scans or reconstructions; or any view representing as closely as possible the appearance of the text, without that layer of editorial interpretation that comes with transcription.

II. **Diplomatic edition**—the transcription that interprets letterforms, but does not expand abbreviations, correct errors or dialect forms, or restore damaged text; most diplomatic transcriptions flatten allographs and elide palaeographical and other information visible in a photograph or the original manuscript.

III. **Interpretive edition** or editorial transcription—designed for *reading* the text, which generally normalises features such as punctuation, word spacing, use of lowercase letters, accentuation and diacritics; the editorial view also uses explicit signs (XML or the Leiden System) to expand abbreviations, restore damaged, omitted or lost characters, correct errors, normalise dialect or idiosyncratic spelling and grammar, and encode other observations about the state of the original.

IV. **Translation** of the text into one or more modern languages—a translation may be anything from a simple updating of the language (e.g. Shakespearean to modern English) to a highly transformative and even speculative rendering of the sense, but every translation is an act of interpretation, and even if aligned to the source, is a barrier between the reader and the original text. One might include multiple translations of a single text into the same language.[5]

V. **Glossaries**, and other indexed, glossed and commented views of the text or key terms within it, take a reader even further from the text, but add interpretive information to aid in understanding, supply expert context, and make a text more accessible to non-specialist readers. It is only a small step from here to the prose commentary or historical discussion of the text and its language, which take us beyond a "view" of the text itself.[6]

There may be more fine-grained taxonomies of views of a text; there are for example several kinds of "diplomatic transcription," ranging from drawings of letter-shapes and surviving fragments, to uncorrected versions of the editorial text. In an EpiDoc edition, it is in principle possible, indeed normal practice, to generate both diplomatic and interpretive views of an edition from the same underlying XML encoding of the transcribed text, given the richness, transparency and redundancy of the markup. As much information as possible to help the reader understand both the state of the surviving text and the editor's reconstruction and interpretation of it, should be accessible to the human reader and explicit in the underlying code (Bodard & Garcés 2006: 92–94; Cayless & Roueché 2009: §26–27).

2.4 Transparency of vocabularies and language

Academic writing relies on specialist, technical vocabulary to communicate clearly and unambiguously the vital concepts that emerge from centuries of

---

[5] See e.g. the Digital Corpus for Graeco-Arabic Studies https://www.graeco-arabic-studies.org/texts.html, which includes original Greek texts, Arabic translations, epitomes, commentaries and secondary sources.

[6] The resources, as we argued, are available. So for Classics, in a broader sense, see e.g. the Ugarit text aligner https://wiki.digitalclassicist.org/Ugarit and for papyrology, see e.g. the new Fachwörterbuch (nFWB): https://www.organapapyrologica.net/receive/PapyrusPortal_dictionary_00000418, a lexicon of papyrological terms, where Arabic and Spanish (beside the traditional English, German, French and Italian) translations of the lemmata are added.

scholarly consensus. While it is important not to use obscure jargon to exclude the uninitiated from our work, it is equally crucial that we use vocabularies—be they terms of art in dating, palaeography, art history or architecture—in a consistent, transparent, and well-documented fashion. Scholars from related fields such as epigraphy and numismatics may understand the same term in subtly different ways, and greater misunderstandings can arise from false-friends across languages.[7]

In digital editing and philology, transparency in terminology is best achieved by the use of recognised taxonomies, thesauri and ontologies, preferably adhering to Linked Open Data standards that allow terms and concepts to be addressed by means of URI—a globally unique string of characters that also serves as the Web-address definition of the concept for which it stands. We discuss in more detail below (§4.3, §4.4) the use of vocabularies and ontologies for consistency, and documentation and training for users and producers of compatible editions. An internal glossary or thesaurus—preferably hyperlinked from the relevant terms in translation and commentary—would be a valuable step in this direction.[8]

2.5 Translation to modern languages

In many contexts, English is a lingua franca of scholarship, even if in archaeology and classics there is more resistance to this monoglossy than in the sciences. It is unfortunate that as a result the vast majority of classical text-bearing objects that originate outside the English-speaking world, are published in a language inaccessible to (much of) the local public. Many Greek and Latin inscriptions and seals, and almost all papyri, originate in parts of the Greco-Roman world that are now Arabic speaking, where English is even less widely spoken than in France or Italy. In digital editions, it becomes more feasible to offer translations into modern languages, and better serve a range of audiences.[9]

It is also conventional to divide texts in different languages—including those from the same support and even in the same hand—into different corpora or databases. For instance the bilingual Greek-Arabic text of *SB* VI.9576 was

---

[7] Lucarelli (Chapter 8 in this volume) discusses the confusion that can arise from technical and discipline-specific terminology in the context of Egyptology.

[8] On the importance of vocabularies in Japanese archaeology, see Baba (Chapter 2 in this volume).

[9] E.g. this edition of an epitaph from Greek Cyrenaica, translated into French, English, Italian and Arabic: https://igcyr.unibo.it/gvcyr001, or this military ostrakon from Roman Tripolitania translated into English and Arabic: https://irt2021.inslib.kcl.ac.uk/en/inscriptions/IRT1518.html.

divided between the (Greek-focussed) Duke Databank of Documentary Papyri (Papyri.info), and the Arabic Papyrology Database (APD), until in 2016 Gad added the Arabic text to the Papyri.info record.[10] The editorial history at the bottom of this record in Papyri.info (compiled from `<change>` tags in EpiDoc XML and Git commit history) makes this entire process more transparent than was possible—or at least the norm—for earlier generations of editors. There remain technical issues for the encoding of (right-to-left) Arabic texts in XML, especially alongside left-to-right languages such as Greek and Latin, primarily with editing the texts in an XML or text editor, but correctly encoded XML can readily be processed and transformed. When Gad approached the editorial team of Papyri.info to propose improving the functionality of the editorial interface for bidirectional texts, to facilitate the addition of Arabic translations of papyri to the collection, the editors were sympathetic, but delayed implementing a technical solution until progress had been made on alignment with the APD. Effectively, the adoption of an approach that would facilitate the engagement of Arabic-speakers with the texts in the collection was not considered high priority at this time, despite the Egyptian origin of almost all papyri, Arabic never having been considered a scholarly language in papyrology, and Arab scholars remaining under-represented and under-served in classics and ancient history (Blouin 2018; Gad 2021: 262–263).

Not all scholars have the capability to translate their work into multiple modern languages, but many digital projects are collaborative endeavours, and opening scholarly works to a range of regional and local audiences may win the attention of the "crowd" of willing contributors, albeit introducing logistical issues of quality control, editorial oversight and consistency. The benefit in removing barriers to both non-Anglophone and non-academic audiences to cultural heritage make this a quintessential example of the transparency we address in this chapter.

2.6 Provision of or linking to supporting materials

Internal or external resources can provide information for the user or reader of an edition, including documentation of technical standards used (discussed further in §4.4); explanation or expansion of technical terms, typographic conventions (e.g. the Leiden System) and abbreviations; historical context or encyclopaedic references for disciplinary issues. Such resources might be provided as supplementary materials, serving a wider audience of the digital publication, scholars from different disciplines, students or non-academic public, via simple links or more direct engagement with external resources and reference works, primary materials and the research tools associated with them, or

[10] *SB* VI.9576, *Papyri.info*: https://papyri.info/ddbdp/sb;6;9576 and CPR III. 38, *Papyri.info:* https://papyri.info/ddbdp/cpr;3;38.

public resources such as Wikipedia articles or supporting data in Wikidata and Wikimedia Commons.

Provision of or reference to supporting materials serves to increase the accessibility of complex digital editions, and improve the transparency of the research process and sources behind the published content. The digital medium facilitates linking and access to external resources, reduces restrictions of space and cost to publish lengthy additional resources alongside often highly abbreviated critical editions (Reggiani 2017: 172).[11]

An editor does not have infinite time on her hands, or even necessarily the skills or inclination to produce unlimited supporting materials for all audiences. As discussed with reference to translations, however, there is the potential for producing better supporting materials than has been the norm, and with community goodwill we can at least begin to achieve more accessible and transparent publications. We discuss further below (§ 4.4) the importance of sustainability of open digital data, which includes supporting materials and publications.

3. Contextual and procedural metadata

Our second axis of openness is the inclusion of information about the creation and origins of digital editions. Such questions were seldom explicitly recorded in print editions, although primary and secondary sources (and less frequently details of archaeological campaigns) were noted. Due to technical and disciplinary features of digital editions, it is possible and should be standard scholarly practice to include procedural metadata (or "paradata") in both print and digital editions to contextualise scholarly editions in their historical moment. The inclusion of such metadata is a recognition of the global digital age, technologically different from earlier generations, with sociological, cultural and most importantly scholarly and ethical implications (Mazza 2021).[12]

As a general disclaimer, the authors are not legal professionals, are making no allegations or preempting the outcomes of legal cases, and nothing written in this chapter should be construed as legal advice or opinion.

[11] Elagina (Chapter 5 in this volume) discusses the advances enabled by digital study of manuscripts in recording material aspects and the role of manuscripts in modern culture.

[12] See also Okorie (Chapter 11 in this volume) on copyright law and local communities.

3.1 Scholarly process, origins, decisions

In the first publication of the Bodmer papyri, a certain vacillation is visible (Robinson 2011: 11). A roll containing documentary texts on the front was later cut into two rolls containing on the back *Iliad* 5 and 6. The two books of the *Iliad* were published with a comment to the effect that, since they are distinct entities, "from a bibliographical point of view," they would be designated P. Bodmer I and II. The single volume in which they were published was however designated *Papyrus Bodmer I* (Martin 1954); this outcome perhaps resulted from the recognition that relatively few fragments remained of the roll that had contained book 6, which did not warrant a whole separate volume, or simply the rationalisation that the documentary texts on the front had been as a single roll, or that the *Iliad* is a single work. The documentary texts will, however, only be published in a concluding volume of miscellanea as Papyrus Bodmer I Recto (Derda 2010). A codex containing only the Gospel of John was then published as Papyrus Bodmer II (Martin 1956–62; see Robinson 2011: 11). The inconsistency is not limited to the first publication of Bibliotheca Bodmeriana, but affects almost every subsequent publication of this important papyrological collection.

In the archive of Papas (P.Apoll.), linguistic barriers between Greek, Coptic and Arabic papyri and papyrology are almost meaningless. The most important factor in these two examples were the sponsors' or collector's involvement in the process of publication, and the degree of expertise of the editors responsible for the publication of the collections. The boundaries between subspecialities of papyrology are blurred, and one can argue that they are meaningless. A lot of codicological and palaeographical information could have been gained from this collection, if the story of its discovery and acquisition were explicitly documented in the first publications.

Such inconsistencies and complexities can just as easily arise in digital editions, but where possible scholarly processes, origins and publication history of the collection and its parts, and decisions made about individual pieces, should not be left for scholars to conjecture, but transparently and explicitly included in the edition.

3.2 Object provenance

Many archaeological associations and publications have strict policies on the publication of unprovenanced or trafficked objects.[13] Such rules are not evenly followed worldwide and in all academic disciplines, but it is increasingly under-

[13] See e.g. the new policy of AJA on the publication and citation of undocumented antiquities https://www.ajaonline.org/submissions/antiquities-policy; good summary of such rules and guidelines now in Nongbri 2022.

stood that encouraging trafficking, looting and unauthorised export, present or past, is irresponsible and dangerous academic behaviour.

Editions of ancient texts traditionally report on the archaeological and custodial provenance of the text-bearing object, even if constrained to a description of original context, place and circumstances of finding, and current location or holding. Questions of context and provenance have wider impact, including legal and ethical, and indeed repercussions on the archaeological and philological disciplines of an editor's engagement with exported, traded and trafficked antiquities. The recent, and still unfolding, scandal involving apparent papyrus theft from the Egypt Exploration Society (EES) collection in Oxford, reported by the EES itself and *The Guardian, Atlantic* and other newspapers (Gad 2019). The equally controversial fake Coptic fragment dubbed the Gospel of Jesus' Wife, whose acquisition history is recounted by Ariel Sabar in works that strip bare the internal workings of our academic field (Sabar 2016; Sabar 2020).

Beyond these blockbuster stories, which harm the public image of the discipline, editions of inscriptions, papyri and related texts will gain much from being explicit about the provenance, acquisition and curation of ancient artefacts, and sensitive to the ethical and intellectual property issues around working with private collections and recently auctioned materials. Such transparency is needed beyond digital editions, but technologies such as Linked Open Data, hypertext, faceted views and Web archives make possible linking to and preserving online resources, holding institutions or auction houses, displaying explicit information without obscuring scholarly edition and commentary, and offering accountability and ethical data reuse.

Given the history of both colonial and post-colonial looting, in which almost all collections in North America, Europe, the Middle East and Japan have been assembled,[14] transparent publication and the use of open data and open licensed materials (where this would not constitute further pillaging of intellectual heritage) becomes an ethical—if not a legal—obligation.[15] It becomes feasible to link editions of text-bearing objects to websites of holding institutions, with precise information about intellectual property; to auction houses or purchase records with dates, provenances, regulations, and other

[14] For more detailed and/or evidence-based research on the illicit trade of cultural objects, see the website of the project "Trafficking Culture" https://traffickingculture.org/projects/.

[15] Pavis & Wallace 2019 discuss the importance of not re-colonising stolen heritage digitally; Okorie (Chapter 11 in this volume) highlights the issue of control; Bianchini (Chapter 4 in this volume) discusses the importance of transcending colonial views of ancient objects.

necessary documentation of the acquisition process.[16] Hypertext, the fundamental and original characteristic of the internet, allows a digital edition to offer information that print editions omit due to limitations of space. We need to take advantage of this medium to add all available, accessible and known information, whether online or in excavation archives (van Minnen 1994). Some sensitive information cannot be shared publicly, but even where a piece is published first in an academic journal or book, when this becomes available online, more information may be added in the process of digitization and analysis.

3.3 Permissions

Historical and contemporary permissions, or indeed denial of such, to publish archaeological finds should be acknowledged in digital editions. Many libraries and museums have made archives wholly or partially available online, making a wealth of information available for editors. With private or not-yet-digitised institutional collections, it is the responsibility of authors and publishers to avoid vague formulations about historical agreements and communications with the source country. In Egypt, for instance, it is increasingly recognised that any text-bearing object not explicitly mentioned in an agreement or correspondence between the holding institution and Service des antiquités de l'Egypte, the Supreme Council of Antiquities, or the Ministry of Culture, is likely trafficked. Given that most of the source countries in the Middle East and North African region use traditional documentation of permissions to track archaeological objects, we must balance the digital divide in the world of online editions by exhausting every avenue to communicate with these institutions to avoid rights encroachment. Simultaneous editions of the same text have been dismissed as "not intentional trespasses on the AIP's guiding principle of *Amicitia Papyrologorum*" (Gad 2016). These unintentional trespasses in printed editions can be avoided in digital editions and databases; the key is transparency and openness concerning assigned numbers and the assignment policies and procedures of the holding institutions, even if there is no explicit metadata field or element for this purpose in our encoding models.[17]

Quite apart from legal copyright issues, the common practice of excavators or museums assigning first-publication rights for a body of texts to a given scholar, also impacts on digital publication. While not a legal barrier to publication by others, the practice can have repercussions on good relations, repu-

---

[16] See the UNESCO's database of legislative texts governing the protection of movable cultural property, e.g. Egypt at: https://unesdoc.unesco.org/ark:/48223/pf0000066629.

[17] This shortcoming is currently under consideration by the EpiDoc community.

tations, and even careers. It is frustrating to see texts that have repeatedly been seen in the field, but are reserved for publication by a scholar who has "sat on" them for years or even decades; many editors are however loath to break such reservation protocols out of politeness or fear of senior colleagues. Even in digital projects, many editors do not question this convention (Feraudi-Gruénais 2020). Equally with coins or lead seals commonly held in private collections, we argue that it is ethically imperative to make such unofficial or "gentlemanly" understandings explicit in the publication of the texts, whether the editor is the beneficiary of such an assignment, or has chosen to circumvent it.

It is critical that the institutional archives of major collections, themselves part of the publication record of papyri, inscriptions and other text-bearing artefacts, follow robust transparent, explicit, openly licensed practices. These holding institutions are best qualified to record and communicate information about acquisition history of collections, correspondence with agents in source countries, and other questions of provenance and materiality. Digitisation of archival materials and their inclusion in canonical text and object records becomes crucial for the interpretation of these ancient texts. The Michigan Papyrus collection exemplifies such practice (Haug 2021) for any other institution that claims to hold scholarly information about ancient heritage, including for instance the collection of papyri at the Egyptian Museum in Cairo. This is not to criticise any institution for their history or question the legality of acquisition, but to preserve all information to recontextualise collection objects in their historical and cultural moments (Hickey 2009).

3.4 Funding and other conflicts of interest

The source of funding for an editorial project, whether institutional budget, public or private grants, is a key element in the power dynamics behind contemporary and historical development of collections. "The shortage of money", as Nongbri put it, was the most likely reason behind Grenfell and Hunt's "hectic working pace and less-than-ideal record keeping" in publishing the early volumes of Oxyrhynchus papyri. Annual reports and letters reveal that financial concerns affected the whole scholarly process: "In Egypt, their goal was to extract as much papyrus as possible for the fund in as short a space of time as possible. [...] Back in England, the objective was to publish the material as quickly as possible. [...] Under these circumstances, it is unsurprising that so little contextual archaeological information was published" (Nongbri 2018: 223). Funding from fossil fuel and arms industries, antiquities dealers, colonising and other repressive regimes, and so forth, are a concern in academia (e.g. Mathiesesn 2021; Khomani 2022; Balter 2006; Vasagar & Syal 2011). Even beyond these overtly problematic cases, all funding carries expectations and agendas, and inclusion of the sources of such funding in editorial metadata should be a default.[18]

One of the goals of Nongbri's project EthiCodex, is to "Make a systematic canvassing of museum and library collections containing ethically acquired early papyrus and parchment books to determine willingness to have AMS radiocarbon analysis carried out on their early codices and then fund this analysis."[19] This strict rule, ensuring that funding is not spent on the study of unethically or illegally acquired texts, is in accordance with UNESCO Conventions.[20] All of the contextual, procedural and ethical concerns discussed in this paper are tied up with sources of funding. Along with overt conflicts of interest, all possible influences from professional relationships, financial benefit, contractual obligations, and the history of institutions and collections, should be flagged as explicitly as possible in digital editions.

4. Documenting digital standards

Our third axis of openness concerns recording, documentation and dissemination of digital standards (including those discussed in §2.1). The implementation of open digital standards strongly incentivises the scholar to make her publication open and transparent, and to convey information explicitly. This task requires digital standards to be employed consistently and accompanied by documentation of practices. In this sense "documentation" includes not only guidelines and recommendations, but also divergences from and customisations of the core standard, and materials for teaching and training.

For the sake of this argument, we shall analyse four features related to the documentation of the digital standards: 1. transparency of practice and code; 2. consistency; 3. training and dissemination; 4. development and sustainability.[21]

---

18 In point: the volume in which this chapter appears could not have been published without the grant of monies from Furman University, a private US institution, and the University of London, a publicly funded university.

19 The Early History of the Codex: A New Methodology and Ethics for Manuscript Studies: https://earlyhistoryofthecodex.com/about/.

20 UNESCO Convention Concerning the Protection of the World Cultural and Natural Heritage: https://whc.unesco.org/en/conventiontext/.

21 For discussion of the FAIR and CARE principles of open publication of cultural heritage materials, see the thorough discussion in Granados & Ashley (Chapter 9 in this volume).

4.1 Transparency of practice and code

Along with transparency of vocabularies and language (§ 2.4 above), an effective community of practice relies on transparency of practice and code, including accessibility of source code and training materials to users and readers of conformant editions. EpiDoc, "an international, collaborative effort that provides guidelines and tools for encoding scholarly and educational editions of ancient documents" (Elliott et al. 2021), is an active and growing community of practice in epigraphic encoding and digital publication, and ensures transparency both among users and in outreach through:

1. creation, maintenance and regular updating of detailed guidelines;
2. presence of code repositories, open licensed and freely available to all users, on free software development platforms;[22]
3. documentation of each new code release;[23]
4. mailing lists and fora for exchange of information, code samples and peer guidance.[24]

Version control is key to transparency and accountability: "by increasing the significance of version control, research transparency and critical discussion could be improved" (Bürgermeister 2019: 187). The EpiDoc community has established versioning practices for source code, documentation and, in most cases, content encoded in EpiDoc. Each release of the source code and of the guidelines is documented in release notes, and available as static XML in a dedicated repository.[25] Within EpiDoc files the element `tei:revisionDesc`, containing one or more `tei:change`, is used for a change log of each file, alongside commit messages in version control repositories.[26]

```
<revisionDesc>
 <change when="2010-08-18" who="#GB">Converted
   from TEI P4 (EpiDoc DTD v. 6) to P5 (EpiDoc
   RNG schema v. 8)</change>
 <change when="2009-05-19" who="#RV">Added Fig-
   ures</change>
 <change when="2008-09-09" who="#ZA">converted
   using CHET-C</change>
</revisionDesc>
```

22 EpiDoc Github repositories: https://github.com/EpiDoc.

23 EpiDoc Release Notes: https://sourceforge.net/p/epidoc/wiki/LatestRelease.

24 Markup list: https://wiki.digitalclassicist.org/Markup_list.

25 The release notes of the latest EpiDoc release, v.9.5, are available here: https://github.com/EpiDoc/Source/releases/tag/v9.5/.

26 This example refers to *IRT2021*, n. 25, available: https://irt2021.inslib.kcl.ac.uk/en/inscriptions/IRT0025.html.

4.2 Enforcing consistency: vocabularies, ontologies and authority files

Indices serve two roles, at the beginning and end of a research process, both helping to ensure internal consistency. An index distils the essence of a larger work by one or more researchers, and constitutes for the user a gateway to the consultation of an edition. Indices of printed volumes meet these two requirements by normalising or lemmatising notable concepts. Creation of indices by hand or assisted by word-processing tools introduces human error (typographical, missed references), as attested in frequent post-publication *addenda et corrigenda*. Digital standards also help to prevent inconsistency in bibliographical abbreviations (Reggiani 2017: 31–32).

Digital standards enable consistency through controlled vocabularies, ontologies and authority files, which provide each term or entity with stable unique identifiers, indicating relations between terms, offering a core of consistency upon which projects may build and inspire new research. The community of digital epigraphists, centred around EpiDoc, are systematising and working toward consistency of data modelling via many projects using the common schema. The Epigraphic Ontology is a first step, proposed by a working group of the Epigraphy.info community (Bodard et al. 2021), building material and solidity through the experience of several projects, in turn providing them with more consistency. The related category of metadata thesauri is served by the EAGLE Vocabularies, structured data designed "to be flexible, align data, and harmonise content without forcing [any] project or publication to change [...] the structure used," in the process of being enhanced and consolidated by the FAIR Epigraphy project.[27] Authority files—external, including VIAF, GeoNames or Pleiades,[28] internal to a project, or developed, shared and extended across projects and communities—enforce consistency within a corpus and between editors. Alignment of domain thesauri and ontologies to massive community resources such as Wikidata would further enhance the sustainability and interoperability of such vocabularies. Authorities signal recurring information pertaining to the text, prevent repeated entry of data and errors that may arise from human input, separate general information from specific textual content, and facilitate linking to external resources.

Consistency allows editors and users to transcend an individual corpus and create larger, connected corpora that add their biological and technological distinctiveness to the collective of reusable tools, going beyond the unique content and behaviour of individual projects, to search and cross-reference among corpora.

---

27 EAGLE Vocabularies: https://www.eagle-network.eu/resources/vocabularies; FAIR Epigraphy https://www.csad.ox.ac.uk/fair-epigraphy.

28 Virtual Internet Authority File: http://viaf.org; GeoNames: http://www.geonames.org; Pleiades Gazetteer: https://pleiades.stoa.org/.

4.3 Dissemination and training, or how to create a broad community of practice

Digital standards depend on wide use and adoption, aided by dissemination and training in scholarly and digital methods. The EpiDoc community of practice considers training provision a major part of its mission to preserve and ensure the sustainable re-use of standards and editions.[29] Training in EpiDoc is participative, learner-focussed and practice-oriented: students learn from hands-on practice with digital encoding, while one-way training delivery from instructors is as concise as possible.[30] Training has been delivered in the framework of university teaching, as one-week intensive courses or as smaller project workshops or crash-courses attached to congresses.[31] Regardless of the setting, training often involves an international audience, with English as lingua franca, although one should be sensitive that this is not the case for all learners; students who are not able to fully follow in English are being failed by a monoglot programme. Community-driven efforts may help to overcome this obstacle, improving the implementation of localised training materials, and making them more accessible, inclusive, sustainable, and effective.

The EpiDoc community represents a positive example in this respect: all pedagogical materials used in training are multi-authored and released under licenses that permit reuse, modification and sharing with others.[32] Training materials include slideshows, short video tutorials, longer lectures on more general features of digital epigraphy, guidelines and code examples, articles and book chapters on methodology. The syllabus of training materials for each workshop offers a gentle and cumulative learning experience, which students are able to consult in the order they prefer.[33]

---

[29] For a broad overview on the embedding of teaching and training within the EpiDoc community see Bodard & Stoyanova 2016: 60–63; and Bodard & Vagionakis 2022.

[30] Amongst the variety of didactic approaches employed, the so-called 'learning by doing' has proven effective in EpiDoc training events over the years, see on this Dee, Foradi, & Šarić 2016: 25–28.

[31] A list of past EpiDoc training events is maintained at: https://wiki.digitalclassicist.org/EpiDoc_Workshops.

[32] The EpiDoc community provides Open Educational Resources (OER)-enabled pedagogy where the "open" indicates that these materials are licensed with copyright licences that provide permission for everyone to participate in the 5R activities: retain, reuse, revise, remix and redistribute (Wiley & Hilton 2018: 134–135).

[33] EpiDoc Tutorials: https://github.com/EpiDoc/Tutorials includes teaching materials and individual syllabi from 2021 onwards.

EpiDoc training practice contributes to and draws on other pedagogical resources and programmes, including Sunoikisis Digital Classics[34] (Vitale, Bodard, & Berti forthcoming 2024), further enhancing durability and sustainability. Transparency is enhanced by inclusivity and accessibility, which implies taking into account (1) disability accommodations, and (2) language barriers.

1. Both the design and delivery of training events will benefit from the expertise of departments or individuals specialised in inclusive learning and e-learning.[35] It is essential to make training materials accessible and inclusive, including through the use of closed captions and translated subtitles on video tutorials, multilingual captions on slides, and slides containing explanations that are friendlier to assistive technology than a parade of images and code snippets (Everett & Oswald 2018; Carballo, Cotán, & Spinola-Elias 2021).
2. Multilingual training materials cater to an ever-expanding community;[36] EpiDoc training is only offered in the main European languages (English, French, Italian, German, Spanish), but we should also consider training materials—including slideshows and captioned videos—in, or enhanced by, further languages.

4.4 Transparency and sustainability

Sustainability of digital content and technical infrastructure within the lifetime of the project depends on maintenance and renewal. It is good scholarly practice to build on and adapt existing, community solutions, avoid bespoke tools and duplication of work. Digital longevity is enabled by community engagement, however small scale: "another important aspect of sustainability that all of these projects [Nomisma, Papyri.info] exemplify is community engagement. Nomisma and Papyri.info have made themselves indispensable tools for the small scholarly communities they represent (Numismatics and Papyrology)" (Cayless 2019: 44).

Beyond the authors' active role in a project, sustainability is better achieved through diversity of hosting and archiving solutions, formats and dissemination strategies. The infrastructures that enable sustainability are seldom managed by the scholars who edit and author ancient editions; a digital humanities

[34] Sunoikisis Digital Classics: https://sunoikisisdc.github.io.

[35] E.g. we have worked with the Competence Center E-Learning (https://elearning.uni-koeln.de/), Center for University Didactics of the University of Cologne (https://zhd.uni-koeln.de/), and Centre for Distance Education, University of London (https://london.ac.uk/centre-for-distance-education).

[36] See section § 2.5 and above for multilingualism respectively in the edition (including text, metadata and commentary) and in the training itself.

centre or lab may provide expertise in data management, a digital library or publisher the physical infrastructure for online publication. A sustainable digital publication needs one or more hosting institution, repositories for data and documentation, user interface, possibly APIs and support for LOD, as well as technical and content maintenance (Aurora & Gasparini 2022). Scholars seeking funding must be explicit about the costs of such infrastructure, support and documentation. Funding bodies as well as editors need to normalise and be transparent about the life-cycle of a project, from grant bid to "graceful shutdown" (Smithies et al. 2019: 24), to avoid the risk of "digital wastelands" (Barats et al. 2020: 33).

Beyond the life of the publication itself, a digital resource may be sustainable because it contributes to scholarship beyond its own existence. Datasets licensed for download, aggregation and reuse, allow easier and more comprehensive access to users, including new avenues of research that the originating authors may not envisage. Open licensing is essential to sustainability in this context, enabling compilation, translation, commentary and other remixing that have allowed ancient texts to be transmitted to us (Cayless 2010).

5. Conclusions

We have outlined multiple axes of transparency and openness in digital editions of ancient text-bearing objects, including inscriptions, papyri, seals and coins. The explicitness enabled by these digital practices serves the reader of the critical edition, the editorial and publication process itself, and the academic obligation to consider ethical and social responsibility in research. Overlying all of the issues we consider is the need to record both materiality and material context (archaeological, geographical and historical) along with text.

The scholarly editor is concerned with all elements of the edition, material and historical information as well as description and transcription of text. Epigraphic scholarship has always included these agendas—these are multidisciplinary and collaborative disciplines, encompassing archaeology and philology; the digital editor is empowered to be more explicit about these features. An account of the scholarly process has always been an important (if under-served) element of epigraphic editing: our current transparency on the contexts of discovery, provenance, curation, access and study of our objects, does not imply that traditional editors were less aware of the colonial legacies, relationships and patronage behind scholarly permissions and access, the intersections between intellectual property and other legal considerations, and more conventional, private and privileged rights of access. The digital medium and standards in use combine to capture and communicate all of the above; we have an obligation to be open and explicit about these methods, through the use of open standards, documentation, training, raising awareness and ensuring sustainability of our digital practices and communities—especially the engagement of local or indigenous communities and cultures in all of these processes.

Digital humanities scholarship brings together interest in historical and literary disciplines with its own research methods and concerns, and is itself as important as traditional epigraphic disciplines—indeed is a more accessible discipline, embodying respect for a wider audience, sustainability of resources, transparency of data and methodology, and social justice. There is no conflict within or between these concerns and 'traditional' scholarship, for they all serve the same ends of academic pursuit: furtherance and communication of knowledge and the betterment of society. These considerations are not new, this chapter is not inventing any wheels. Digital methods and approaches merely enable (and therefore oblige) us to be explicit in all features of our scholarly editing work, making that work more accessible, inclusive, sustainable, ethical, and in all senses more scholarly.

6. References

Aurora, F., & Gasparini, A. (2022). The Crowd of Resources: Thoughts About Sustainability and Access. Paper presented at *Papyri and Crowdsourcing* (conference of the ENCODE project), February 2022, Würzburg, Germany.

Balter, M. (2006, March 31). $200 Million Gift for Ancient World Institute Triggers Backlash. *Science*. DOI: https://doi.org/10.1126/science.311.5769.1846.

Barats, C., Schafer, V., & Fickers, A. (2020). Fading Away... The Challenge of Sustainability in Digital Studies. *Digital Humanities Quarterly, 14*(3). Retrieved from: http://www.digitalhumanities.org/dhq/vol/14/3/000484/000484.html.

Bauman, S. (2001). Interchange vs. Interoperability. In *Proceedings of Balisage: The Markup Conference 2011*. Balisage Series on Markup Technologies 7, DOI: https://doi.org/10.4242/BalisageVol7.Bauman01.

Bleier, R., & Winslow, S. M. (2019). *Versioning Cultural Objects: Digital Approaches*. Norderstedt: Books on Demand.

Blouin, K. (2018). Wonder How Male & Eurocentric Your Antiquity-Related Field Is? Try the Committee Test!, *Everyday Orientalism* 2018-02-13. Retrieved from: https://everydayorientalism.wordpress.com/2018/02/13/wonder-how-male-eurocentric-your-antiquity-related-field-is-try-the-committee-test/.

Bodard, G., Cayless, H., Cenati, C., Cooley, A., Elliott, T., Evangelisti, S., Felicetti, A., Granados García, P., Grieshaber, F., Gruber, E., Hershkowitz, A., Hill, T., Kiiskinen, H.,Kollatz, T., Levivier, A., Liuzzo, P., Luciani, F., Mannocci, A., Mataix, E., Murano, F., Murphy, O., Mylonas, E., Prag, J., Razanajao, V., Stoyanova, S., Tsolakis, G., Tupman, C., Vagionakis, I., Vitale, V., & Weise, F. (2021). Modeling Epigraphy with an Ontology. DOI: https://doi.org/10.5281/zenodo.4639508.

Bodard, G., & Garcés, J. (2009). Open Source Critical Editions: A Rationale. In M. Deegan & K. Sutherland (Eds.), *Text Editing, Print, and the Digital World* (pp. 84–98). Farnham: Ashgate Press. Retrieved from: https://blog.stoa.org/files/2010/09/Bodard-Garces_2009_Open-source-digital-editions.pdf.

Bodard, G., & Stoyanova, S. (2016). Epigraphers and Encoders: Strategies for Teaching and Learning Digital Epigraphy. In Bodard, G., & Romanello, M. (Eds.) *Digital Classics Outside the Echo-Chamber: Teaching, Knowledge Exchange & Public Engagement* (pp. 51–68). London: Ubiquity Press. DOI: http://dx.doi.org/10.5334/bat.d.

Bodard, G., & Vagionakis, I. (2022). EpiDoc and Epigraphic Training in the Era of Remote and Hybrid Teaching. *Digital Classics Online* 8, 108–122. DOI: https://doi.org/10.11588/dco.2022.8.90358.

Bodard, G., & Yordanova, P. (2020). Publication, Testing and Visualization with EFES: A tool for all stages of the EpiDoc editing process. *Studia Digitalia Universitatis Babeș-Bolyai, 65*(1), 17–35. DOI: https://doi.org/10.24193/subbdigitalia.2020.1.02.

Brusuelas, J. (2016). Engaging Greek: Ancient Lives. In G. Bodard, & M. Romanello (Eds.), *Digital Classics Outside the Echo-Chamber: Teaching, Knowledge Exchange & Public Engagement* (pp. 187–204). London: Ubiquity Press. DOI: https://doi.org/10.5334/bat.k.

Brodie, N. (2016). Scholarly Engagement with Collections of Unprovenanced Ancient Texts. In K. Almqvist, & L. Belfrage (Eds), *Cultural Heritage at Risk* (pp. 123–142). Stockholm: Ax:son Johnson Foundation.

Bürgermeister, M. (2019). Extending Versioning in Collaborative Research. In R. Bleier, & S. M. Winslow (Eds.). *Versioning Cultural Objects: Digital Approaches* (pp. 171–190). Norderstedt: Books on Demand.

Bürgermeister, M. (2020). An Empirical Study of Versioning in Digital Scholarly Editions. In Marras, C., Passarotti, M., Franzini, G., & Litta, E. (Eds.), *Atti del IX Convegno Annuale AIUCD. La svolta inevitabile: sfide e prospettive per l'Informatica Umanistica* (pp. 55–60). Bologna. DOI: https://doi.org/10.6092/unibo/amsacta/6316.

Carballo, R., Cotán, A., & Spinola-Elias, Y. (2021). An Inclusive Pedagogy in Arts and Humanities University Classrooms: What Faculty Members Do, *Arts and Humanities in Higher Education, 20*(1), 21–41. DOI: https://doi.org/10.1177/1474022219884281.

Carlin, C., Czaykowska-Higgins, E., Jenstad, J., & Grove-White, E. (2016). The Endings Project, *The Endings Project*, 2016 – https://projectendings.github.io (accessed February 21, 2022).

Cayless, H. (2010). *Ktema es aiei*: Digital Permanence from an Ancient Perspective. In G. Bodard, & S. Mahony (Eds.), *Digital Research in the Study of Classical Antiquity* (pp. 139–150). Farnham-Burlington (VT): Routledge.

Cayless, H. (2019). Sustaining Linked Ancient World Data. In Berti, M. (Ed.) *Digital Classical Philology: Ancient Greek and Latin in the Digital Revolution* (pp. 35–50). Berlin-Boston: De Gruyter. DOI: https://doi.org/10.1515/9783110599572-004.

Cayless, H., Roueché, C. M., Bodard, G., & Elliott, T. (2009). Epigraphy in 2017. *Digital Humanities Quarterly, 3*(1). Retrieved from: http://digitalhumanities.org/dhq/vol/3/1/000030/000030.html.

Chue Hong, N. P., Katz, D. S., Barker, M., Lamprecht, A.-L., Martinez, C., Psomopoulos, F. E., Harrow, J., Castro, L. J., Gruenpeter, M., Martinez, P. A., Honeyman, T., Struck, A., Lee, A., Loewe, A., van Werkhoven, B., Jones, C., Garijo, D., Plomp, E., Genova, F., Shanahan, H., Leng, J., Hellström, M., Sandström, M., Sinha, M., Kuzak, M., Herterich, P., Zhang, Q., Islam, S., Sansone, S.A., et al. (2021). FAIR Principles for Research Software (FAIR4RS Principles). DOI: https://doi.org/10.15497/RDA00065.

Dee, S., Foradi, M., & Šarić, F. (2016). Learning By Doing: Learning to Implement the TEI Guidelines Through Digital Classics Publication. In Bodard, G., & Romanello, M. (Eds.) *Digital Classics Outside the Echo-Chamber: Teaching, Knowledge Exchange & Public Engagement* (pp. 15–32). London: Ubiquity Press. DOI: http://dx.doi.org/10.5334/bat.b.

Derda, T. (2021). *P. Bodmer I Recto: A Land List From the Panopolite Nome in Upper Egypt (After AD 216/7).* Journal of Juristic Papyrology Supplement 14. Warsaw: Institute of Archeology, University of Warsaw & Taubenschlag Foundation.

Dobusch, L., & Kapeller, J. (2018). Open Strategy-Making With Crowds and Communities: Comparing Wikimedia and Creative Commons, *Long Range Planning, 51*(4), 561–579, DOI: https://doi.org/10.1016/j.lrp.2017.08.005.

Elliott, T., Bodard, G., Mylonas, E., Stoyanova, S., Tupman, C., & Vanderbilt, S., (lead authors) (2007–2021), *EpiDoc Guidelines: Ancient documents in TEI XML* (Version 9). Retrieved from: https://epidoc.stoa.org/gl/latest (v.9.3).

Everett, S., & Oswald, G. (2018). Engaging and training students in the development of inclusive learning materials for their peers, *Teaching in Higher Education, 23*(7), 802–817, DOI: https://doi.org/10.1080/13562517.2017.1421631.

Feraudi-Gruénais, F., Kruschwitz, P., Orlandi, S., & Prag, J. (2020). Statement of Intent on the Handling of Unpublished Inscriptions. *Epigraphy.info*. DOI: https://doi.org/10.11588/heidok.00027952.

Fickers, A. (2020). Update für die Hermeneutik. Geschichtswissenschaft auf dem Weg zur digitalen Forensik?, *Zeithistorische Forschungen/Studies in Contemporary History, 17*(1), 157–68. DOI: https://doi.org/10.14765/zzf.dok-1765.

Gad, U. (2016). A Checklist of the Egyptian Museum's Unpublished Greek Papyri. *AWOL – The Ancient World Online*. Retrieved from: http://ancientworldonline.blogspot.com/2016/03/a-checklist-of-egyptian-museums.html.

Gad, U. (2019). Decolonizing the Troubled Archive of Egyptian Papyri. *Everyday Orientalism*. Retrieved from: https://everydayorientalism.wordpress.com/2019/08/05/decolonizing-papyrology.

Gad, U. (2021). Receptions of Classical Antiquity in Egypt and the Arab World: Parallel Narratives, Invisible Corpora and a Troubled Archive. In Baadji, A.S.

(Ed.) *A Handbook of Modern Arabic Historical Scholarship on the Ancient and Medieval Periods* (pp. 249–293). Leiden: Brill. DOI: https://doi.org/10.1163/9789004460089007.

Haug, B. (2021). Politics, Partage, and Papyri: Excavated Texts Between Cairo and Ann Arbor (1924–1953). *American Journal of Archaeology, 125*(1), 143–163. DOI: http://doi.org/10.3764/aja.125.1.0143.

Hickey, T. (2009). Writing Histories from the Papyri. In Bagnall, R. (Ed.) *The Oxford Handbook of Papyrology* (pp. 495–520). Oxford: Oxford University Press. DOI: https://doi.org/10.1093/oxfordhb/9780199843695.013.0021.

Hoekstra, R., Koolen, M., & van Faassen, M. (2018). Data Scopes: Towards Transparent Data Research in Digital Humanities, *DH2018*, Mexico City. Retrieved from: https://dh2018.adho.org/en/data-scopes-towards-transparent-data-research-in-digital-humanities.

Jacobsen, A., Miranda Azevedo, R., Juty, N., Batista, D., Coles, S., Cornet, R., Courtot, M., Crosas, M., Dumontier, M., Evelo, C. T., Goble, C., Guizzardi, G., Hansen, K. K., Hasnain, A., Hettne, K., Heringa, J., Hooft, R. W. W., Imming, M., Jeffery, K. G., Kaliyaperumal, R., Kersloot, M. G., Kirkpatrick, C. R., Kuhn, T., Labastida, I., Magagna, B., McQuilton, P., Meyers, N., Montesanti, A., van Reisen, M., Rocca-Serra, P., et al. (2020). FAIR Principles: Interpretations and Implementation Considerations. *Data Intelligence 2*, 10–29. DOI: https://doi.org/10.1162/dint_r_00024.

Khomami, N. (2022, April 19). Climate and heritage experts call on British Museum to end BP sponsorship, *The Guardian*. Retrieved from: https://www.theguardian.com/culture/2022/apr/19/climate-and-heritage-experts-call-on-british-museum-to-end-bp-sponsorship.

Koller, D., & Levoy, M. (2006). Computer-aided Reconstruction and New Matches in the Forma Urbis Romae. *Bullettino della Commissione Archeologica Comunale di Roma*, Supplementi 15, 103–125. Retrieved from: http://graphics.stanford.edu/papers/forma-bullcom/.

Lewis, A. W. (2015). The Reconstruction of Virtual Cuneiform Fragments in an Online Environment. PhD thesis, University of Birmingham. Retrieved from: https://etheses.bham.ac.uk/id/eprint/6714/1/Lewis16PhD_Redacted.pdf.

Martin, V. (1954). *Papyrus Bodmer 1. Iliade: chants 5 et 6*. Cologny-Genève: Bibliotheca Bodmeriana.

Mathiesen, K. (2021, July 30). London Science Museum signed gagging order with Shell over climate change exhibition, *Politico*. Retrieved from: https://www.politico.eu/article/london-science-museum-shell-gagging-order-climate-change-exhibition-carbon-capture/.

Mazza, R. (2021). Descriptions and the Materiality of Texts. *Qualitative Research, 21*(3), 376–393. DOI: http://doi.org/10.1177/1468794121992736.

Morley, J., Widdicks, K., & Hazas, M. (2018). Digitalisation, Energy and Data Demand: The Impact of Internet Traffic on Overall and Peak Electricity Consumption, *Energy Research & Social Science, 38*, 128–137. DOI: https://doi.org/10.1016/j.erss.2018.01.018.

Nongbri, B. (2018). *God's Library: The Archaeology of the Earliest Christian Manuscripts*. New Heaven, CT: Yale University Press.

Nongbri, B. (2022). The Ethics of Publication: Papyrology. *Bryn Mawr Classical Review* 2022.05.25. Retrieved from: https://bmcr.brynmawr.edu/2022/2022.05.25/.

Pavis, M., & Wallace, A. (2019). Response to the 2018 Sarr-Savoy Report: Statement on Intellectual Property Rights and Open Access relevant to the digitization and restitution of African Cultural Heritage and associated materials. *Journal of Intellectual Property, Information Technology and E-Commerce Law, 10*(2), 115–129. Retrieved from: https://zenodo.org/record/2620597.

Reggiani, N. (2017). *Digital Papyrology I: Methods, Tools and Trends*. Berlin/Boston: De Gruyter. DOI: https://doi.org/10.1515/9783110547474.

Robinson, J. M. (2011). *The Story of the Bodmer Papyri: From the First Monastery's Library in Upper Egypt to Geneva and Dublin*. Eugene, OR: Wipf and Stock Publishers.

Sabar, A. (2016). The Unbelievable Take of Jesus's Wife. *The Atlantic*, 2016. Retrieved from: https://www.theatlantic.com/magazine/archive/2016/07/the-unbelievable-tale-of-jesus-wife/485573.

Sabar, A. (2020). *Veritas: A Harvard Professor, a Con Man and the Gospel of Jesus's Wife*. New York: Doubleday.

Smithies, J., Westling, C., Sichani, A.-M., Mellen, P., & Ciula, A. (2019). Managing 100 Digital Humanities Projects: Digital Scholarship & Archiving in King's Digital Lab. *Digital Humanities Quarterly, 13*(1). Retrieved from: http://www.digitalhumanities.org/dhq/vol/13/1/000411/000411.html.

Toler-Franklin, C., Brown, B., Weyrich, T., Funkhouser, T., & Rusinkiewicz, S. (2010). Multi-feature matching of fresco fragments. *ACM Transactions on Graphics, 29*(6), 1–12. DOI: https://doi.org/10.1145/1882261.1866207.

van Minnen, P. (1994). House-to-House Enquiries: An Interdisciplinary Approach to Roman Karanis. *Zeitschrift für Papyrologie und Epigraphik, 100*, 227–251.

Vasagar, J., & Syal, R. (2011, March 4). LSE head quits over Gaddafi scandal. *The Guardian*. Retrieved from: https://www.theguardian.com/education/2011/mar/03/lse-director-resigns-gaddafi-scandal.

Vitale, V. (2016). Transparent, Multivocal, Cross-disciplinary: The Use of Linked Open Data and a Community-developed RDF Ontology to Document and Enrich 3D Visualisation for Cultural Heritage. In Bodard, G., & M. Romanello (Eds.) *Digital Classics Outside the Echo-Chamber* (pp. 147–168). London: Ubiquity Press. DOI: https://doi.org/10.5334/bat.i.

Vitale, V., Bodard, G., & Berti, M. (Forthcoming 2024). Collaborations and Relationships with the Sunoikisis Digital Classics Open Teaching Programme.

Wiley, D., & Hilton, J.L., III. (2018). Defining OER-enabled pedagogy. *The International Review of Research in Open and Distance Learning, 19*(4), 133–147.

CHAPTER 4

Looking beyond the text: Opportunities and challenges in the digitisation of Sanskrit inscriptions

Francesco Bianchini
King's College, University of Cambridge

Abstract

This chapter provides an introduction to the main digital repositories of inscriptions from South and Southeast Asia. The digitisation of epigraphs in Sanskrit and other languages has found considerable impetus in recent years, being the focus of two ERC Synergy projects as well as a number of other scholarly initiatives. While producing reliable editions and comprehensive metadata remains a central concern, the digital environment brings unique opportunities to move beyond traditional printed editions. The repositories introduced below already offer some practical solutions as to how this may be achieved, especially through a more integrated approach to the epigraphic object as a whole. This includes, among other aspects, recording object data as well as the physical layout of the inscriptions, and the integration of GIS technologies. Despite recent progress, the chapter argues that more can be done in this direction. Another aspect that deserves further attention is the development of the database itself,

How to cite this book chapter:

Bianchini, F. 2023. Looking beyond the text: Opportunities and challenges in the digitisation of Sanskrit inscriptions. In: Palladino, C. and Bodard, G. (Eds.), *Can't Touch This: Digital Approaches to Materiality in Cultural Heritage*. Pp. 77–93. London: Ubiquity Press. DOI: https://doi.org/10.5334/bcv.e. License: CC BY 4.0

especially in terms of advanced search and query capabilities, as well as cross-database communication. Lastly, the chapter raises the issue of the historical complexities involved in standardisation and efforts towards decolonisation. It suggests that a diversified approach involving independent teams that nonetheless communicate with one another may be a viable way forward.

Abstract (Italiano)

Il presente capitolo offre una panoramica delle principali collezioni epigrafiche digitali riguardanti l'Asia meridionale e sudorientale. La digitalizzazione di fonti epigrafiche in sanscrito e altre lingue ha di recente ricevuto una notevole attenzione, trovandosi al centro di ben due ERC Synergy projects nonché di altre iniziative accademiche. Certamente il miglioramento delle edizioni e delle banche dati attualmente disponibili rimane uno scopo importante. Tuttavia è imperativo sfruttare al massimo le opportunità offerte dal contesto digitale rispetto alle tradizionali edizioni cartacee. Le collezioni descritte qui sotto già offrono varie soluzioni pratiche in questo senso, in particolare tramite un approccio integrato all'oggetto epigrafico, che non consiste certo di solo testo. Tra i vari aspetti menzioniamo la registrazione di dati relativi all'oggetto stesso, nonché il formato del testo come appare sulla superficie iscritta, oppure la mappatura digitale che posiziona l'artefatto all'interno di un contesto archeologico e paesaggistico. Nonostante i risultati già raggiunti, il presente capitolo suggerisce che le possibilità non sono per nulla esaurite e guarda con trepidante attesa ai risultati di certi progetti attualmente in corso. Un altro aspetto da considerare è lo sviluppo delle banche dati e soprattutto degli strumenti di ricerca e interrogazione dei dati stessi. In ultima istanza, vanno anche considerate le varie complessità storiche che possono sorgere nel contesto post-coloniale, in cui la standardizzazione delle banche dati presenta sia opportunità che problemi. Si suggerisce qui sotto un approccio che valorizzi la diversità e allo stesso tempo la collaborazione tra team indipendenti di studiosi.

1. Introductory remarks

The study of pre-modern inscriptions in Sanskrit and other languages of Southern Asia has made great progress in recent years.[1] On the one hand, epigraphists have focused on what might be considered 'groundwork', i.e. producing reliable editions—in many cases for the very first time—and recording metadata systematically and comprehensively. On the other hand, scholars have also explored new ways and techniques for dealing with epigraphic texts and associated objects. This is particularly true of efforts towards the digitisation

[1] For an introduction to these sources see Salomon 1998; Francis 2018. On Sanskrit inscriptions from Southeast Asia see Griffiths & Lammerts 2015.

of Sanskrit corpora, with a number of epigraphic repositories now accessible online—each showcasing a different set of strategies, methods and techniques.

Improving the reliability of edited texts remains a key aim for epigraphists. In the digital environment, this process can be supported by the adaptation of EpiDoc XML encoding to the specific features and needs of Asian languages and scripts. However, the digital environment and EpiDoc itself also offer various opportunities to think beyond traditional printed editions.[2] Epigraphists have already started to explore a range of possibilities, for example in terms of documenting visual features, creating searchable databases of object metadata, and exploring digital mapping technologies (GIS).

Furthermore, the digitisation of Sanskrit inscriptions offers an opportunity to reflect upon a number of social and cultural issues. This involves reflecting on and transcending colonial and eurocentric ways of approaching Asian cultural heritage. Possible strategies include encouraging more inclusivity within epigraphic task-forces, welcoming the formation of digital repositories across multiple institutions, and proposing new ways of cataloguing and describing objects, not necessarily based on pre-existing colonial archival practices. On the other hand, there is also the question of how emerging Asian nationalisms can impact historical and cultural studies, and more specifically of how Asia-based digital repositories can come into a constructive dialogue with Western scholarship.[3]

The present chapter aims at highlighting and discussing these issues, without claiming to be comprehensive or conclusive. In introducing various online repositories, it seeks to highlight the positive, while also indicating where more progress could be made. In terms of methodology, the main suggestion made in this chapter can be summarised as follows: the digital environment can help revolutionise the way we think about inscriptions as well as the way we study them. In order to achieve this, I suggest focusing on what is not immediately visible, on what surrounds the 'text' and would otherwise remain implicit in most traditional printed editions. This includes recording the links between texts and textual layouts; texts and objects; objects and their monumentalized environment, and even monuments and (inter)regional cultural networks. Furthermore, there is an increasing need to build extensive databases that can be queried in advanced ways, not only in terms of locating textual strings, but also in terms of retrieving object features, as well as geographical and chronological parameters. Digital repositories that meet such criteria would significantly improve our ability to develop a more compelling—and in fact decolonised—form of historiography.

---

[2] On digital editions of inscriptions see also Filosa, Gad & Bodard (Chapter 3 in this volume).

[3] See sections 4 and 5 below for further comments on these issues, and Baba (Chapter 2 in this volume) for further discussions on cultural heritage and digitisation.

2. Digitised palm-leaf manuscripts

Before diving into epigraphic sources, it is helpful to look at digital manuscript repositories, for these offer a range of digitisation strategies that are also relevant to inscriptions.[4] For example, a number of Sanskrit manuscripts—mostly palm-leaf or paper—are available on the Cambridge Digital Library.[5] One may access the specimen called *Suvarṇaprabhāsottamasūtra* (CUL MS Add.875), an 18th century paper manuscript copied in Kathmandu and preserving the text of a major Buddhist scripture.[6] The interface presents high-quality zoomable images on the left, with detailed metadata on the right side of the screen (Figure 4.1). Both images and metadata (XML) can be downloaded by the user.[7] The metadata offers a general description of the specimen and the text it contains, before listing various specifications, many of which address the physical object and its characteristics. Then, incipit, rubrics, and colophon are presented in roman transliteration, followed by bibliographic details. The user is thus presented with what appears to be meticulously collected and systematically arranged data.

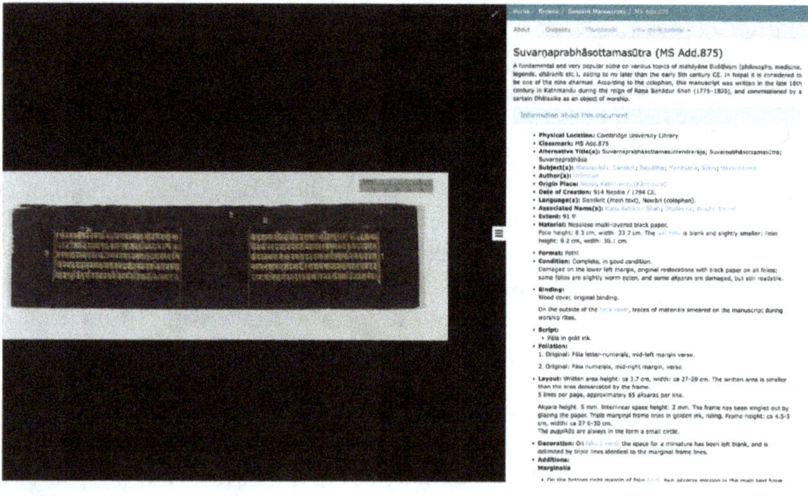

Figure 4.1: CUL, digitised Sanskrit MS (image and metadata).

---

[4] On manuscript digitisation see also Woodward, Offner & Blackwell (Chapter 6 in this volume).

[5] https://cudl.lib.cam.ac.uk/collections/sanskrit/1 (Accessed January 2023).

[6] https://cudl.lib.cam.ac.uk/view/MS-ADD-00875/1 (Accessed January 2023).

[7] In this chapter, I will not dwell on copyright issues, which represent of course a key aspect of digitisation.

The carefully edited texts can be easily checked on the basis of the images on the left side of the page. Editions also include punctuation marks, symbols, folio numbers, fillers, string holes, substrate defects and annotations, with conventions listed in a separate PDF.[8]

One may now ask which features make fuller use of the digital platform and the opportunities that come with it. For example, folio specifications within the edited texts link directly to the relevant image, which saves the user time; metadata often also includes hyperlinks. Indications about illuminations, bindings and marginalia link directly to the relevant folios. Authors and toponyms are part of the database. One interesting consequence of this is that by clicking on a place name one gets results from across the entire library, not just the Sanskrit section (clicking on 'Nepal' will bring up a number of Darwinian letters, for example). This might not always be useful to subject specialists but it can produce new insights and unexpected associations. The final portion of the metadata provides links to other specimens of the *Suvarṇaprabhāsottamasūtra* from two separate digital manuscript repositories (the International Dunhuang Project and the Nepalese German Manuscript Cataloguing Project). There is thus—to some extent—a synergy across different databases and platforms. This is in my opinion one of the key features to look for in digital collections, and a stepping stone towards more ambitious efforts, such as Open Linked Data.

Finally, each manuscript is arranged through 'subjects'. This allows one to view the entire list of manuscripts associated in terms of genre, subject, language and so on. For example, opening the database link for *Vyākaraṇa* (a term indicating the emic grammatical tradition), the researcher has a glimpse of all relevant texts across the collection, arranged according to sub-topics and with indication of the number of available specimens. The drop-down menu 'date' gives the number of specimens available for each century. Taken with all due caution, this is information that can be interpreted and used in research, with potential implications that may transcend the history of the Cambridge collection itself.[9]

There is much about this database one would wish to find in repositories dedicated to epigraphic texts. However, epigraphic texts are in a way even more complex, for they are more intimately linked with landscapes and monuments, making GIS and in-situ photography quite indispensable.

---

8 https://www.repository.cam.ac.uk/handle/1810/326907 (Accessed January 2023).

9 https://cudl.lib.cam.ac.uk/search/advanced/results?subject=vyakarana (Accessed January 2023).

3. Two pioneering repositories of Sanskrit inscriptions

The first digital epigraphic repository to adopt EpiDoc XML encoding was the *Corpus of Inscriptions of Campa* (2012), thanks to the efforts of Arlo Griffiths and various other scholars.[10] This was then followed by a second repository called the *Early Inscriptions of Āndhradeśa* (2017).[11] In both cases, the EFEO (École française d'Extrême-Orient) collaborated with various partners, based in France or overseas.

The two repositories are similar enough in concept to justify treating them together. One can perhaps conceptualise the key aims of the editors as follows: achieving reliability, transparency, and comprehensiveness.[12] Reliability is particularly important here, for many of the previously available editions were simply faulty. In the field of Sanskrit epigraphy, investing time, efforts and resources into improving editions is still a valuable and legitimate enterprise, however unambitious this might seem from the perspective of more advanced historiographical research. As for transparency, the idea in both repositories is to provide the reader with an image against which they can readily check the edition. As for comprehensiveness, the repositories collect secondary sources that are scattered across old and rare journals, with information often found in archaeological notes, the retrieval of which can be very time consuming. Corpora that provide such valuable contributions are definitely to be welcomed.

The *Corpus of the Inscriptions of Campā* presented about 50 records, including inscriptions on steles, pedestals, door jams, dishes and vases. The website names at least three Asian specialists who acted as collaborators to the project.[13] Although simple and somewhat rudimentary, it is a must-go for any scholar interested in the inscriptions of this ancient kingdom. The website has been discontinued but the materials continue to be expanded under the framework of an ongoing ERC Synergy project introduced below.

The key part of each record appears to be the edition, which is usually very detailed and accompanied by an apparatus with copious notes (Figure 4.2). Translations in both English and French are also offered. For our present purposes, it is important to note that the pictures usually cover not only estampages but also the objects themselves. Thus, one gets a clear idea of the substrates on which the texts have been inscribed and their architectonic, monumental, or utilitarian functions. The metadata is somewhat minimal but it includes

---

[10] https://isaw.nyu.edu/publications/inscriptions/campa/index.html (Accessed January 2023).

[11] http://hisoma.huma-num.fr/exist/apps/EIAD/index2.html (Accessed January 2023).

[12] Read the author's statement here: https://isaw.nyu.edu/publications/inscriptions/campa/about.html (Accessed January 2023).

[13] https://isaw.nyu.edu/publications/inscriptions/campa/credits.html (Accessed January 2023).

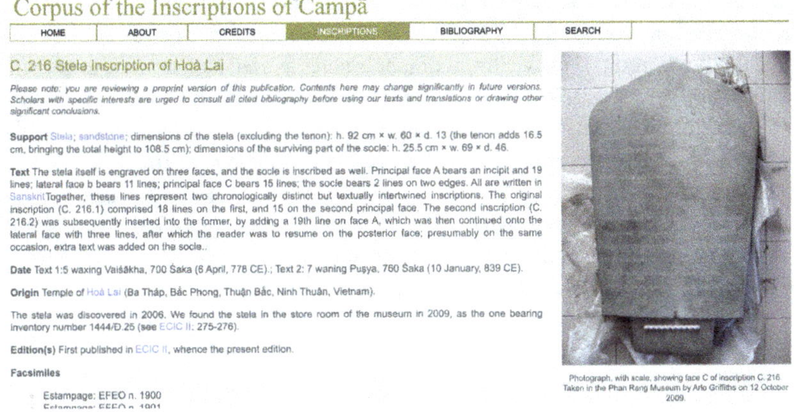

Figure 4.2: Sample inscription from Vietnam (metadata and image).

a description of the support and used to comprise various hyperlinks which are now inactive. As per the original intention, by clicking on 'gilded silver' one could have viewed all the objects made of or covered in silver. The search engine itself seems rather limited and mostly oriented at finding text strings present within the corpus.

The EpiDoc XML file can be downloaded, but the website interface does not include the familiar toggle option between diplomatic and critical editions. It appears to me that the main reason—although certainly not the only one—for adopting EpiDoc encoding here is that it allows the editors to update the editions and keep improving the records as new information becomes available. Printed editions simply do not offer this kind of flexibility, whose implications are in my opinion mostly positive. For example, an editor may be reluctant to publish a corpus of inscriptions in print unless convinced that the readings are definitive. This may in some cases result in long delays to publications despite the fact that the editions have already reached a very high standard. The digital environment allows some of these valuable results to be shared with others (with provision of DOIs for example), leaving open the possibility of an update to a record where this becomes necessary. However, potential pitfalls of a more flexible environment include: the inability to bring the editorial process to a conclusion (returning again and again to the same record, switching between possible interpretations rather than actually improving the readings); the digital publication of records that are not sufficiently precise or mature (in the absence of a balanced supervision of the platform); a reluctance to pay more attention to other important aspects, such as metadata, GIS, or the development of search engines. These considerations do not relate in any way to this very useful digital collection and are meant to be general remarks based on my own experience of epigraphic digitisation.

Although similar, the *Early Inscriptions of Āndhradeśa* corpus presents further features of interest. It is a larger repository consisting of 173 records. The careful editing and the provision of object images as well as estampages provide both reliability and transparency. Here we see the toggle options, which allow one to switch between 'logical' and 'physical' versions of the text, as well as the XML markup itself.[14] Some features related to textual layout are also recorded systematically, which is particularly welcome. For example, a diamond shape (◊) indicates blank space used as a punctuation mark (Figure 4.3).[15] Unfortunately the metadata does not present hyperlinks, except for bibliographical entries. Perhaps the most exciting feature is an exploratory GIS page which presents both a drawn map and a link to a QGIS cloud. Lastly, a number

Metadata

Support	Āyaka pillar; h. 275 × w. 47 × d. 36 cm.
Text	Middle Indo-Aryan, Southern Brāhmī script. h. 66 × w. 51 cm .
Date	Sixth regnal year of Siri-Vīrapurisadatta, approximately between 225 and 275 CE.
Origin	Erected originally at findspot.
Provenance	Discovered between March 1926 and October 1927 at Nagarjunakonda, Site 1, on the South side of the Mahācaitya. Mistakenly, Raghunath 2001: 197 indicates Site-2 instead of Site-1. Identified at Nagarjunakonda Museum (acc. no. 285) in February 2016.
Visual Documentation	Photo(s): photos AL 2017 Photo(s) of estampage(s): estampage Leiden N8 Vogel Raghunath
Editors	Stefan Baums, Arlo Griffiths, Ingo Strauch and Vincent Tournier.
Publication history	First described and edited by Vogel 1929–30a: 13, 18-9 (B4). Re-edited here from the Leiden estampage and after autopsy of the stone.

Edition

Logical Physical XML

(1) sidhaṁ namo bhagavato devarājasakatasa supabudhabo⟨dhino⟩ savaṁñuno sava[sa] (tā) (2)nukaṁpakasa jitarāgadosamohavipamutasa mahāgaṇivasabhagaṁdhaha[thi] (sa) (3) saṁmasaṁbugasa dhātuvaraparigahitasa mahācetiye kulahakānaṁ bālikā (4) mahāsenāpatisa mahātalavarasa vāsiṭhīputasa hirañaṁkānaṁ khaṁdacalikikaṁmaṇakasa (5) bhayā mahāsenāpatini culacātisiriṇikā °apano °ubhayalokahitasukhani(6)vāṇathanāya °imaṁ selakhaṁbhaṁ patiṭhapitaṁ ti raṁño sirivirapurisadatasa (7) ◊ sava 6 vāpa 6 diva 10

Figure 4.3: Metadata and 'logical' edition of inscription from Southern India. Note use of diamond-shaped symbol to indicate blank space.

[14] http://hisoma.huma-num.fr/exist/apps/EIAD/works/EIAD0008.xml?&odd=teipublisher.odd (Accessed January 2023).

[15] http://hisoma.huma-num.fr/exist/apps/EIAD/conventions.html (Accessed January 2023).

of Indian scholars and institutions are mentioned for their role in facilitating access to various resources and sites, although no South Asian scholar is mentioned among the main editors (Credits page).

Generally speaking, both corpora seem to have been designed primarily by philologists whose focus is to edit and interpret the inscriptions. This, to some extent, is to be expected. And yet one of the main opportunities provided by a digital environment is that the digitisation process can lead to something much more comprehensive. It is very encouraging in this regard to see that GIS was added to one of the corpora (albeit in an exploratory way), and that great care was taken into providing pictures of the objects. Some art historians were also involved in various capacities, which is a further positive sign.

Arguably, however, these very valuable repositories are not yet fundamentally different from printed editions, at least not in a way that revolutionises how these fascinating sources are approached and studied.

4. Digital epigraphy and two recent ERC Synergy projects

The digitisation of Sanskrit epigraphy has been a central component of two ERC Synergy projects: Asia-Beyond Boundaries (2014–2020) and DHARMA (2019–2025). For both projects, it is still too early to offer a comprehensive evaluation of how deeply and substantially they have changed the way we look at Sanskrit epigraphy, or the extent to which 'synergy' has been achieved. This term in my opinion implies both bringing together scholars who work on different corpora or regions, as well as scholars who work in different ways, transcending the disciplinary boundaries between philology, archaeology, or art history. For our present purposes, it will suffice to offer a few introductory remarks on the breadth of possible digitisation strategies, mostly based on my experience as a student collaborator of the former of these two projects.

When it comes to the digital repository of Asia Beyond Boundaries, I would like to focus on the current *Siddham.network*[16] online repository, not its earlier incarnation as *Siddham*.[17] The reason is that the current version offers some tentative alternative approaches to some of the issues outlined above. The earlier *Siddham* was the almost singlehanded achievement of Dániel Balogh, who—along with Arlo Griffiths—should be mentioned among the currently leading (digital) Sanskrit epigraphists (Balogh 2019). In many ways, *Siddham* continued along the lines of the corpora outlined in the preceding section. One additional feature was that a separate entry was provided for each object (assigned with a unique object identifier). Thus, text and object were given almost equal weight in the Siddham system. The main way of recording metadata was through detailed spreadsheets, which could to some extent be queried

[16] https://siddham.network/ (Accessed January 2023).

[17] http://siddham.uk/ (Accessed January 2023).

(or sorted). The internal EpiDoc encoding guidelines prepared by Balogh were reasonably robust and detailed and yet also manageable and could be mastered in a relatively short period by dedicated students.[18] The encoder was still able to navigate and follow the Sanskrit text of a fully marked-up edition, due to the relatively limited amount of code.

The current *Siddham.network* repository represents primarily the vision and ideas of one of the ERC project's PIs, Michael Willis (Figure 4.4).[19] To put it simply, the repository hands over control to the user, who is free to create their own 'community' (a curated group of epigraphs which are mutually related, e.g. by dynasty or place) and adopt whatever editorial policies seem appropriate. Very few of the communities being developed currently use EpiDoc at all. The user might also be surprised to see a 'Google search' box on the opening page. This indicates an intention to gradually move away from expensive custom-search engines that attempt to predict what a user will input, in favour of something more dynamic, that may slowly and gradually 'learn on its own'. For example, there are a number of ways a Sanskrit term can be romanised. Therefore, expensive search engines could be designed to automatically include the most common alternative spellings. Alternatively, one could put trust in a search engine that learns over time as more user data makes itself available. This of course remains more of an aspiration than a reality at present, for epigraphists are likely to ask very specific phonological questions that require an equally precise answer.

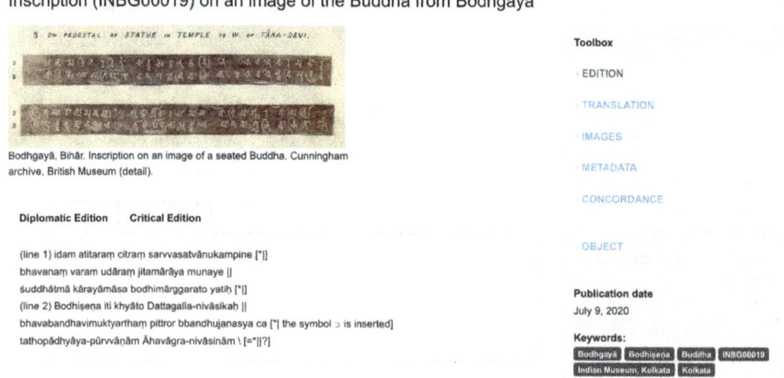

Figure 4.4: Image, 'toolbox' and edition (not encoded in EpiDoc) of sample inscription on *Siddham.network*.

---

[18] For an overview of markup strategies developed by epigraphists working on Sanskrit and other South and Southeast Asian languages, please refer to the DHARMA EpiDoc guidelines quoted below.

[19] Willis has authored a monograph on the cultural landscape of the Gupta period, covering many key epigraphic sources (2009).

These policies mean that *Siddham.network* is particularly useful as a note-taking tool to be used while researching or even while conducting fieldwork. In short, quality will vary depending on the editor(s) of the individual communities and their standards and methods of work. Furthermore, many texts and records can still be very hard to find and query. Currently, there is no way for the external user to view all of the communities present within the repository (there are plans to achieve this through the introduction of a drop-down menu).

Be that as it may, *Siddham.network* does encourage us to ask a number of deeper questions. This can be a very useful exercise for scholars and project managers alike. Can we ever and should we ever attempt to control or predict the way people work? Should we let people take control, as long as there is a way of bringing each other's work into dialogue (for example via sets of keywords)? In the longer term, is it not more appropriate to expect AI to learn by itself, rather than marking up every single element of a sentence manually? Perhaps such approaches need not result in decreased quality and reliability, provided there are ways for scholars to interact and build on each other's efforts.

Incidentally, the approach just outlined could prove particularly useful when it comes to the heritage of countries which have experienced colonisation. There seems to be an intrinsic problem with scholars and institutions imposing a top-down approach in terms of mark-up guidelines, unique identifiers, and database structures. *Siddham.network* does not solve any of these issues but its flexible, user-based approach can at least inspire a certain form of inclusivity.

Be that as it may, how does *Siddham.network* attempt to build a database? This is mostly achieved via hyperlinks and sets of keywords, which should in time generate an underlying network.[20] In practice, keywords are often either too generic or too specific (e.g. the name of a remote Indian village associated with a single copper-plate inscription). Another interesting aspect is that the 'Concordance' window provides links to the PDFs of open access articles, which makes it a very valuable instrument for research. Links to other repositories can also be provided and although no proper GIS is in place, recording map coordinates is possible and encouraged.

One example of a community that has reached a good state of development is the one labelled 'Bodhgaya epigraphy', which collects inscriptions from the site associated with the Buddha's awakening.[21] This has been prepared not by an epigraphist but by an archaeologist, Daniela De Simone.[22] It is particularly encouraging to see that other professional figures can find the repository useful enough to dedicate considerable time to it. De Simone has collected not only the editions, but plenty of photographic evidence of objects (with dedicated

20 https://siddham.network/inscription/inbg00014/ (Accessed January 2023).

21 https://siddham.network/community/bodhgaya-epigraphy/ (Accessed January 2023).

22 De Simone is the PI of the project *Excavations at Bodhgaya*, sponsored by the Shelby White and Leon Levy Program for Archaeological Publications (2021–2023).

pages and IDs), as well as estampages. Most of the secondary literature can now be accessed directly through the links in the concordance. Plenty of other communities have achieved significant results and can already be of great use to students and researchers alike.

The ERC Synergy project DHARMA has recently taken off and can only be mentioned in passing here. Within a comprehensive and nuanced approach to epigraphy and its archaeological contexts, it seems to place particular importance on the reliability of edited texts and the consistency of a highly developed system of EpiDoc mark-up. A large number of encoded epigraphs are already available for consultation.[23] The mark-up guidelines, co-authored by Balogh and Griffiths, have already been published and encompass more than 150 pages.[24] These guidelines are now the go-to resource for anyone interested to know more about the Indological contributions to EpiDoc mark-up.

One of the interesting aspects of the DHARMA project is that it employs a large number of scholars from South and Southeast Asia. The project offers opportunities for young scholars to gain professional training and academic qualifications within the EU, for example at universities in Paris. This form of partnership based on the provision of 'training' can be seen as part of the wider Western move towards trading in consultancies and knowledge-based products, given that Asian nations now increasingly have their own experts, infrastructures and cultural institutions in place.

In conclusion, the amount of resources provided for the study of Sanskrit epigraphy by these two ERC projects represents nothing less than a once-in-a-generation opportunity to change the way we think and study epigraphic texts from Southern Asia.

5. A Thai epigraphic project

In practical terms, the best results in the digitisation of inscriptions—both academically and in terms of the decolonisation of heritage—are probably achieved by fostering a variety of approaches. The repositories mentioned above are very different from one another, and that is arguably a good thing. But for the range of opportunities to be fully explored, there need to be repositories developed independently from each other, by different teams and institutions. This is particularly true of repositories designed and run in Asian countries. For example, Indian scholars have taken major steps towards the digitisation of an immense

[23] The DHARMA project team has recently made available a significant number of digital editions, meticulously edited and often accompanied by English and/or French translations: https://erc-dharma.github.io/#tfc-collection (Accessed July 2023).

[24] https://hal.archives-ouvertes.fr/DHARMA/halshs-02888186v1 (Accessed January 2023).

cultural heritage. The focus has been on manuscripts and art-historical artefacts, although some epigraphic sources can already be consulted too. The Museums of India repository allows one to view object images as well as basic metadata.[25]

A fascinating Thailand-based epigraphic database is the "Inscriptions in Thailand" project by Princess Maha Chakri Sirindhorn Anthropology Center, built in collaboration with Silpakorn University, Bangkok.[26] The website calculates the number of available records at 2456. Opening sample records, one finds basic metadata, alongside estampages and photos of the objects (Figure 4.5). There is some interlinked data, for example according to scripts, places and languages. Editions and translations are provided—although sometimes only in Thai script and Thai language—and can be downloaded as PDF (EpiDoc encoding is generally not employed by this particular project). While the website interface is available both in Thai and English, the reliance on Thai for deciphering the records sends a strong signal in terms of the repository being primarily meant for a local readership. One fascinating element, which one may take as decolonising, is the systematic use of the Buddhist Era in the metadata, instead of the Christian/Common one. Also,

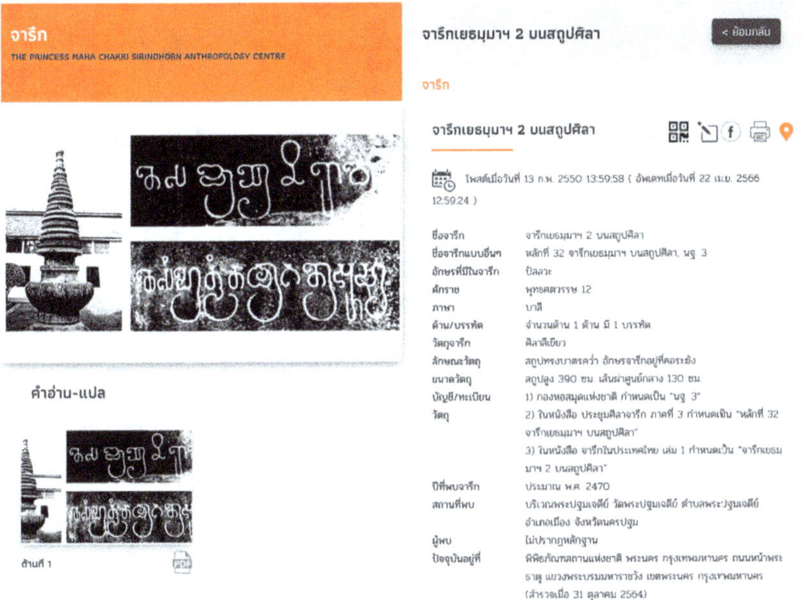

Figure 4.5: Metadata and photographic samples of inscription on the Inscriptions in Thailand database.

[25] http://museumsofindia.gov.in/repository/record/nat_del-92-53-29127 (Accessed January 2023).

[26] https://db.sac.or.th/inscriptions/ (Accessed January 2023).

it appears that only occasional use is made of the French system of cataloguing Southeast Asian and specifically Khmer inscriptions. While many Western scholars would be quite willing to adopt new cataloguing guidelines set in place in collaboration with Asian colleagues and their institutions, at the same time there is a need to avoid unnecessary confusion. How a new system might work in practice remains obscure, although it would certainly require considerable international cooperation (Khmer/Angkorian inscriptions alone have been found across a number of modern nations, including Cambodia, Thailand, and Laos). As a regular user of the database, I found dealing with Thai scripts, the Buddhist Era and the lack of familiar inscriptions IDs rather challenging.

Another valuable aspect of the Anthropology Center's repository is that it provides a map interface which is searchable.[27] For example, one can search for the Sanskrit inscriptions in the Northeastern Thai province of Buriram, after which one currently gets three hits which are pin-pointed on the map and can be then browsed on separate windows. The editions themselves are currently being improved and published in a separate series edited by Thai epigraphist Ajahn Sombat Mangmeesukhsiri at Silpakorn University.

6. Database, query, analysis

So far I have primarily examined website interfaces, encoding, and inclusivity within digital projects. However, one aspect which none of the above repositories has fully mastered so far is in a way the most basic one: the database itself. If we are to move beyond printed editions in a true 'epistemic turn', the database itself would need to be at the centre of attention, rather than the edited text. Keywords and (hyper)links are certainly useful, and so are edition-image interactions and powerful GIS. However, one should also focus on the range of search options. For example, a particularly useful digital tool available to Sanskritists is Harry Falk's Indoskript (Figure 4.6).[28] This is essentially a palaeographic database that allows one to search for a certain letter (or, more precisely, a syllable graph) and view how it appears on a variety of manuscripts and epigraphs over various centuries. The search function allows one to narrow it down to certain centuries and to select certain areas of the map. For example, one can search for the syllable 'ka' from 300 BCE to 100 BCE, focusing on witnesses from Western India. This is a simple and yet powerful way of making data accessible. Ideally, the records digitised through the repositories mentioned above, should also be searchable palaeographically or at least integrated with Indoskript. It may not be enough to offer an image so that the edition can be checked against it. Various parts of that image could be actively integrated within the database itself.[29]

---

27 https://db.sac.or.th/inscriptions/map (Accessed January 2023).

28 http://www.indoskript.org/letters (Accessed January 2023).

29 An attempt can be found in Bianchini 2023, based on a seventh century Maitraka inscription from Gujarat. On the vast epigraphical corpus of the Maitrakas see Schmiedchen 2018.

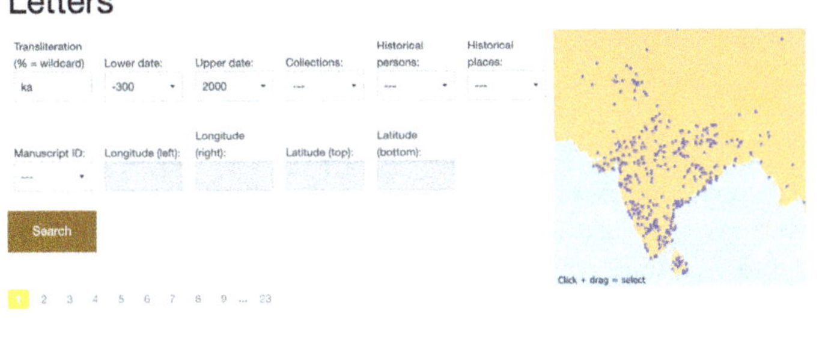

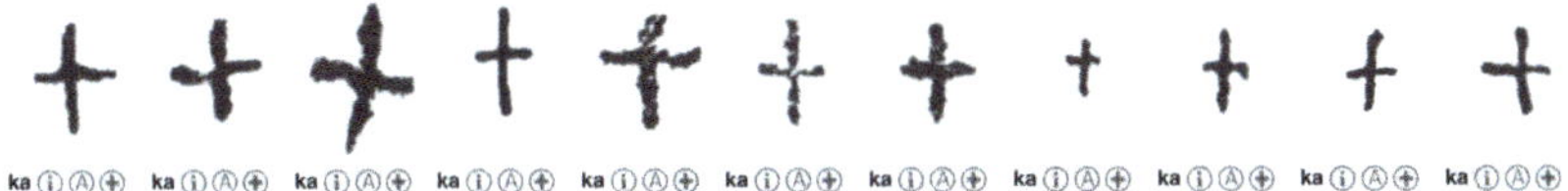

Figure 4.6: Partial overview of letter 'ka' in Western India, date range 300 BCE-200 CE.

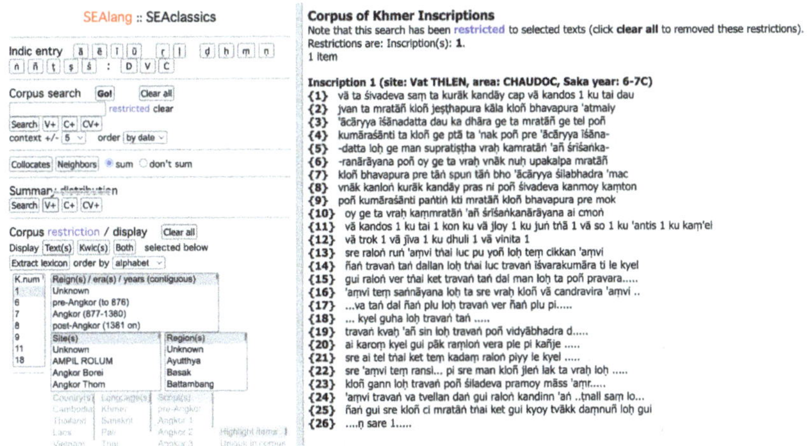

Figure 4.7: The search engine of SEAlang, Corpus of Khmer Inscriptions.

Another example are the records on SEALang Classics, particularly the *Corpus of Khmer Inscriptions*, based on the extensive work on Old Khmer by Phillip Jenner.[30] Much effort seems to have gone into designing the search engine here, although primarily for philological purposes. Apart from a very precise way of searching for text strings, the site offers the ability to narrow it down by region, site, time period, reigning monarch, language, and script (Figure 4.7). It should be feasible for repositories of Asian inscriptions to offer at least this much in terms of querying possibilities as well as further options.

30 http://sealang.net/classic/khmer/ (Accessed January 2023).

7. Conclusion

To sum up, the digitisation of inscriptions from Southern Asia is an ongoing and complex process, although some very valuable results have already been achieved. The availability of readily accessible, reliable, and open-access digital records represents an advantage to both scholars and students of South and Southeast Asia. While one should keep in mind the contingencies and requirements of funding bodies, as well as realistically attainable goals, a fascinating question is to what extent digitisation practices actually reach beyond traditional printed editions, opening the door to new ways of thinking. In this regard, I think it is crucial to gauge how the multidimensionality of artefacts is represented—i.e. if text, objects, and archaeological landscapes are integrated—and thus the extent to which collaborative interdisciplinarity is achieved. Powerful search engines and GIS tools that explore the whole scale of epigraph multidimensionality are further desirable components of an ideal database that could potentially revolutionise research.

Last but not least, a plurality of voices, methods and approaches can help ensure that we do not fall back on unequal ways of engaging with Asian cultural heritage. Multiple databases, no matter how different, can still link to each other and need not be isolated. Ultimately, the digitisation of Asian inscriptions should be a way to celebrate our shared passion for history and historiography, enhancing it with the valuable tools offered by modern-day technology.

8. References

Balogh, D. (2019). *Inscriptions of the Aulikaras and their associates.* Berlin: De Gruyter.

Balogh, D., & Griffiths, A. (2020). DHARMA Encoding Guide for Diplomatic Editions. [Technical Report] EFEO; Humboldt-Universität (Berlin); CEAIS – Centre d'Études de l'Inde et de l'Asie du Sud. Retrieved from: https://hal.archives-ouvertes.fr/DHARMA/halshs-02888186v1.

Bianchini, F. (2023). Legally binding: the textual layout of a copper-plate grant from South Asia. *Manuscript and Text Cultures 2*(1). https://doi.org/10.56004/v2.1fb.

Cambridge Digital Library – Sanskrit Manuscripts. (2015). Retrieved from: https://cudl.lib.cam.ac.uk/collections/sanskrit/1.

Corpus of the Inscriptions of Campā. (2012). Retrieved from: https://isaw.nyu.edu/publications/inscriptions/campa/index.html.

ERC DHARMA. (2020). Github Repository. Retrieved from: https://github.com/erc-dharma.

Early Inscriptions of Āndhradeśa. (2017). Retrieved from: http://hisoma.huma-num.fr/exist/apps/EIAD/index2.html.

Francis, E. (2018). Indian Copper-Plate Grants: Inscriptions or Documents? In: A Bausi, C Brockmann, M Friedrich and S Kienitz (Eds.), *Manuscripts and Archives: Comparative Views on Record-Keeping*. (Studies in Manuscript Cultures). Berlin: De Gruyter, 387–417.

Griffiths, A., & Lammerts, Ch. (2015). Epigraphy: Southeast Asia. In J. Silk, O. von Hinüber & V. Eltschinger (Eds.), *Brill's Encyclopaedia of Buddhism: Volume One, Literature and Languages* (pp. 988–1009). Leiden: Brill.

Indoskript 2.0. (2017). URL: http://www.indoskript.org/.

Museums of India. National Portal and Digital Repository. (2020). Retrieved from: https://museumsofindia.gov.in/repository/home.

Salomon, R. (1998). *Indian Epigraphy: A Guide to the Study of Inscriptions in Sanskrit, Prakrit, and the Other Indo-Aryan Languages*. New York; Oxford: Oxford University Press.

Schmiedchen, A. (2018). Kings, authors and messengers: The composition of the Maitraka copper-plate charters. In B. Shelat and T. Parmar (eds), *New horizons in Indology. Prof. Dr. H.G. Shastri commemoration volume*. Ahmedabad: Shri Nandan H. Shastri, 35–41.

SEAlang. SEAclassics: Corpus of Khmer Inscriptions. Retrieved from: http://sealang.net/classic/khmer/.

Siddham. The Asia Inscriptions Database. Retrieved from: https://siddham.network/.

The Inscriptions in Thailand Database. (2019). The Princess Maha Chakri Sirindhorn Anthropology Centre. Retrieved from: https://db.sac.or.th/inscriptions/.

Willis, M. (2009). *The Archaeology of Hindu Ritual : Temples and the Establishment of the Gods*. New York; Cambridge: Cambridge University Press.

CHAPTER 5

Materiality and community: Digital approaches to Ethiopic manuscript culture

Daria Elagina
University of Hamburg

Abstract

The manuscript tradition of Ethiopia and Eritrea extends from the beginning of the first millennium CE until the present and bears witness not only to a large corpus of texts of various genres and origins, but also to diverse aspects of the social, economic, religious, and cultural life of the region. Each manuscript has a particular role in the life of the society and thus embodies diverse social and cultural practices. Besides intellectual content, much information on the actual role of manuscripts in the life of the societies of Ethiopia and Eritrea is delivered by their material features. Consequently, collection and processing of codicological data on Ethiopic manuscripts is essential for understanding their social lives. This data can be approached from two different but complementary perspectives, the so-called New Philology and Quantitative Codicology. Both of these approaches might profitably be combined with digital research methods, enhancing the ways in which collected data can be processed and interpreted.

How to cite this book chapter:
Elagina, D. 2023. Materiality and community: Digital approaches to Ethiopic manuscript culture. In: Palladino, C. and Bodard, G. (Eds.), *Can't Touch This: Digital Approaches to Materiality in Cultural Heritage*. Pp. 95–119. London: Ubiquity Press. DOI: https://doi.org/10.5334/bcv.f.

Digital research methods foster a formalised description of many codicological and paratextual features of Ethiopic manuscripts and their quantitative and qualitative analysis and consequently promote the study of the role of manuscripts in the societies of Ethiopia and Eritrea. The multi-media research environment for the study of the rich manuscript culture of that region developed in the context of the project *Beta maṣāḥəft: Manuscripts of Ethiopia and Eritrea* might serve as a solid and flexible platform for the study of the role of manuscripts in society.

Zusammenfassung

Die Manuskriptkultur Äthiopiens und Eritreas reicht vom Beginn des ersten Jahrtausends n. Chr. bis in die Gegenwart und zeugt nicht nur von einem großen Korpus an Texten unterschiedlicher Gattungen und Ursprünge, sondern auch von vielfältigen Aspekten des sozialen, wirtschaftlichen, religiösen und kulturellen Lebens der Region. Jede Handschrift hat eine besondere Rolle im Leben der Gesellschaft und verkörpert somit vielfältige soziale und kulturelle Praktiken. Neben dem Inhalt liefern ihre materiellen Eigenschaften viele Informationen über die tatsächliche Funktion der Handschriften im Leben der Gesellschaften Äthiopiens und Eritreas. Folglich ist die Sammlung und Verarbeitung kodikologischer Daten zu äthiopischen Manuskripten für das Verständnis ihres Sitzes im Leben unerlässlich. Diese Daten können aus zwei unterschiedlichen, aber einander ergänzenden Perspektiven angegangen werden, der sogenannten ‚New Philology' und der quantitativen Kodikologie. Beide Ansätze können gewinnbringend mit digitalen Forschungsmethoden kombiniert werden, um die Art und Weise zu verbessern, wie gesammelte Daten verarbeitet und interpretiert werden können. Digitale Forschungsmethoden begünstigen eine formalisierte Beschreibung vieler kodikologischer und paratextueller Merkmale äthiopischer Handschriften und deren quantitative und qualitative Analyse und fördern folglich die Erforschung der Rolle von Handschriften in den Gesellschaften Äthiopiens und Eritreas. Die im Rahmen des Langzeitvorhabens *Beta maṣāḥəft: Die Schriftkultur des christlichen Äthiopiens und Eritreas: Eine multimediale Forschungsumgebung* entstandene und weiter entstehende multimediale Forschungsumgebung zum Erforschen der reichen Manuskriptkultur dieser Region soll als solide und flexible Plattform für die Untersuchung der Rolle von Manuskripten in der Gesellschaft dienen.

1. The Manuscript Culture of Ethiopia and Eritrea

The written tradition of Ethiopia and Eritrea has survived uninterrupted from the first millennium BCE until today (Bausi 2014; Bausi 2015).[1] The first

[1] I would like sincerely to thank Gabriel Bodard and Chiara Palladino for inviting me to contribute to this volume and for their competent and

evidence for written tradition in the region is in inscriptions (Avanzini et al. 2007); the introduction of manuscripts happened at an early date, apparently no later than the third century CE.[2] The process of Christianization, which took place as early as in the fourth century CE, fostered a diffusion of manuscripts—and consequently their production—in the region, at least for religious services and liturgical practices (Uhlig & Bausi 2007). Manuscript production has survived in some regions to the present. Most manuscripts are written in Ethiopic, a considerably smaller number in Amharic; Arabic and Harari are used in the Islamic context. Most of the manuscripts, at least those described and available for study, are datable to rather recent times (a significant number of manuscripts is attested from the fourteenth century onwards), with, however, some prominent exceptions.[3]

Having most probably started as an indispensable part of religious practice, manuscript culture in Ethiopia and Eritrea expanded its role during its long life in the region: new translations and local literary production (for example, hagiographical texts or royal chronicles), church education and healing practices, archiving and correspondence practices, and numerous other activities moulded the manuscript culture of Ethiopia and Eritrea into a multi-faceted and multi-dimensional phenomenon that became an integral part of the social, economic, religious and cultural life of the region.

According to approximate estimates the number of codices in Ethiopia and Eritrea may be as high as ca. 200,000, excluding scrolls and other manuscript forms (Sergew Hable Selassie 1981: 35). Several thousand manuscripts are also housed in museums, libraries, and other collections outside the region (Uhlig & Bausi 2007). The actual number of manuscripts might be even higher when taking less-explored monasteries of the region into consideration

---

patient editorial work and valuable remarks. I would also like to extend my thanks to Usama Gad for his helpful comments. I am extremely grateful to Steve Delamarter, George Fox University, Denis Nosnitsin, University of Hamburg, and Sisay Sahile, University of Gondar, for their permission to publish photographic material. My special thanks go to Sean M. Winslow, University of Graz, for his valuable comments on this chapter.

2 For the list of bibliographic references, see Bausi, 2014: 41, n. 9. The earliest specimen of manuscripts being represented by codices, the time of introduction of other manuscript forms, such as scrolls, can hardly be determined. Contrary to the situation, for example, in Egypt, where a substitution of (papyrus) scrolls through parchment codices might be traced back (Bülow-Jacobsen 2009: 18–25), no such observations can be made for Ethiopia and Eritrea with certainty.

3 For example, the famous ʾAbbā Garimā Gospels are dated to the ca. 6th–7th century CE at the latest by radiocarbon dating. See the comprehensive monograph by Judith S. McKenzie and Francis Watson (2016), and the review of it by Bausi (2017; 2011).

(Bausi 2014: 37).[4] An unknown number of manuscripts are also kept in private collections, which largely remain uncatalogued and unstudied. From this number of manuscripts only a portion have been documented,[5] let alone digitised and thoroughly catalogued, although digitization and cataloguing projects are core activities in the field of Ethiopian Studies.[6]

2. Digital approaches in cataloguing

2.1 From traditional to digital cataloguing

Scholarly cataloguing practices for Ethiopic manuscripts in the West have undergone several changes since the first catalogue descriptions by Heinrich von Ewald in the 1840s (Ewald 1844; Ewald 1847). From the mid-nineteenth to the second half of the twentieth century, catalogues were mainly concerned with philological and comparative aspects, with little attention paid to the material features (Witakowski 2015). The 1978 catalogue by Stefan Sterlcyn (Strelcyn 1978) heralded a new approach to the cataloguing of Ethiopic manuscripts, with much more advanced physical description, including details of decorations, layout, and palaeography. Subsequently, the late twentieth century saw catalogues which are excellent in their descriptions of both intellectual content and material features (Marrassini 1984; Marrassini 1987; Hammerschmidt 1973; Hammerschmidt 1977; Hammerschmidt and Six 1983; Six 1989; Six 1994; Six 1999). Since that time physical descriptions of manuscripts have

---

[4] These treasures are, however, endangered due to the complexity of the political situation. To draw attention on the problem, members of the Hiob Ludolf Centre for Ethiopian and Eritrean Studies and associated scholars issued an appeal for salvation of the cultural heritage of Tigray: https://www.aai.uni-hamburg.de/en/ethiostudies/news/appeal2021.html. See also Hagos Abrha Abay and Flanagan (2022).

[5] For example, the database of the project *Beta maṣāḥǝft: Manuscripts of Ethiopia and Eritrea (Schriftkultur des christlichen Äthiopiens: eine multimediale Forschungsumgebung)* contains over 18,000 entries for manuscripts at the time of writing. For more details on the project see below.

[6] For copyright issues of digitised cultural heritage consider Okorie (Chapter 11 in this volume). In addition to digitization projects of collections of Ethiopic manuscripts (or their microfilms) kept in Europe or North America, several digitization projects have been conducted in Ethiopia in recent years, for example, the Project Ethio-SPaRe, HLCEES, University of Hamburg (PI Denis Nosnitsin; ERC Starting Grant 240720). For one of the most recent cataloguing projects of the uncatalogued collection of Ethiopic manuscripts of Dayr as-Suryān, see Nosnitsin and Reule 2021.

become an important part of catalogue descriptions. Summarising some experience of the last years, Witold Witakowski argues that 'in order to achieve a satisfactory description of a collection of manuscripts collaboration between textual scholars and codicologists, and where necessary art historians and conservators, is desirable' (Witakowski 2015: 487).

An excellent opportunity for such a collaboration is offered by the multimedia research environment for the study of Ethiopic manuscripts of the project *Beta maṣāḥəft:*[7] *Manuscripts of Ethiopia and Eritrea* (*Schriftkultur des christlichen Äthiopiens: eine multimediale Forschungsumgebung*).[8] One of the project's main objectives is the digital provision of manuscript descriptions based on existing catalogues of Ethiopic manuscripts, enhanced by consulting digitised images if available or occasionally physical manuscripts.[9] Born-digital descriptions of uncatalogued manuscripts are also amongst the project's activities.

Although it is not the first digital project in the field,[10] *Beta maṣāḥəft* is an innovative endeavour in Ethiopian Studies, establishing a collaborative platform for manuscript catalogue records, text editions, and authority lists. The data architecture uses XML (Extensible Markup Language) as a data entry format. There are records for manuscripts, works (of literature), persons and places which are connected with one another and validate to the schema, which is a customization of TEI (Text Encoding Initiative). Hosting data on GitHub allows for continuous and collaborative editing and quality control. This workflow, on the one hand, fosters work with heterogeneous sources of information and, on the other hand, allows cataloguers to make individual decisions on the depth of cataloguing.

---

7 *Beta maṣāḥəft*, literally meaning 'house of books', stands for 'library' in the Ethiopic language.

8 *Beta maṣāḥəft* is a long-term project funded within the framework of the Academies' Programme (coordinated by the Union of the German Academies of Sciences and Humanities) hosted by the Akademie der Wissenschaften in Hamburg. The PI is Alessandro Bausi, the Technical Lead was Pietro Maria Liuzzo until 2022, the Project Coordinator is Eugenia Sokolinski. The project website is: https://www.betamasaheft.uni-hamburg.de/. For the digital research environment: https://betamasaheft.eu/. For a detailed description including technical aspects see Liuzzo (2019), for a more concise overview see Reule (2018). I had the joy of working for this project as a cataloguer and of experiencing the inspiring and enriching atmosphere of a collaborative work process in 2018–2021. For a list of contributors visit: https://betamasaheft.eu/team.html.

9 For the list of digitised manuscripts maintained by the team of *Beta maṣāḥəft* visit: https://github.com/BetaMasaheft/Manuscripts/wiki/List-of-digitized-Ethiopic-manuscripts-available-online.

10 For a list of projects see Liuzzo 2019: xxv–xxxii.

Amongst the many advantages of the project, one of the most valuable is the possibility of collaboration and easy and straightforward discussion of questions arising from the process of cataloguing using the Issues feature in GitHub.[11] Through a digital collaboration on manuscript descriptions between scholars at different career stages, interests, and cultural and academic backgrounds, flexible and editable Guidelines for cataloguing manuscripts of Ethiopia and Eritrea are being continuously developed (Liuzzo et al. 2018),[12] that highlight and formalise their various features. Many features (frequently material ones), which have been neglected in printed catalogues due to the limit of space, focus of the cataloguers on intellectual content, or other reasons, are coming to light, revealing the multiple dimensions of manuscript culture of the region, and illuminating many aspects of the real lives of manuscripts within the community. This is a result of scholarly collaboration which would barely have been possible without modern digital approaches to the study of manuscript cultures.

However, this is not the only advantage of applying digital approaches to the study of the manuscript culture of Ethiopia and Eritrea. In addition to the opportunity for collaboration and knowledge exchange, digital methods allow for processing large amounts of formalizable and quantifiable data pertaining to the materiality of manuscripts, which is indispensable in the field given the overall number of manuscripts and the number of already catalogued and digitised ones. This data can be approached from two different but complementary perspectives: the so-called 'New Philology' or 'Material Philology,' and 'Quantitative Codicology' (also known as 'statistical codicology').[13] New Philology, a term officially launched in *Speculum* in 1990 (Nichols 1990), advocates for the primary significance of a manuscript and its material settings for the study of texts and regards each manuscript as an individual written artefact with its own history of transmission. Quantitative Codicology, a term coined by Ezio Ornato in 1990s (see, for example, Ornato 1997), focuses on a systematic study of a statistically significant number of samples and uncovering overall phenomena of long-term trends, and aims at setting each manuscript against the backdrop of a considerable number of other manuscripts (for an overview see Maniaci 2022). Both approaches can profit significantly from the application of digital research methods, which enhance the ways in which collected data can be processed and interpreted. In the following, I will demonstrate based on examples, the advantages, challenges, and new perspectives that arise from the application of digital research methods to the study of the manuscript heritage of Ethiopia and Eritrea within the project *Beta maṣāḥəft* and beyond.

[11] *Beta maṣāḥəft* GitHub Issues: https://github.com/BetaMasaheft/Documentation/issues.

[12] For the Guidelines visit: https://betamasaheft.eu/Guidelines/.

[13] For history, methods, and challenges of this approach see Maniaci (2022).

2.2 *Formalisation of data: size of codices*

The number of Ethiopic manuscripts available, their diversification in materiality and content allows for posing of diverse research questions. In the meantime, formalisation and documentation even of very basic material settings such as book form and size for a statically relevant number of manuscripts,[14] alongside their intellectual content, might provide information for the role of many manuscripts in the community. For example, the discussion on the so-called 'monumental' codices in the Ethiopian context (Bausi 2008: 517; Bausi 2014: 42–44; Brita 2015), which appear to play a specific social role being a sign of the richness and religious devotion of the community, might profit considerably from encoding of codex sizes in a consistent manner and from a possibility of filtering codices according to facets including height and width. Collection of the same data from printed catalogues would be a monumentally more time-consuming task, not least because some catalogues provide measurements in units other than centimetres.[15] None of the catalogues of Ethiopic manuscripts known to me arrange manuscripts exclusively according to their size. Thus, filtering of manuscripts according to their size changes the research approach from sporadic case study observations to much more statistically reliable data.

2.3 *Digital scientific methods and parchment description*

For features of manuscripts which require more skill to define and formalise precisely than size, specific knowledge and expertise are necessary. These features, not commonly mentioned in catalogues, include the quality of parchment used in the production of manuscripts and the material characteristics of textiles in bindings. The overwhelming majority of Christian manuscripts in Ethiopia and Eritrea are made from parchment (Balicka-Witakowska et al. 2015: 154–156). Although information on the costs for manuscript production in the course of the history is sparse (Platonov 2017: 102–105), the expenses connected to the production of parchment would have represented a considerable (and along with the work of the scribe(s), completely indispensable) part of the production costs. Thus, a private manuscript of the kind shown in Figure 5.1, a small magic text most probably meant for private use (MS SSB-015) shows lower parchment quality than a manuscript produced, for example, for a monastic community or to serve political goals, such as the Four Gospel manuscript (MS Ef. n.s. 22), which was presented to the Russian Emperor Nikolay II by the Emperor Menelik II in 1895 (Dege-Müller et al. 2020a;

---

[14] See also Filosa, Gad & Bodard (Chapter 3 in this volume) on machine-actionable encoding.

[15] For example, the catalogue by William Wright (1877) utilised inches for measurements.

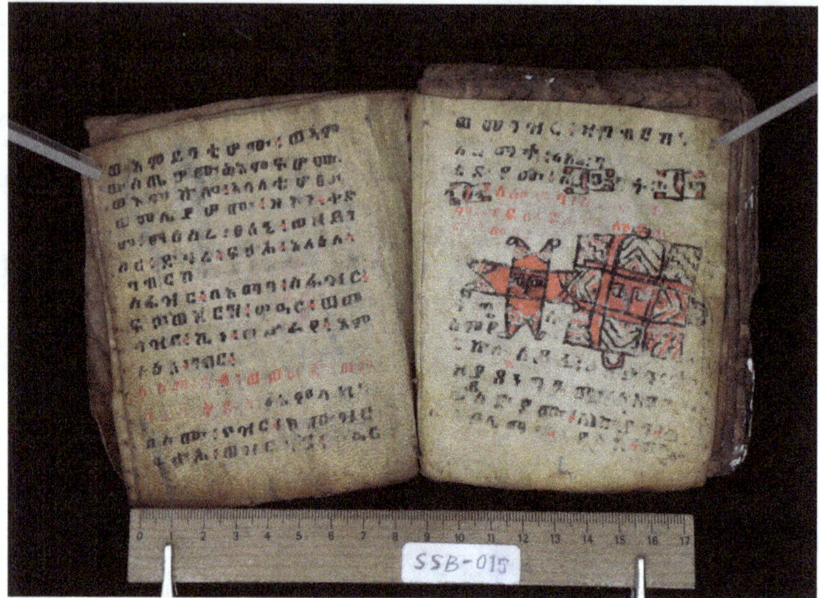

Figure 5.1: Poor parchment quality: MS SSB-015, fols. 3v-4r. MS Bet Ḥāwāryāt (Ethiopia), SSB-015, Maftəḥe śərāy, 19th century (catalogued for Ethio-SPaRe by S. Dege-Müller; now also accessible in the database of the project *Beta maṣāḥəft*: https://betamasaheft.eu/manuscripts/ESssb015/main). (Photo Ethio-SPaRe).

Platonov 1996: 9–11; Elagina 2019). The latter attests such a high quality of parchment (white and thin) that it was specifically (and exceptionally) mentioned in the catalogue (Platonov 1996: 9–11). In this respect, manuscripts that simultaneously attest various qualities of parchment within a single codicological unit are of special interest.[16] Additionally parchment quality might give us insight to the craftsmanship and production techniques which in their turn might attest to a particular centre of manuscript production.[17] These aspects make a description of the parchment quality of manuscripts a scholarly desideratum.

[16] For an example of a manuscript with a change of parchment quality within the text block see MS AM-008 (Dege-Müller et al. 2020b). Sometimes protective leaves are made of lower quality parchment than the rest of the text block (Tomaszewski & Gervers 2015: 37).

[17] For some hints on centres of high-quality parchment production, see, for example, Pankhurst 1983: 207. Reportedly, scribes or parchment makers could use individual recipes for occasional parchment whitening (Balicka-Witakowska et al. 2015: 155).

Parchment quality depends on two main aspects: the quality of animal skin (including species, overall health condition, insect bites, rubs)[18] and the parchment production techniques and skills of a parchment maker. The description of both aspects requires specific expertise.[19] The assessment of the quality of parchment requires not only the possibility of checking a physical manuscript, expertise in the parchment production of the region (Faqāda Śellāsē Tafarrā 2002: 94–126; Sergew Hable Selassie 1981: 9–12; Godet 1980, Mellors and Parsons 2003),[20] and the ability to distinguish between initial lack of quality and signs of deterioration, but is also quite problematic in formalisation. The quality of parchment within a particular manuscript culture is not an absolute but a relative characteristic, and it requires the preliminary examination of a considerable amount of data and the definition of a "standard", deviations from which might be considered as peculiarities.

Concerning the stage of parchment production, much data can be obtained through the application of modern scientific and digital methods (Rabin 2015), such as digital microscopy, for example, the Dino Lite digital stereomicroscopy (UV/VIS/NIR), which helps detect, on the one hand, the remains of hair, blood, and other marks that might give us some clues to the process of parchment production (Liszewska and Tomaszewski 2016: 187). On the other hand, a microscopic examination can also reveal the initial colour of a manuscript, detecting spots with no discoloration (Liszewska 2017: 268). Much more advanced technologies, such as infrared spectroscopy or SEM-EDS might detect specific substances (for example, kaolin) used in the manufacturing process at different stages (Liszewska & Tomaszewski 2016: 187; Liszewska 2017: 266; Bicchieri et al. 2019: 8–11).[21] Several technologies might be applied for defining the species of animal whose skin was used to produce parchment. Although these technologies are very advanced and might provide reliable and formalisable data, it is unreasonable to rely on collecting such data for a considerable number of Ethiopic manuscripts (especially of those kept in monastic libraries of Ethiopia and Eritrea) due to the human, technological, and financial resources such an enterprise would require.

---

[18] The quality of skin was even dependent on the climate zone in which the animal was bred (Assefa Liban 1958: 11–12).

[19] A proper description of parchment quality requires an expertise on the production techniques pertaining specifically to the region. Thus, for example, gelatinization on surfaces is rather normal and typical for the parchment production technique in Ethiopia and Eritrea without strong chemical processing (Tomaszewski and Gervers 2015: 17).

[20] For a summary of the evidence of parchment manufacturing in Ethiopia and Eritrea see, for example, Bausi (2008: 531–536); Balicka-Witakowska et al. (2015: 154–155); Winslow (2015: 69–112).

[21] For detection of substances on Ethiopic manuscripts using X-ray fluorescence method (XRF) see Richardin and et al. (2006), Nosnitsin et al. (2014).

2.4 Statistical analysis and textiles in manuscripts

Another material feature of Ethiopic manuscripts to which I want to draw attention is the presence of different types of textiles as inlays,[22] attached to the inner surfaces of the binding boards. These elements are important from different perspectives. Originating from different parts of the world, these pieces of textile are material evidence for the trade and cultural relations between Ethiopia and other countries (Pankhurst 1980; Pankhurst 1981; Pankhurst 1985–1986); on the other hand the presence and choice of textiles in codices might have had meaning within the manuscript culture of the region (Fee, Gervers & Melis 2022). The importance of collecting data pertaining to the presence and character of textile inlays has provoked a fruitful discussion between the members of the *Beta maṣāḥəft* project on the depth of description and formalisation plausible in cataloguing such material features.[23] Since a detailed description of historical textiles requires specific expertise, it has been decided to limit the documentation to the general presence of textile inlays and not to distinguish between the origin and type of textile. The only exception is for silk, which might represent material with a specific meaning in the culture of Ethiopia and Eritrea, since the acquisition, distribution, and use of silk was a royal prerogative for several centuries (Gervers 2010). One might try to trace this relationship based on the data of *Beta maṣāḥəft*.

At the time of writing, the database contains entries for 18,177 manuscripts. A considerable proportion of those are automatically generated stubs or entries not encoded according to the standards of the project's Guidelines.[24] Accordingly, the following analysis is a very preliminary attempt at analysing data collected in the database and should not be considered as a final result; the restrictions of this analysis will be presented below.

According to the search function of the web application,[25] 695 manuscripts contain textiles in their binding and 66 (under 10%) of those attest the presence of silk. The list of manuscripts with silk inlays is of much interest. Except for one manuscript from Grottaferrata, MS Crypt. Aet. 7 (Dal Sasso 2018), the other 65 manuscripts are from the so-called Maqdalā collection stored

---

[22] The term 'textile inlay' is used by the team of *Beta maṣāḥəft* (https://betamasaheft.eu/Guidelines/?id=bindingDescription). The new *Textiles in Ethiopian Manuscripts* project applies the term 'textile pastedowns'. I stick to the term 'inlay' because that was the term I was searching in the database of *Beta maṣāḥəft*. Textile inlays are not the only cases of application of textiles in manuscripts of Ethiopia and Eritrea. Sometimes textile pieces are also used as protective curtains for miniatures, textile bags or wraps for keeping manuscripts are attested as well.

[23] https://github.com/BetaMasaheft/Documentation/issues/1337.

[24] For example, due to automatic creation of stubs from printed catalogues.

[25] https://betamasaheft.eu/newSearch.html?searchType=text&mode=any&work-types=mss.

today in the British Library.[26] The Maqdalā collection was a rich collection of manuscripts (reportedly over one thousand) which the Emperor Tewodros (1855–68) took from churches all over his empire, especially from Gondar. The collection was housed at the natural fortress of Maqdalā (Pankhurst 1973; Pankhurst 2007). In 1868, the manuscripts of this royal library were looted by the British Napier expedition and 400 were brought to Britain. 350 are kept today in the British Library (Wright 1877: iv). Not all of those manuscripts have been fully included in the database; nevertheless, the search results, despite almost exclusively returning manuscripts from the collection, are still of interest.

These results might point to the association of silk inlays in codices with a high social status of the manuscript's owner or of the hosting institution, the Maqdalā collection being a royal library. Indeed, some of the pieces from this collection with silk inlays were even produced personally for the members of the royal family. For example, a beautiful, richly illuminated manuscript of Four Gospels (CAe 1560)[27] from the Maqdalā collection, MS Oriental 510 (Wright 1877: 24b-25a; Reule et al. 2022), was in the possession of Sabla Wangel, wife of the Emperor Yoḥannəs I (1667–1682). Another example is a manuscript containing a collection of magical texts known as *Maftəḥe śərāy* ('Undoing of charms', CAe 1824), MS Oriental 566 (Wright 1877: 113b; Elagina et al. 2022), which belonged to the ruler of Shoa Wasan Sagad (1808–1812/13).

Another possible explanation might pertain to the character of data that is collected in the database. The sources for the data in the database are very heterogeneous. I have already outlined at the beginning of this contribution that the standards for cataloguing Ethiopic manuscripts have varied considerably over the course of time. Since the main source for data at this stage of the project is historical catalogues of Ethiopic manuscripts, it is not impossible that the search results represent the cataloguing practices of William Wright in particular, whose catalogue, enhanced with analysis of available digitised material, is the source for the encoding of this collection.[28] Moreover, the catalogue of Wright is one of the catalogues on which the team of *Beta maṣāḥəft* has been working most actively. In other words, it is at this stage not possible to decide whether the search results are based on the absence of silk inlays in other manuscripts or on the absence of recording of them. This observation sheds light, in

[26] The list of manuscripts in a concise form is the following: MSS London, British Library, Oriental 78, 483, 488, 508, 509, 510, 513, 517–522, 533, 534, 536, 539, 542, 545, 547, 549, 552, 554, 555, 557, 562, 566, 591, 596, 598, 599, 603, 607, 608, 615, 616, 617, 658, 660, 661, 666, 670, 685, 686, 696, 701, 708, 715, 723, 727, 730, 732, 739, 741, 742, 744, 751, 752, 776, 777, 778, 781. All these numbers fall within the numbers ascribed to the Maqdalā collection (Wright 1877: iii).

[27] CAe stands for Clavis Aethiopica, a repertory of works of the literature of Ethiopia and Eritrea, and refers to the individual identifier of a text.

[28] http://www.bl.uk/manuscripts/Default.aspx.

my opinion, on some limitations of editable digital cataloguing, flexible in depth and scope, which I have highlighted above. A statistical analysis, one of the main tools of Quantitative Codicology, requires data of a specific quality. Missing or incomplete data inevitably leads to distortion of analysis results. In cases when the absence of a feature in encoding does not explicitly document the absence of the feature, statistical analysis becomes a very unreliable instrument. This is not to be considered critical of the strategy of the project *Beta maṣāḥəft*, which I find very balanced and sensible, since much of the data just cannot be retrieved from historical catalogues, and there should be a scholarly freedom in the decision making on the depth of cataloguing.

2.5 Closed lists in digital cataloguing: book forms

The recording of the type of textile might appear as a less important material feature for many cataloguers, or a feature requiring special expertise, and therefore neglected. However, the categorization of either of the two most widespread types of book forms in Ethiopia and Eritrea, codex and scroll, is inevitably documented by any cataloguer, and a definition of the object form in the object description of each manuscript is required by the project's schema.[29] This serves to the advantage of the study of scrolls, which are still understudied. Scrolls have almost exclusively been described in the literature as text carriers for magic texts (Balicka-Witakowska et al. 2015: 158–159; Nosnitsin 2020: 295). Indeed, the so-called *kətābs*, scrolls containing magic texts and pictures used as apotropaic objects, are still quite widespread in Ethiopia and Eritrea today (Chernetsov 2007). However, this is apparently not the only context in which scrolls as text carriers have been circulating in the region.

Scrolls have also been used in the traditional system of church education as didactic tools for learning to read. In this case scrolls contain, according to current knowledge, two types of texts: traditional Ethiopic syllabaries, *ʾAbugidā* (CAe 5913) and *Hahu* (CAe 5914) (Chernetsov 2003), and *Fidala ḥawārəyā* ('Apostle's Alphabet', CAe 5905), an excerpt from the First Epistle of John. There is hardly any information on this type of scroll in Western literature,[30] probably because such scrolls, which I call student scrolls, are almost absent in the collections of Ethiopic manuscripts outside Ethiopia and Eritrea. I know so far of only six specimens kept in three different institutions. The Museum of Anthropology and Ethnography of the Russian Academy of Sciences 'Kunstkamera' in Saint-Petersburg holds the 'largest' collection of four items: MSS 2103–21 (Platonov 1996: 67; Elagina 2020a), 2103–25 (Platonov 1996: 68; Elagina 2020b), 3052–887a (Platonov 1996: 70; Elagina 2020c) and 3052–887b (Platonov 1996: 70–71; Elagina

29 https://betamasaheft.eu/Guidelines/?id=objectDescription.

30 The only exception known to me is the posthumous monograph on the manuscript culture of Ethiopia by Platonov (2017: 26–29).

2020d). The British Museum in London has in its collection one student scroll (Af1893,0715.7),[31] and one single scroll is kept in Paris (MS Éthiopien 521).[32]

Other than student scrolls, there is another more enigmatic category of scrolls or similar objects representing parchment strips or leaves, ca. 50–60 cm long and ca. 36–55 cm wide, with narrow strips of parchment possibly meant to keep them rolled. I know so far of two examples of such objects digitised in the frames of the Endangered Archives Programme of the British Library, project EAP286:[33] one (MS British Library EAP286/1/1/121) transmitting *Mystagogia* (CAe 3978),[34] and another one (MS British Library EAP286/1/1/152) transmitting *Malkəʾa Tewodros* (*Image of Tewodros*, CAe 6389).[35] The purpose and use of these manuscripts has not been determined with certainty so far.[36]

These types of scrolls, including the student scrolls, might be very underrepresented in digital or analogue collections, due to the very private character of such manuscripts, their modest physical features (for example, the lack of decoration in contrast to the magic scrolls), or their overall scarcity. Being very rare they often remain unnoticed. The idea of a digital hyper-catalogue, which stores information from different catalogues, pointing to the *Beta maṣāḥəft* project would create much more visibility for such objects and would widen our understanding of the manuscript culture. Additionally, this would provide grounds for analysis of the distribution of texts amongst different text carriers and subsequently the role of texts in different aspects of the community's life.

2.6 Encoding the interaction with manuscripts: navigation systems

In Ethiopia and Eritrea manuscripts have often been witnesses to the social practices connected to the texts they contain. Regular use of a manuscript quite often presupposed the existence of elements that assisted in navigation through volumes and structuring their content. In Ethiopic manuscript culture, there are many ways in which manuscripts were adapted for the specific purposes of reading, chanting, or other practices. This 'system of navigation', or 'finding aids,'

---

[31] The digital image of the scroll is available online: https://www.britishmuseum.org/collection/object/E_Af1893-0715-7.

[32] I express my gratitude to my colleague Dorothea Reule, who has discovered this manuscript in the large collection of Bibliothèque Nationale de France. A digital image of the manuscript is available at: https://gallica.bnf.fr/ark:/12148/btv1b531151467.

[33] Grant holders are Ato Demeke Berhane Teffera and Stephen Delamarter. For more details on the project visit: https://eap.bl.uk/project/EAP286.

[34] https://eap.bl.uk/archive-file/EAP286-1-1-121.

[35] https://eap.bl.uk/archive-file/EAP286-1-1-152.

[36] Although both texts transmitted in these artefacts are known in the context of magic, these scrolls do not show typical features of protective artefacts (for example, they lack protective pictures).

can take different forms: textual or non-textual; pertaining to the stage of production or of secondary nature. The complexity of this phenomenon deserves special attention. It is a case where there is still room for improvement in encoding strategies and an active collaboration with colleagues, fostering best practices and the collection of experiences and opinions, which I demonstrate by referring to the relevant GitHub Issues in the following section.

Textual elements that seem to serve as navigation through a volume can take various forms, such as tables of contents, titles of texts or text parts written in the margins, as well as running titles throughout a text unit. Their categorization and attribution to a certain stage of production is a complex task. Even more so defining a strategy for their consistent and sustainable encoding.[37] Interestingly, such elements appear alongside other structuring elements in Ethiopic manuscripts belonging to the initial stage of production, such as rubrication and aniconic decorations at the beginning of texts and text sections. Quite often, liturgical manuscripts contain indications for readings at the beginning of textual units, which tell on which day or holiday the text should be read.[38]

A non-textual form of finding aid, the bookmark, is normally represented by small pieces of threads (silk in case of *deluxe* manuscripts), textile ribbons, or pieces of leather attached to folio margins (Balicka-Witakowska et al. 2015: 174; Figure 5.2). They might be attached to different parts of a leaf and be of different colours. This is a phenomenon which is close in its functionality to the textual finding aids but is different in its expression and possibly also purpose.[39] As pointed out by Di Bella and Sarris (2014: 303), such elements are not infrequent, especially in liturgical manuscripts, and a thorough study of them would also contribute to the study of liturgical practices. However, bookmarks are attested in manuscripts transmitting different texts. The above-mentioned manuscript with magic (or medical) text belonging to Wasan Sagad also attests such elements[40] —undoubtedly a fascinating topic for research, which might reveal much on the intended usage of the manuscript.

Finding the right strategy for encoding such phenomena, which represent the connecting element between the materiality of a codex and its contents and might serve as a witness to the way a codex was used, is a complex task. The Guidelines of *Beta maṣāḥəft* provide a solution which differentiates between a leaf string marker and a leaf tab marker;[41] however, some further physical

[37] I have tentatively proposed for discussion an approach for encoding at least some cases of such phenomenon: https://github.com/BetaMasaheft/Documentation/issues/1765.

[38] A GitHub Issue concerning formalisation of their encoding was created by Marcin Krawczuk: https://github.com/BetaMasaheft/Documentation/issues/1804.

[39] For the GitHub Issues concerning these elements see: https://github.com/BetaMasaheft/Documentation/issues/972; https://github.com/BetaMasaheft/Documentation/issues/1130.

[40] For example, MS Oriental 566, fols. 1, 6, 11, 18, 30, 36.

[41] https://betamasaheft.eu/Guidelines/?q=tab&id=bindingDescription.

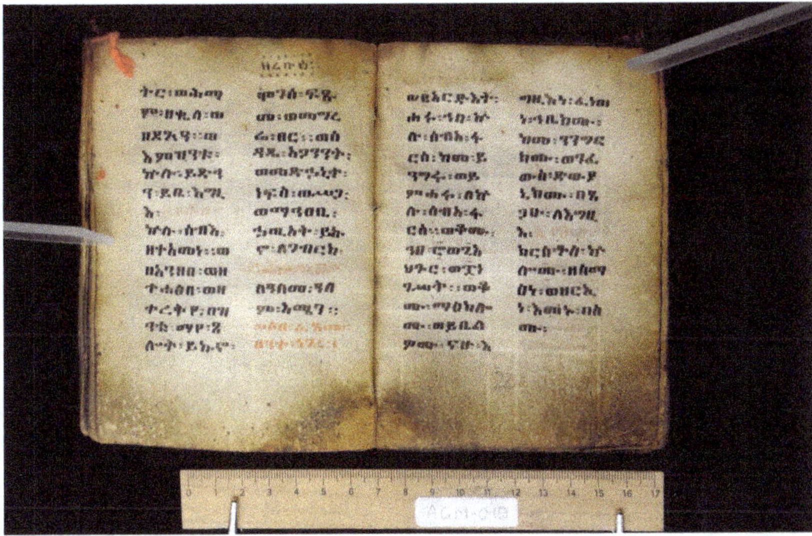

Figure 5.2: Red thread, MS AGM-010, fol. 21. MS ʾAgamyo Qəddus Mikāʾel (Ethiopia), AGM-010, Collection of texts, 19th century (catalogued for Ethio-SPaRe by S. Dege-Müller; now also accessible in the data base of the project *Beta maṣāḥəft*: https://betamasaheft.eu/manuscripts/ESagm010/main). (Photo Ethio-SPaRe).

aspects, such as material or colour in case of textiles or threads, should probably receive more attention in the future, especially in cases of the use of several colours for bookmarks throughout a codex, which might represent a further level of structuring.

2.7 Digital approach to seals and sealing practices

Ethiopic manuscripts, including personal letters, are witnesses to another fascinating but often neglected practice: sealing.[42] While the presence of seals in Ethiopia and Eritrea is first attested in the sixteenth century at the latest (Sohier 2010), their use flourished in the nineteenth and early twentieth centuries. The functions of seals in the manuscript culture of the region are manifold; they were used as signatures, to authenticate documents and letters; in codices, they were supposed to declare ownership of a volume; in the system of traditional education, seals were used to certify students by putting a seal impression

42 The study of seals and sealing practices in Ethiopic manuscripts would also open new perspectives in comparative studies of the same phenomenon in neighbouring regions, for example, with seals in Greco-Roman Egypt (Vandorpe 1997). For an online database, see https://www.trismegistos.org/seals/overview_A.html.

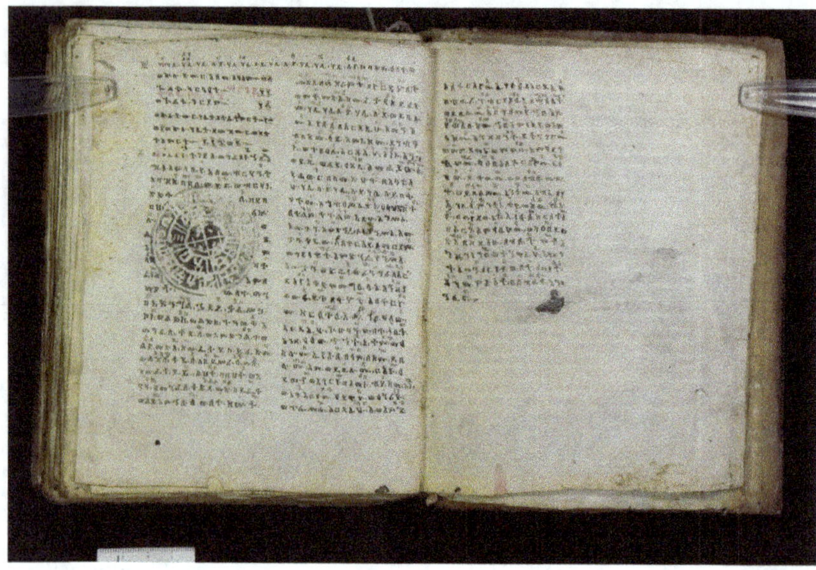

Figure 5.3: Seal impression. MS Portland, Ethiopic Manuscript Imaging Project, Weiner Codex 74, fols. 119v-120r. Image courtesy of Ethiopic Manuscript Imaging Project, Director Steve Delamarter.

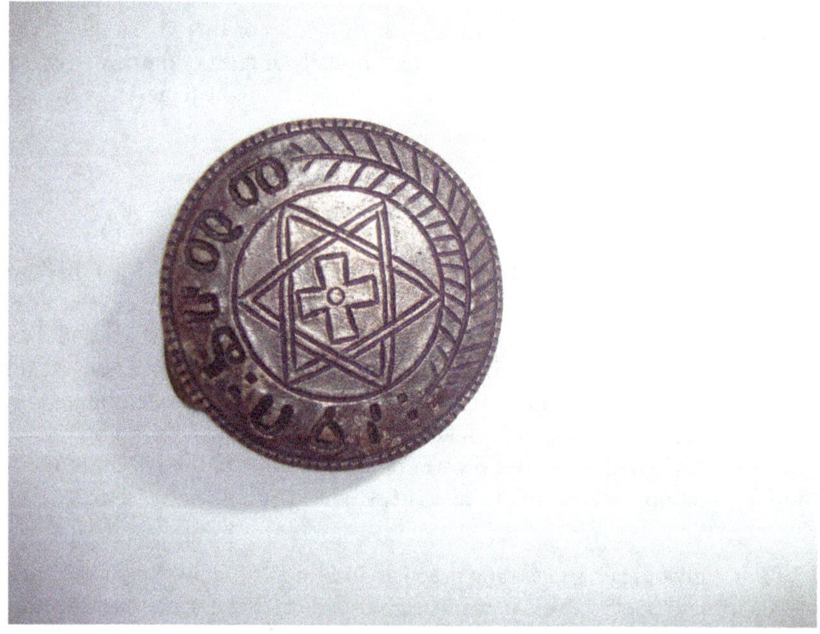

Figure 5.4: Seal matrix. A bronze seal of Mamhər Bayyana, a notable clergy from Gondar, 19th–20th century. Image courtesy of Sisay Sahile Beyene.

in their codices (Figure 5.3) and issuing parchment certificates (Platonov 2017: 40); signet rings were apparently used to seal imperial messages with wax or another substance. Not only the sealing practices are of interest, but also the design and manufacturing techniques of seals. Seals have always been precious and expensive objects that represented their owners and their status. The design of seals is therefore also a topic that can tell us a lot about self-representation, aesthetics, and symbolism, but also about craftsmanship and artistry.

However, seals as surviving physical objects (matrices) are extremely rare (Figure 5.4), which is most probably connected to the practice of destroying seals after the death of the owner to prevent their misuse. In this situation, seal impressions are in many cases the only source for the study of sealing practices, as well as of the materiality of seals. The latter is of course very restricted, but much valuable information on the materiality of matrices can be inferred from their impressions: size (which defines the relative size of a matrix), basic information on manufacturing techniques (engraved vs. *champlevé*), designs, and legends. At the current state of research, seal impressions are mostly treated in isolation, each seal impression is described on its own with sporadic references to other publications of impressions of the same seal (Tornay & Sohier 2007). In the Guidelines of *Beta maṣāḥəft*, seal impressions can be described in each manuscript.[43] I believe, however, that using TEI XML for separation of features pertaining to seals as material objects[44] (size, design, legends, ownership, bibliography) and seals as impressions (position, quality, accompanying elements, ink colour, etc.) could benefit to the study of the usage of seals in Ethiopia and Eritrea considerably.[45]

What I tentatively propose in the case of seal impressions, is inspired by the way in which texts are treated in the frames of the project *Beta maṣāḥəft*, that is the distinction between 'text-as-witness' and 'text-as-opus' (Liuzzo 2019: 79). I would suggest treating any seal impression as a witness to the existence of a (lost) material matrix, which should be created as a separate record with an individual identifier. The record should contain information pertaining to the material object it represents, that is: size of the impression surface, description

[43] https://betamasaheft.eu/Guidelines/?id=additionsVaria.

[44] For a XML-based and TEI-compliant standard for the encoding of Byzantine seals see SigiDoc by Alessio Sopracasa and Martina Filosa (http://sigidoc.huma-num.fr). This approach focuses on seals as individual objects given the state of Byzantine sigillography. For a different approach to markup of seal impressions as authenticating elements in TEI see Winslow (2021) and GitHub TEI Issue #1851: https://github.com/TEIC/TEI/issues/1851. For treatment of seal impressions as distinct objects associated with manuscripts see the GitHub Issue #2376: https://github.com/TEIC/TEI/issues/2376.

[45] For more observations on digital editions of text-bearing objects, including seals, see Filosa, Gad & Bodard (Chapter 3 in this volume).

of its design, ideally marked up with keywords, legends, ownership,[46] time of use, and any other information. This would allow for identification of impressions of this seal scattered amongst codices, documents, and letters, and to point to the one and the same ID of a record, which would aggregate information on a matrix from different evidence of its existence. Given that identification of some features of a seal might be easier in some cases (for example, existence of additional information on the owner of a seal, or better quality of an impression), and much more difficult in another (isolated, destroyed, or unclear impression), such approach would minimise the existence of impressions left without identification.[47] Description of seal impressions in manuscripts would then be limited to the actual sealing practice: function of the impression, its position in the manuscript, existence of hand-drawn doublets of impressions, colour of the ink, etc. This approach would not only help create a repository of the seal matrices attested in the manuscript culture, documenting their design and symbolism in a more consistent way, but would also help identify persons who were authorised to own and use seals, and to study their individual sealing practices.

3. Conclusion

To conclude, I want to stress once more that Ethiopian Studies currently profits significantly from the introduction of digital tools and technologies into its scholarly practices. Digital research methods allow for structuring, documenting, and exchanging information, for exploring manuscript culture from different scientific perspectives, as well as fruitful cooperation between scholars of different disciplines from all over the world. They have their restrictions, but also provide new ways of addressing research questions.

The study of material aspects of manuscripts especially benefits from the application of digital research methods and tools. Hyper-cataloguing draws attention to lesser-known aspects of manuscript culture of Ethiopia and Eritrea by aggregating information on them. The need for formalisation and classification of some material aspects of manuscripts will create new

[46] For declaring of ownership the project *Beta maṣāḥəft* has a repository for persons (https://betamasaheft.eu/newSearch.html?searchType=text&mode=any&work-types=pers).

[47] The Digital Sigillography Resource (DIGISIG) project by John McEwan on seals in England has very similar objectives, namely, linking multiple descriptions of the same seal (McEwan 2022). The project is launched online: https://www.digisig.org/home. It uses the opensource Python-based web framework Django and a PostgreSQL database. The main source of data for this project are, however, sigillographic reference works almost absent in the case of Ethiopian Studies, except Tornay & Sohier (2007).

standards for cataloguing and shed light on important neglected features. Digital approaches to organisation and storing of data open new perspectives in the creation of repositories of material objects which have been lost but are documented from the evidence of their use. All these aspects allow us to learn more about the life of the community and the role of the manuscripts.

4. References

Assefa Liban. (1958). Preparation of Parchment Manuscripts. *University College of Addis Ababa Ethnological Society Bulletin, 8*: 85–21.

Avanzini, A., Nebes, N., Müller, W., Fiaccadori, G., Frantsouzoff, S., & Gori, A. (2007). Inscriptions. In S. Uhlig (Ed.), *Encyclopaedia Aethiopica III* (pp. 152a–167b). Wiesbaden: Harrassowitz Verlag.

Balicka-Witakowska, E., Bausi, A., Bosc-Tiessé, C., & Nosnitsin, D. (2015). Ethiopic Codicology, in A. Bausi, P.G. Borbone, F. Briquel-Chatonnet, P. Buzi, J. Gippert, C. Macé, M. Maniaci, Z. Melissakis, L.M. Parodi, W. Witakowski & E. Sokolinski (Eds.) *Comparative Oriental Manuscript Studies. An Introduction* (pp. 154–174) Hamburg: Tredition.

Bausi, A. (2008). La tradizione scrittoria etiopica. *Segno e Testo, 6*, 507–557

Bausi, A. (2011). The 'True Story' of the Abba Gärima Gospels. *Comparative Oriental Manuscript Studies Newsletter, 1*, 117–20.

Bausi, A. (2014). Writing, Copying, Translating: Ethiopia as a Manuscript Culture. In J. Quenzer, D. Bondarev & J.-U. Sobisch (Eds.) *Manuscript Cultures: Mapping the Field.* Studies in Manuscript Cultures 1 (pp. 37–77). Berlin—New York: De Gruyter.

Bausi, A. (2015). The manuscript traditions: Ethiopic manuscripts. In A. Bausi, P.G. Borbone, F. Briquel-Chatonnet, P. Buzi, J. Gippert, C. Macé, M. Maniaci, Z. Melissakis, L.M. Parodi, W. Witakowski & E. Sokolinski (Eds.), *Comparative Oriental Manuscript Studies: an Introduction* (pp. 46–49) Hamburg: Tredition.

Bausi, A. (2017). Review of J. S. McKenzie & F. Watson, The Garima Gospels: Early Illuminated Gospel Books from Ethiopia, with Preface and Photographs by Michael Gervers and Contributions by Matthew R. Crawford, Linda R. Macaulay, Sarah S. Norodom, Andres T. Reyes, and Miranda E. Williams, Manar al-Athar Monograph, 3 (Oxford: Manar al-Athar, 2016). *Aethiopica, 20*, 289–292.

Bicchieri, M., Biocca, P., Colaizzi, P., & Pinzari, F. (2019). Microscopic Observations of Paper and Parchment: the Archaeology of Small Objects. *Heritage Science, 7*: 47. DOI: https://doi.org/10.1186/s40494-019-0291-9.

Brita, A. (2015). The manuscript as a leaf puzzle: the case of the Gädlä sämaʿtat from ʿUra Qirqos (Ethiopia). *Comparative Oriental Manuscript Studies Bulletin, 1*(1), 7–20.

Bülow-Jacobsen, A. (2009). Writing Materials in the Ancient World. In R. S. Bagnall (Ed.), *The Oxford Handbook of Papyrology* (pp. 3–29). Oxford–New York: Oxford University Press.

Chernetsov, S. (2003). Abugida and Hahu. In S. Uhlig (Ed.), *Encyclopaedia Aethiopica I* (pp. 55a–55b). Wiesbaden: Harrassowitz Verlag.

Chernetsov, S. (2007). Magic Scrolls. In S. Uhlig (Ed.), *Encyclopaedia Aethiopica III* (pp. 642a–643b). Wiesbaden: Harrassowitz Verlag.

Dal Sasso, E. (2018). Grottaferrata, Exarchic Greek Abbey of St. Mary of Grottaferrata, Crypt. Aet. 7. In A. Bausi (Ed.), *Beta maṣāḥǝft: Manuscripts of Ethiopia and Eritrea. Catalogue of Ethiopian Manuscripts.* https://betamasaheft.eu/manuscripts/GAet7/main, accessed 19 October 2022.

Dege-Müller, S., Liuzzo, P. M., Sokolinski, E., & Nosnitsin, D. (2020a). Bǝḥerāwi Kǝllǝlāwi Mangǝśti Tǝgrāy, Bet Ḥāwāryāt, SSB-015. In A. Bausi (Ed.) *Beta maṣāḥǝft: Manuscripts of Ethiopia and Eritrea. Catalogue of Ethiopian Manuscripts.* https://betamasaheft.eu/manuscripts/ESssb015/main, accessed 18 October 2022.

Dege-Müller, S., Villa, M., Reule, D., Liuzzo, P. M., Sokolinski, E., & Nosnitsin, D. (2020b). ʿAddigrat, ʿĀddigrāt Madḫāne ʿĀlam, AMM-008. In A. Bausi (Ed.) *Beta maṣāḥǝft: Manuscripts of Ethiopia and Eritrea. Catalogue of Ethiopian Manuscripts.* https://betamasaheft.eu/manuscripts/ESamm008/main, accessed 18 October 2022.

Di Bella, M., & Sarris, N. (2014). Field Conservation in East Tigray, Ethiopia. In M.J. Driscoll (Ed.) *Care and Conservation of Manuscripts 14. Proceedings of the fourteenth international seminar held at the University of Copenhagen 17th–19th October 2012* (pp. 271–307), Copenhagen: Museum Tusculanum Press.

Elagina, D. (2019). Saint Petersburg, Rossijskaja Nacionalnaja Biblioteka, RNB Ef. n.s. 22. In A. Bausi (Ed.), *Beta maṣāḥǝft: Manuscripts of Ethiopia and Eritrea. Catalogue of Ethiopian Manuscripts.* https://betamasaheft.eu/manuscripts/RNBEfns22/main, accessed 18 October 2022.

Elagina, D. (2020a). St Petersburg, Etnografičeskij Muzej Akademii Nauk, 2103–21. In A. Bausi (Ed.), *Beta maṣāḥǝft: Manuscripts of Ethiopia and Eritrea. Catalogue of Ethiopian Manuscripts.* https://betamasaheft.eu/manuscripts/InEtn210321/main, accessed 19 October 2022.

Elagina, D. (2020b). St Petersburg, Etnografičeskij Muzej Akademii Nauk, 2103–25. In A. Bausi (Ed.), *Beta maṣāḥǝft: Manuscripts of Ethiopia and Eritrea. Catalogue of Ethiopian Manuscripts.* https://betamasaheft.eu/manuscripts/InEtn210325/main, accessed 19 October 2022.

Elagina, D. (2020c). St Petersburg, Etnografičeskij Muzej Akademii Nauk, 3052–887a. In A. Bausi (Ed.), *Beta maṣāḥǝft: Manuscripts of Ethiopia and Eritrea. Catalogue of Ethiopian Manuscripts.* https://betamasaheft.eu/manuscripts/InEtn3052887a/main, accessed 19 October 2022.

Elagina, D. (2020d). St Petersburg, Etnografičeskij Muzej Akademii Nauk, 3052–887b. In A. Bausi (Ed.), *Beta maṣāḥǝft: Manuscripts of Ethiopia and*

Eritrea. Catalogue of Ethiopian Manuscripts. https://betamasaheft.eu/manuscripts/InEtn3052887b/main, accessed 19 October 2022.

Elagina, D., Reule, D., & Solomon Gebreyes. (2022). London, British Library, BL Oriental 566. In A. Bausi (Ed.), *Beta maṣāḥǝft: Manuscripts of Ethiopia and Eritrea. Catalogue of Ethiopian Manuscripts.* https://betamasaheft.eu/manuscripts/BLorient566/main, accessed 19 October 2022.

Ewald, H. von. (1844). Ueber die Aethiopischen Handschriften zu Tübingen. *Zeitschrift für die Kunde des Morgenlandes 5*, 164–201.

Ewald, H. von. (1847). Ueber eine zweite Sammlung Aethiopischer Handschriften in Tübingen. *Zeitschrift der Deutschen Morgenländischen Gesellschaft 1*, 1–43.

Faqāda Śellāsē Tafarrā. (2002). ጥንታዊ የብራና መጻሕፍት አዘጋጃጀት (Ṭentāwi yaberānnā maṣāḥeft azzagāǧāǧat, 'The ancient manner of preparing parchment books'). Addis Ababa: Addis Ababā Yunivarsiti Press.

Fee, S., Gervers, M., & Melis, C. (2022). Uncovering History from Textile Pastedowns in Ethiopian Manuscripts: A Singular and Complex Research Project. *Rassegna Di Studi Etiopici 3ª Serie, 6*(53), 295–310.

Gervers, M. (2010). Silk. In S. Uhlig (Ed.), *Encyclopaedia Aethiopica IV* (pp. 659b–661b). Wiesbaden: Harrassowitz Verlag.

Godet, É. (1980). La préparation du parchemin en Éthiopie. *Abbay, 11*, 203–210.

Hagos Abrha Abay, & Flanagan, J. (2022, February 8). Ethiopian relics on eBay may have been looted from Tigray, experts fear. *The Times*. Retrieved from: https://www.thetimes.co.uk/article/ethiopian-relics-on-ebay-may-have-been-looted-from-tigray-experts-fear-2w2rbjsdx.

Hammerschmidt, E. (1973). Äthiopische Handschriften vom Ṭānāsee 1: Reisebericht und Beschreibung der Handschriften in dem Kloster des Heiligen Gabriel auf der Insel Kebrān. Verzeichnis der orientalischen Handschriften in Deutschland 20/1. Wiesbaden: Franz Steiner Verlag GmbH. DOI: https://doi.org/10.26015/adwdocs-1657.

Hammerschmidt, E. (1977). Äthiopische Handschriften vom Ṭānāsee 2: Die Handschriften von Dabra Māryām und von Rēmā. Verzeichnis der orientalischen Handschriften in Deutschland 20/2. Wiesbaden: Franz Steiner Verlag GmbH. DOI: https://doi.org/10.26015/adwdocs-1658.

Hammerschmidt., E., & Six, V. (1983). Äthiopische Handschriften 1: Die Handschriften der Staatsbibliothek Preussischer Kulturbesitz. Verzeichnis der orientalischen Handschriften in Deutschland 20/4. Wiesbaden: Franz Steiner Verlag. DOI: https://doi.org/10.26015/adwdocs-1660.

Liszewska, W. (2017). New Methods of Leafcasting in the Conservation of Historic Parchments. Technologia-Sztuka-Konserwacja, 1. Warszawa: Akademia Sztuk Pięknych w Warszawie.

Liszewska, W., & Tomaszewski, J. (2016). Analysis and conservation of two Ethiopian manuscripts on parchment from the collection of the University Library in Warsaw. In M.J. Driscoll (Ed.) *Care and Conservation of Manuscripts 15: Proceedings of the fifteenth international seminar held at the*

University of Copenhagen 2nd–4th April 2014 (pp. 183–201). Copenhagen: Museum Tusculanum Press.

Liuzzo, P. M., Reule, D., Dal Sasso, E., Elagina, D., Nosnitsin, D., Sokolinski, E., & Solomon Gebreyes Beyene. (2018). *Beta maṣāḥəft Guidelines.* Retrieved from: http://betamasaheft.eu/Guidelines/ (Accessed 7 February 2020).

Liuzzo, P. M. (2019). *Digital Approaches to Ethiopian and Eritrean Studies.* Supplement to Aethiopica 8. Wiesbaden: Harrassowitz Verlag.

Maniaci, M. (2022). Statistical Codicology: Principles, Directions, Perspectives. In M. Maniaci (Ed.), *Trends in Statistical Codicology*. Studies in Manuscript Cultures 19 (pp. 1–32). Berlin—Boston: De Gruyter.

Marrassini, P. (1984). I manoscritti etiopici della Biblioteca Medicea Laurenziana di Firenze. *Rassegna di Studi Etiopici, 30,* 81–116.

Marrassini, P. (1987). I manoscritti etiopici della Biblioteca Medicea Laurenziana di Firenze. *Rassegna di Studi Etiopici, 31,* 69–110.

McEwan, J. (2022). New Approaches to Old Question: Digital Technology, Sigillography, and DIGISIG. In Morreale, L., & Gilsdorf, S. (Eds.), *Digital Medieval Studies: Practice and Presevation* (pp. 33–48). Leeds: ARC Humanities Press.

McKenzie, J. S., & Watson, F. (2016). The Garima Gospels: Early Illuminated Gospel Books from Ethiopia, With Preface and Photographs by Michael Gervers and contributions by Matthew R. Crawford, Linda R. Macaulay, Sarah S. Norodom, Andres T. Reyes, and Miranda E. Williams. Manar al-Athar Monograph 3. Oxford: Manar al-Athar.

Mellors, J., & Parsons, A. (2003). Manuscript and Book Production in South Gondar in the Twenty-First Century. In Birhanu Teferra & R. Pankhurst (Eds.), *Proceedings of the Sixth International Conference on the History of Ethiopian Art, Addis Ababa, 5–8 November 2002* (pp. 85–99). Addis Ababa: Institute of Ethiopian Studies, Addis Ababa University.

Nichols, S. (1990). Introduction: Philology in a Manuscript Culture. *Speculum, 65*(1), 1–10. DOI: https://doi.org/10.2307/2864468.

Nosnitsin, D., Kindzorra, E., Hahn, O., & Rabin, I. (2014). A "Study Manuscript" from Qäqäma (Təgray, Ethiopia): Attempts at Ink and Parchment Analysis. *Comparative Oriental Manuscript Studies Newsletter,* 7, 28–31.

Nosnitsin, D. (2020). Christian Manuscript Culture of the Ethiopian-Eritrean Highlands: Some Analytical Insights. In Kelly S. (Ed.), *A Companion to Medieval Ethiopia and Eritrea* (pp. 282–32). Leiden–Boston, MA: Brill.

Nosnitsin, D., & Reule, D. (2021). The Ethiopic Manuscripts of Dayr as-Suryān: A Catalogue. Supplement to Aethiopica 10. Wiesbaden: Harrassowitz Verlag.

Ornato, E. (1997). L'histoire du livre et les méthodes quantitatives: bilan de vingt ans de recherche. In Ornato, E. et al. (Eds.), *La face cachée du livre médiéval. L'histoire du livre vue par Ezio Ornato, ses amis et ses collègues. Avec une préface d'Armando Petrucci.* I libri di Viella 10 (pp. 607–679). Roma: Viella.

Pankhurst, R. (1973). The Library of Emperor Tewodros II at Mäqdäla (Magdala). *Bulletin of the School of Oriental and African Studies, 36*(1), 15–42.

Pankhurst, R. (1980). Imported Textiles in Ethiopian Sixteenth and Seventeenth Century Manuscripts in Britain. *Azania, 15*, 43–55.

Pankhurst, R. (1981). Imported Textiles in Ethiopian Eighteenth Century Manuscripts in Britain. *Azania, 16*, 131–150.

Pankhurst, R. (1983). Ethiopian manuscript bindings and their decoration. *Abbay, 12*, 205–257.

Pankhurst, R. (1985). Imported cloth in early 19th century Ethiopian bindings. *Quaderni di Studi Etiopici, 6–7*, 105–114.

Pankhurst, R. (2007). Mäqdäla. In S. Uhlig (Ed.), *Encyclopaedia Aethiopica III* (pp. 763a–765a). Wiesbaden: Harrassowitz Verlag.

Platonov, V. (1996). Efiopskie rukopisi v sobranijakh Sankt-Peterburga: Katalog. (Ethiopic Manuscripts in the Collections of Saint-Petersburg: Catalogue). St Petersburg: Rossijskaja natsional'naja biblioteka.

Platonov, V., & Gusarova E. (Eds.) (2017). Rukopisnaja kniga v traditsionnoj kulture Efiopii. (Manuscripts in the Traditional Culture of Ethiopia). Sankt-Peterburg: Rossijskaja natsional'naja biblioteka.

Rabin, I. (2015). Digital and scientific approaches to oriental manuscript studies: Instrumental analysis in manuscript studies. In A. Bausi P.G. Borbone, F. Briquel-Chatonnet, P. Buzi, J. Gippert, C. Macé, M. Maniaci, Z. Melissakis, L.M. Parodi, W. Witakowski & E. Sokolinski (Eds.), *Comparative Oriental Manuscript Studies: An Introduction* (pp. 27–30). Hamburg: COMSt.

Reule, D. (2018). Beta Maṣāḥəft: Manuscripts of Ethiopia and Eritrea. *Comparative Oriental Manuscript Studies Bulletin, 4*(1), 13–28. DOI: https://doi.org/10.25592/uhhfdm.247.

Reule, D., Sokolinski, E., & Solomon Gebreyes. (2022). London, British Library, BL Oriental 510. In A. Bausi (Ed.), *Beta maṣāḥəft: Manuscripts of Ethiopia and Eritrea. Catalogue of Ethiopian Manuscripts.* https://betamasaheft.eu/manuscripts/BLorient510/main, accessed 19 October 2022.

Richardin, P., Mercier, J., Tieu, G., Elarbi, S., & Legrand-Longin, S. (2006). Les rouleaux protecteurs éthiopiens d'une donation au Musée du quai Branly. Étude historique, scientifique et interventions de conservation-restauration. *Technè, 23*, 79–84.

Sergew Hable Selassie. (1981). *Bookmaking in Ethiopia.* Leiden: Karstens Drukkers.

Six, V. (1989). Äthiopische Handschriften 2: Die Handschriften der Bayerischen Staatsbibliothek. Verzeichnis der orientalischen Handschriften in Deutschland 20/5. Stuttgart: Franz Steiner Verlag Wiesbaden GmbH. DOI: https://doi.org/10.26015/adwdocs-1661.

Six, V. (1994). Äthiopische Handschriften 3: Handschriften deutscher Bibliotheken, Museen und aus Privatbesitz. Verzeichnis der orientalischen Handschriften in Deutschland 20/6. Stuttgart: Franz Steiner Verlag. DOI: https://doi.org/10.26015/adwdocs-1662.

Six, V. (1999). Äthiopische Handschriften vom Ṭānāsee 3: Nebst einem Nachtrag zum Katalog der äthiopischen Handschriften Deutscher Bibliotheken und Museen. Verzeichnis der orientalischen Handschriften in Deutschland 20/3. Stuttgart: Franz Steiner Verlag. DOI: https://doi.org/10.26015/adwdocs-1659.

Sohier, E. (2010). Seals. In S. Uhlig (Ed.), *Encyclopaedia Aethiopica IV* (pp. 585a–587a). Wiesbaden: Harrassowitz Verlag.

Strelcyn, S. (1978). Catalogue of Ethiopian Manuscripts in the British Library acquired since the Year 1877. London: British Museum.

Tomaszewski, J., & Gervers, M. (2015). Technological aspects of the monastic manuscript collection at May Wäyni, Ethiopia. In M. Kominko (Ed.), *From Dust to Digital. Ten Years of the Endangered Archives Programme.* Cambridge: Open Book Publishers.

Tornay, S., & Sohier, E. (2007). Empreintes du temps: Le sceaux des dignitaires éthiopiens du règne de Téwodros à la régence de Täfäri Mäkonnen. Études éthiopiennes 3. Addis Ababa: Institute of Ethiopian Studies, Addis Ababa University.

Uhlig, S., & Bausi, A. (2007). Manuscripts. In S. Uhlig (Ed.), *Encyclopaedia Aethiopica III* (pp. 738a–744a). Wiesbaden: Harrassowitz Verlag.

Vandrope, K. (1997). Seals in and on the Papyri of Greco-Roman and Byzantine Egypt. In M.-Fr. Boussac & A. Invernizzi (Eds.), *Archives et Sceaux du monde hellénistique*. Bulletin de Correspondance Hellénique. Supplément. (pp. 231–291). Athènes-Paris: École française d'Athènes.

Winslow, S. M. (2015). *Ethiopian Manuscript Culture: Practices and Contexts* (Doctoral dissertation, University of Toronto, Medieval Studies, Toronto).

Winslow, S. M. (2021). Authenticating Features in the TEI. *Journal of the Text Encoding Initiative*, [Online], *Issue 13*, May 2020–November 2022, Online since 23 September 2021, connection on 27 March 2023. URL: http://journals.openedition.org/jtei/3608; DOI: https://doi.org/10.4000/jtei.3608.

Witakowski, W. (2015). Catalogues of Ethiopic manuscripts. In A. Bausi P.G. Borbone, F. Briquel-Chatonnet, P. Buzi, J. Gippert, C. Macé, M. Maniaci, Z. Melissakis, L.M. Parodi, W. Witakowski & E. Sokolinski (Eds.), *Comparative Oriental Manuscript Studies. An Introduction.* (pp. 484–487). Hamburg: Tredition.

Wright, W. (1877). Catalogue of the Ethiopic Manuscripts in the British Museum Acquired since the Year 1847. London: Gilbert and Rivington.

Manuscripts abbreviated in text:

MS Crypt. Aet. 7 = MS Grottaferrata, Exarchic Greek Abbey of St. Mary of Grottaferrata, Crypt. Aet. 7

MS Ef. n.s. 22 = MS Saint-Petersburg, Rossijskaja Nacionalnaja Biblioteka, Ef. n.s. 22

MS Éthiopien 521 = MS Paris, Bibliothèque nationale de France, Éthiopien 521

MS Oriental 510 = MS London, British Library, Oriental 510

MS Oriental 566 = MS London, British Library, Oriental 566
MS AMM-008 = MS ʿĀddigrāt Madḫāne ʿĀlam (Ethiopia), AMM-008
MS SSB-015 = MS Bet Ḥāwāryāt (Ethiopia), SSB-015
MSS 2103-21 = MS Saint-Petersburg, Etnografičeskij Muzej Akademii Nauk, 2103-21
MSS 2103-25 = MS Saint-Petersburg, Etnografičeskij Muzej Akademii Nauk, 2103-25
MSS 3052-887a = MS Saint-Petersburg, Etnografičeskij Muzej Akademii Nauk, 3052-887a
MSS 3052-887b = MS Saint-Petersburg, Etnografičeskij Muzej Akademii Nauk, 3052-887b

CHAPTER 6

Collaborative editing of sixteenth century Indigenous graphic manuscripts from Central Mexico

Hayley Woodward
Tulane University
Jerome A. Offner
Houston Museum of Natural Science
Christopher W. Blackwell
Furman University

Abstract

Understanding the messaging of an Indigenous graphic manuscript from early colonial Central Mexico requires the accumulation and amplification of many voices. Restricting interpretation to a single expert or academic discipline, without the input of descendant communities for whom these objects held and hold significant valency, stifles the communicative potential of such manuscripts. This chapter highlights a collaborative, replicable, flexible, and linkable solution to presenting such objects online to an open audience of users: the CITE Architecture. This chapter begins with a brief overview of this Indigenous

---

How to cite this book chapter:
Woodward, H., Offner, J. A. and Blackwell, C. W. 2023. Collaborative editing of sixteenth century Indigenous graphic manuscripts from Central Mexico. In: Palladino, C. and Bodard, G. (Eds.), *Can't Touch This: Digital Approaches to Materiality in Cultural Heritage*. Pp. 121–139. London: Ubiquity Press. DOI: https://doi.org/10.5334/bcv.g.

manuscript painting tradition, demonstrating its unique challenges to reading, interpreting, and citing its narrative structures. It then demonstrates how producing collaborative editing frameworks is necessary to caption, interpret, and link information to visual documents such as the objects in question. It then introduces how an existing solution—the CITE Architecture—can be leveraged to facilitate new collaborations between scholars and Indigenous communities for whom these manuscripts hold living meaning.

Nahuatl by Abelardo de la Cruz de la Cruz, Chicontepec de Tejada, Veracruz

Hueli mocuamachiliz tlen quihtoznequi ce macehualixcopincayotl tlen Mexcotlalli tlen ipehuayan caxtolli huan ce hueyixihuicahuitl monequi oncaz huan mopazoloz miac tlahtolli.

Tlan zan ce acahya zo ce tlamachtiliztli quichihuaz ni tequitl, huan tlan macehualmen tlen naman axcanah tlapalehuizceh, huan ni ixcopincayotl nochipa quipixtihualtoc ipatiuh, quiixtzacua iquihtoznequiliz ica nochi ni amatlahcuilolli.

Ni tequitl quipannextia ce tlamapalehuiliztli, hueli quichihuaz ceyoc, amo ohuih, huan mohuicaltia para mopannextiz pan tepoztlamahuizolli tlen motequihuiah naman: Arquitectura CITE.

Ni amatequitl pehua ica ce tlacuamachiliztli ica queniuhqui mochiuhtihualtoc macehualixcopincayotl, campa quipannextia ohuihcayotl para ce quipohuaz, quicuamachiliz huan quimatiz cualli queniuhqui moxeloa tlahtolli.

Teipan mopannextia queniuhqui monequi mochihchihuaz tequitl para tlahcuilolli, mocuamachiliz huan mohuicaltiz tlamatiliztli ica amaixcopincayotl.

Teipan monextia queniuhqui hueli motequihuiz, ni Arquitectura CITE, para mochihuaz yancuic tequitl ica coyotlamachtianih huan macehualaltepetzitzin tlen ininaxca ni amatlahcuilolli huan quipiyah hueyi ipatiuh naman tonatiuh.

Nahuatl by Gaby Citlahua Zepahua, Tequila, Veracruz

Kampa ma moyekmati se tlahkuilolneskayotl masewal tlen opankiskih itlahkotipan Mexihko tlalnantli ihkuak yekintzin oahsikoyah pinomeh, moneki, ma molochokan iwan ma mokalakikan tlatlamantli tlahtolmeh.

Tla san se ixtlamatke noso san se temachtilistli moaxkatilis nin yekmatilistli noso tlahtolkuepalistli, iwan amo kitlakamatis itlachialis masewalaltepemeh tlen ich walkisah, akinmeh melahka kiyekmatiwitzeh nin tlatlamanyotl, kiehtlakowa iwan kiaxkayotia iteixpantilis inin tlahkuilolli.

Inin tlahkuilolli kiyektenewa se sekantlachiwalli, tlen kualtis oksekan mochiwas, tlen kualtis san akin kinehnekis iwan noihki motexpantihtos noso tesalohtos kampa ma monextikan nin tlatlamanyotl kampa ma kittakah san akin: Tekalchihyehyekolistli CITE.

Inin tlahkuilolli pewa kampa kiteixpantia san yehyektzin kenin yiwehkika mochihtiwitz non masewal tlahkuilolneskayotl iwan kinextia iowihkayo kampa ma moamapowa iwan ma motlahtolkuepa, noihki kenin moneki momehtoltis noso ipan motlahtos kenin machiohtiwitz.

Noihki ihkon, kinextia kenin moyektlalia sekan kanin kualtis motlahkuilos tlen motlahtowa, noihki kampa ma motlahtolkuepa iwan ma mo panoltili tlhkuilolli, noso tlatehyekolli ich okse amatepostlahkuillolli ipan uñinin tlatlamanyotl.

Nimantzin, kiteixpantia kenin kualtis monehnekis inin tlapalewilistli tlen yi kahki Tekalchihyehyekolistli CITE, kampa ma mopalewi olocholistli ipan tleyehyekoltlahkuilowani inawak masewalaltepemeh akinmeh ipampa ininkeh tlahkuilolneskayomeh ok moyolitihtokeh.

Spanish by Elizabeth Baquedano

Entender el mensaje de un manuscrito gráfico indígena del México central colonial temprano requiere, la acumulación e inclusión de muchas voces. Restringir la interpretación a un solo experto o disciplina académica, sin el aporte de las comunidades descendientes para quienes estos objetos tenían y tienen un valor significativo, restringe el potencial comunicativo de tales manuscritos. Este capítulo destaca una solución colaborativa, replicable, flexible y de vinculación para presentar tales objetos en línea a un público abierto de usuarios: la Arquitectura CITE. Este capítulo comienza con una breve descripción de esta tradición de manuscritos indígenas y demuestra los retos únicos para su lectura e interpretación, así como para citar y explicar sus estructuras narrativas. Así mismo, demuestra cómo produciendo marcos de trabajo de edición colaborativa para subtítulos, así como para interpretar y vincular información a documentos visuales como los objetos en cuestión. Posteriormente se presenta cómo se puede aprovechar una solución existente, la Arquitectura CITE, para facilitar nuevas colaboraciones entre académicos y comunidades indígenas para quienes estos manuscritos tienen un significado vivo.

1. Indigenous Graphic Manuscripts

Many centuries before the Spanish invaded what is now the nation-state of Mexico, Indigenous makers across time and space encoded information on a variety of supports including *amatl* paper and animal hide, employing conventionalized semasiographic and glottographic communication systems (Boone & Urton 2011; Mikulska & Offner 2019).[1] Works on paper

[1] The authors would like to thank Patricia Murrieta-Flores for her generous contributions to this chapter.

and hide often took the form of accordion-style books, and contained divinatory, historical, and calendrical information with Indigenous, rather than Western, categorical boundaries. In the wake of the Spanish Invasion of 1519, nearly all pre-Hispanic books and manuscripts were destroyed or lost, although fourteen survive today. Despite this large-scale destruction, the manuscript-making tradition did not end in 1519, but instead proliferated in the early colonial period, often in response to the challenges of the new legal system imposed by the Spanish, but also for the internal needs of Indigenous communities.

Today very few such manuscripts remain in the possession of living communities. One example is the Tlalamatl Cuaxicalan ("Land Paper of Cuaxicala" in Nahuatl), held for four and one-half centuries by the town of Cuaxicala, to the east-northeast of Mexico City (Figure 6.1). This five-meter-long manuscript, painted on animal skin, divided into twenty-four sections, and executed in the graphic non-alphabetic Aztec style, tells the history of the surrounding region, including two more powerful neighboring cities expelling rival Huastecs in previous centuries. The manuscript includes Nahuatl-based glyphs and notation specifying personages, geographic locations, and dates, although at least one glyph can be read in two additional languages, Totonac and Otomi (Stresser-Péan 1995; Offner 2010). Alphabetic annotations in Nahuatl were added at least once in the late seventeenth century and perhaps later by members of the community to repurpose it as a boundary statement for their community in colonial legal struggles with neighboring communities (Offner 2021a). The manuscript continues to be a "living document", celebrated and consulted by this community as a touchstone of identity. After a campaign initiated and led by the community, it was recognized as a "Memoria del Mundo México" in 2018 by UNESCO Mexico, the first time that it had recognized an artifact held by a living community rather than by a cultural institution. Even before UNESCO recognition, the town had a long history of people interpreting their manuscript, with notes on copies of it more than four inches thick observed by Offner in 2019.

In 2019, the local school produced a sophisticated map of their community, based on the alphabetic glosses in Nahuatl added to the manuscript in 1698 and conventional colonial legal records, including several pages of Nahuatl brought to light by Sr. Nabor Garcia, a former official of the town at the time of the UNESCO recognition (Figure 6.2 is a recent iteration). Research recently presented by Offner (2021a), on behalf of longstanding friends of Cuaxicala, Guillermo Garrido Cruz and the late Nohemí Leticia Ánimas Vargas, provides numerous examples of improvements in understanding of the manuscript through direct engagement with the community (cf. Offner 2010). Key community figures have also voluntarily permitted recorded video and audio interviews in Nahuatl and Spanish providing their thoughts on growing up with such an extraordinary manuscript in their community.[2] The additional insights already

---

[2] The video interviews are in several private hands as are the later audio interviews, with plans to archive them in an online repository in the coming few years.

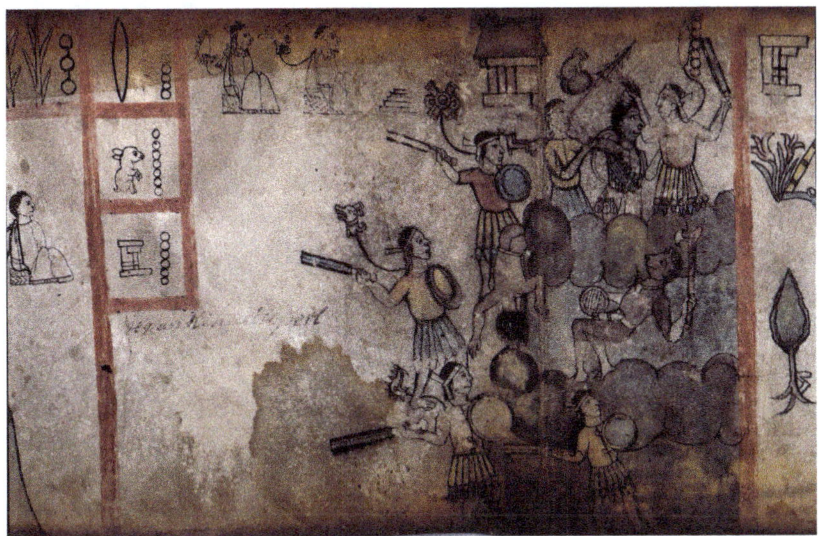

Figure 6.1: Section 10 of twenty-four graphic sections of the five-meter long Cuaxicala manuscript on animal skin known as the Tlalamatl Cuaxicalan or Códice de Cuaxicala. Nahuas from two cities in the region expel Huastecs from their fortified site of Tuzapan. Three dates when this happened are shown in Indigenous notation in the upper left. Courtesy: Comunidad de Cuaxicala, Guy and Claude Stresser-Péan.

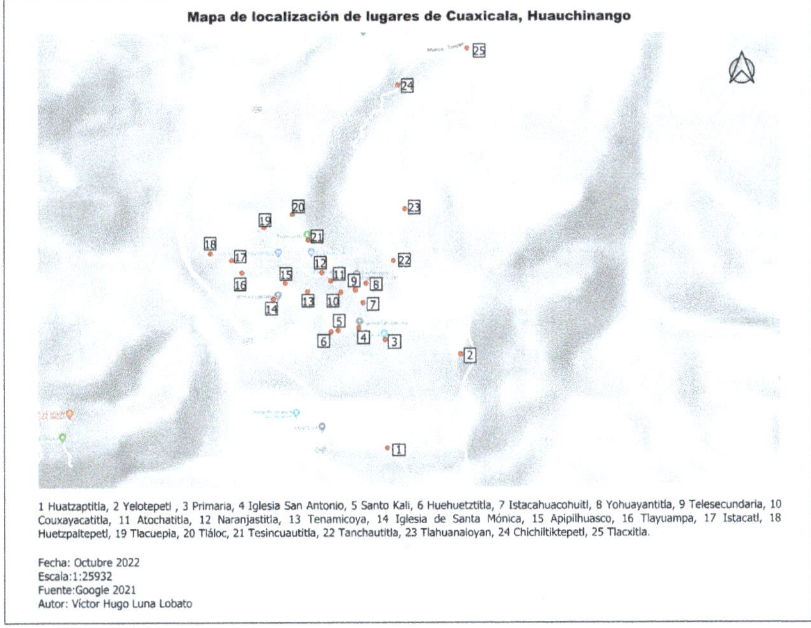

Figure 6.2: Digital map of Cuaxicala produced by and courtesy of Victor Hugo Luna Lobato.

obtained directly benefit anthropology, archaeology, art history, history, and other fields of study (Garrido Cruz, Animas Vergas & Offner, forthcoming).

Another group of manuscripts in the graphic Aztec style, the *Papers of Itzcuintepec* is held by the British Museum (Figure 6.3).[3] While no longer *in situ*,

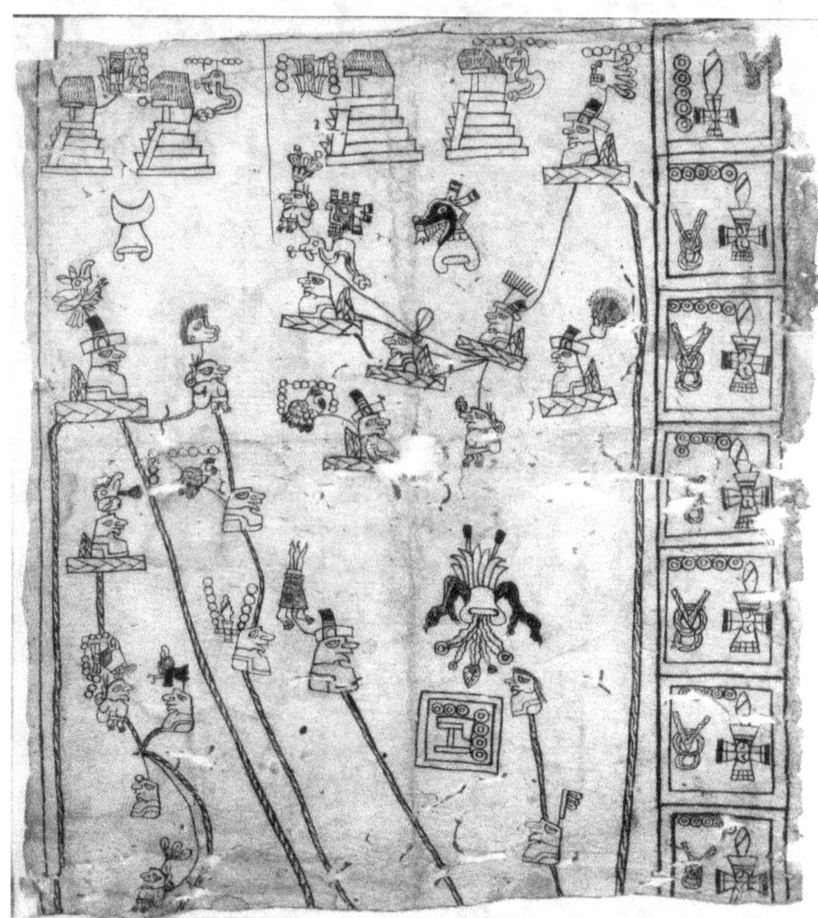

Figure 6.3: Part of the Papers of *Itzcuintepec*, Egerton 2897(2). Courtesy British Museum. https://www.britishmuseum.org/collection/object/E_Am2006-Drg-2897.

[3] See https://www.britishmuseum.org/collection/object/E_Am2006-Drg-2897, and https://www.britishmuseum.org/collection/object/E_Am2006-Drg-2896. Oudijk (2009) proposes they come from the Huauchinango region and references and evaluates earlier work by Brotherston and Berger. A later work by Ortiz Arroyo (2010) seeks incorrectly to localize these manuscripts in Oaxaca. Offner (2012) localized them more precisely in the area of Xolotla

these documents have begun to play a similar role for the nearby communities of Xolotla and Metztla, as Garrido Cruz reports intense interest from the people of Xolotla in viewing and understanding their past as depicted in these documents.

Although a few Mexican Indigenous manuscripts remain in their original communities, many others are held in museums and libraries across the Atlantic. The provenance histories of such manuscripts are varied and often fraught with colonial circumstances. The Bibliothèque nationale de France now holds the Codex Xolotl, which is well outside of its original context, the eastern Basin of Mexico (Dibble 1951; Offner 2021b). It is a group of similar documents that recount several centuries of Aztec history ending about ninety years *before* the Spanish invasion, executed in Indigenous and non-alphabetic form, according to expert, but non-Western, historiographic conventions (Figure 6.4). Over the

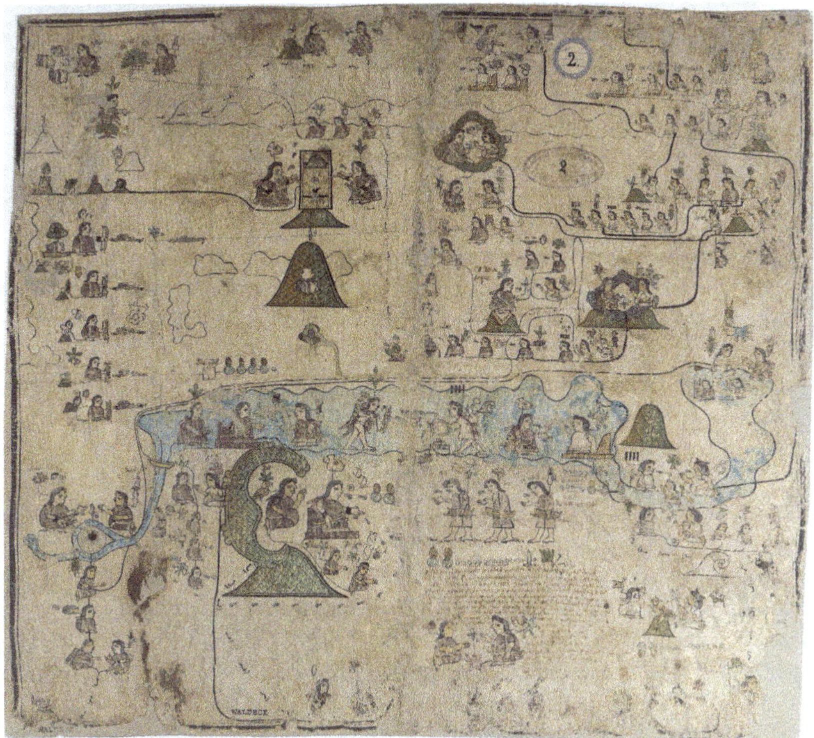

Figure 6.4: Codex Xolotl, page 2, ca. 1540s, carbon black ink and other pigments on *amatl* paper, 42 x 48 cm. Bibliothèque nationale de France, Mexicain 2.

and Metztla-Copila, Huauchinango, Puebla. Garrido Cruz and Offner have been conducting research "on the ground" in this area recently and hope to publish their findings in the coming years.

course of ten pages and three fragments of Indigenous *amatl* paper, it displays hundreds of scenes of precontact history. It records several centuries of histories and stories culminating in about 1431. It begins *in medias res* tracing a Chichimec migratory group, helmed by its first ruler Xolotl (the manuscript's namesake), as they enter the Basin of Mexico.

Within the *Xolotl*'s pages, we learn how some of these gathering and hunting groups become acculturated to sedentary, agricultural practices. The narrative goes on to record the intermarriages and acculturation among many of the groups that ultimately coalesce as the Aztec Empire at the time of European contact. Marriages, births, deaths, as well as both community and individual tales of conflict, concordance, heroism, avarice, cowardice, good, and evil play out as scores of characters swarm over the densely-packed, interrelated leaves of this engaging series of compositions.

The *Xolotl* is unusual in the corpus of Mesoamerican manuscripts because of its iterative cartographic organizational framework; over the course of nine of the ten pages, its makers arranged the historical narrative with regional maps of the Basin of Mexico. Thus, the map-histories of the *Xolotl* present complex historical and geographical information from a uniquely Indigenous perspective.

Understanding the *Xolotl*'s complex narrative requires an acknowledgement of its geographic armature and the nature of its reading practices. The Xolotl's spatial framework, which presents the historical narrative of each page simultaneously, means the reader approaches all the content synchronously; there is no single reading order, as multiple perspectives exist contemporaneously within and between pages. Portions of the story may be read or orated, depending on the needs or circumstances of the intended audience, and narrative threads across the page(s) could be tailored and tied together or neglected, depending on the intention of the orator.

This fact has largely been ignored by scholars who have interpreted the Codex Xolotl. The Xolotl's role as a prime source of the precontact past has made many want to dive into its narrative, interpreting it into linear, alphabetic prose to which Western, scholarly writing is confined. This inclination is not novel, since a few hundred pages of Spanish and Nahuatl texts survive from the sixteenth and early seventeenth centuries (including Fernando de Alva Ixtlilxochitl's *Obras históricas* [1975], Juan de Torquemada's *Monarquía Indiana* [1969], a Nahuatl source known as the *Anónimo Mexicano* [2005], and *Anales de Cuauhtitlan* [Bierhorst 1992a, b]) that use the Codex Xolotl (among other graphic manuscripts) as source material, but they only succeed in describing some aspects of its content and meaning.

Given the tension between an overarching map-like framework and the individual strands of narrative that can be pulled out of a given page, the *Xolotl*'s historical narrative challenges traditional assumptions about interpreting, editing, and publishing this manuscript. The *Codex Xolotl*, taken together with the colonial texts that report on it, constitute the ideal laboratory for the collaborative interpretation of Indigenous texts that privileges how these manuscripts were intended to be read: via multiple voices and agendas. It is a manuscript that speaks to the scholarly concerns of a multidisciplinary audience. Its large collection of glyphs, including the longest strings of Aztec language glyphs, fascinates linguists and students of writing, while its complex semasiography challenges and informs investigators of indigenous artistic expression and practice.

The holding institution of the *Codex Xolotl* has done an excellent job of curating and presenting the manuscripts in electronic form for visual inspection by an English-speaking audience, within accepted expectations of professional museum exhibitions, while the town of Cuaxicala has not been able to afford its own online presentation for its manuscript. Moreover, broadly speaking, silos exist between the institutions that steward these (and other) graphic manuscripts and the communities from which they originate. It would be ideal to go beyond this creditable stage of conventional, Western exhibition of such artifacts to a new stage of curated, collaborative, evolving, online presentation in languages accessible to the communities indelibly linked to them. This would require supporting relationships with these communities in order to cultivate new pathways and infrastructures of scholarly contributions to the study of such manuscripts. It would present certain challenges for editing, datamanagement, and would certainly require a re-thinking of "citation" both in the technological sense of "how to connect information together" and in the human sense of "how to give credit and assert authority for insights and ideas."

2. Challenges of Digitally Editing Mesoamerican Manuscripts

The obvious first steps towards preparing digital editions of these manuscripts are the preparation of catalogs of personages, locations, glyphs, and scenes, defined as labeled regions-of-interest on page images. Because "scenes" on the manuscripts often consist of smaller scenes, and because "scenes" are matters of scholarly assertion and may therefore be contentious, no edition of these texts can expect to be definitive but will represent one moment in an ongoing conversation about the meaning of the manuscript.

In fact, the sixteenth and seventeenth century Spanish and Nahuatl texts narrating the history of the hero Xolotl, based on manuscript evidence, represent the first voices in that conversation, and would be the basis for an initial body of image-aligned commentary.

These manuscripts are an open-world problem, as they treat mythology, history, and geography. Because they challenge modern assumptions and conventions of narrative (given the push-pull between the totality and the detail of each page), they are not well suited to any data organization that depends on a predefined schema or that places restrictions on overlapping hierarchies (as XML does).

Furthermore, these manuscripts are living documents, actively participating in the communities, both Indigenous and academic, that have possessed them for centuries. When living communities are involved, it would be presumptuous for any professional scholars to "edit" these artifacts, making positive assertions, without at least giving equal voice to the people whose communities, history, and identity are based on these documents. When, inevitably, scholarly understanding may conflict with local understanding on some points of interpretation, the utmost delicacy will be necessary. Of course, scholars edit texts that are important to communities or faith-groups all the time, and propose new understandings of history that differ, for example, from the Vulgate. With these Mesoamerican texts, however, the potential disparity of wealth and power, and the history and even current relationships between the Spanish and Indigenous language speakers of Mexico, not to mention the United States, the United Kingdom, and Europe, amplify the ethical considerations. Furthermore, for a digital project, issues of wealth and access to technology come to the fore via questions of who can contribute to an editorial project focused on these texts, and who will profit from that project.

To take the *Codex Xolotl*, for example, the manuscript has always presented challenges for publication, analysis, and presentation, prompting the need for a new solution. The undisputed starting point for analysis is the print publication by the American Charles Dibble (1951), whose exceptional book included high quality black and white photographs of the *Codex Xolotl*, expert commentary, analytical indices, genealogy, a study of chronology and a bibliography. While vital to any student of the *Xolotl*, Dibble's reliance on earlier historians' interpretations betrays its limitations.

In terms of digital projects, beginning in 1994 and based on the program Windev, France's Marc Thouvenot pioneered electronic presentation of *Codex Xolotl*, and indeed, many Mesoamerican graphic manuscripts, with his program Tlachia, using 72 and later 300 dpi visible light images and a robust method of glyphic analysis. Complemented by an available PDF version of his 1987 dissertation, he created downloadable catalog files of the Codex Xolotl and other graphic manuscripts that were made available at SUP-INFOR.[4] These have since been put online in a browser-based edition, as a part of a revamped platform called the Compendio Enciclopédico Náhuatl (CEN), which has fixed many of the issues of the original Tlachia program (which did not run on Apple devices and had user-generated installation issues on PCs).[5] Care has been taken to make CEN available on smartphones, a device available to more people than computers and increasingly flexible search capabilities have been added. Unfortunate intradisciplinary doctrinal divisions over methods for Aztec glyphic analysis and antipathy to the method developed by the Mexican scholar Joaquín Galarza and used, in adapted form, for Tlachia, have sharply reduced its use (Oudijk

[4] http://www.sup-infor.com/.

[5] https://cen.sup-infor.com/home/tlachia. CEN is available at: https://cen.sup-infor.com/home/hellow.

2008). However, Thouvenot's body of work in glyphic decipherment, although necessarily Procrustean and often decontextualized, remains unmatched in breadth and accuracy. Overall, Thouvenot's Tlachia remains underutilized and underappreciated outside of France and Mexico, but the authors nonetheless find it indispensable for study of the *Codex Xolotl.*

Beyond the *Xolotl*, additional high-quality pioneering work in Mesoamerican digital humanities has been led by Stephanie Wood with the online Nahuatl (Aztec language) dictionary.[6] This Drupal-based site is searchable using open methods, linguistically-informed methods, and a developing list of preset themes. It is an indispensable tool for the study of Nahuatl, along with the Gran Diccionario Náhuatl (GDN), an older, more comprehensive, less flexible, but searchable compilation of four centuries of dictionaries developed by Sybille de Pury and Marc Thouvenot (also now integrated into Thouvenot's CEN). None of these, however, contains images or glyphs. Graphic manuscripts are presented in high-definition visible light images in Wood's "The Mapas Project", again using Drupal.[7] On this site, areas per page are "clickable" to bring up brief commentary on the specific area. As with Thouvenot, we hold Wood's work in high regard.

Another early effort to share digital copies and translations of Mesoamerican manuscripts, largely based on Thouvenot's program and work, is Amoxcalli, spearheaded by Luz María Mohar Betancourt in 1999.[8] It also uses 72 dpi visual light images linked to commentary of each manuscript. However, currently, there is no ability to see text and commentary on a single webpage and it is not interactive beyond clicking through set menus.

In recent years, there are excellent online editions of single Mesoamerican manuscripts, such as the Codex Mendoza and the Lienzo de Tlaxcala. Both of these feature a user-friendly presentation of high definition images of a manuscript with a promise, not yet realized, of interactivity and further content development.[9] In the former, the ability to mouse over sections of the Spanish text on the manuscript to bring up an easily-read Spanish transcription is a notable feature, but other aspects, such as mapping of toponyms, are undeveloped.

For non-alphabetic manuscripts, such as the aforementioned manuscripts, where the *images* must be central, any analysis of them is inevitably controversial, or at least multivalent (with professional scholarly and historical perspectives not necessarily aligning with the received understanding of the communities that own the manuscripts). A "multi-textual" approach is most

6 https://nahuatl.uoregon.edu/.
7 https://mapas.uoregon.edu/.
8 https://amoxcalli.org.mx/.
9 https://codicemendoza.inah.gob.mx/inicio.php?lang=english; https://lienzodetlaxcala.unam.mx/lamina-0-alegoria/.

appropriate, which allows the relation of graphic images to each other without the interference of alphabetic text, while preserving and enhancing the ability to summon up alphabetic sources that are dependent on the graphic surface, along with later critical commentaries (explanations, analyses, stories). This will place the graphic material in the center of perception, appreciation and analysis, where it has always belonged. In so doing, we believe that realizing an accelerated understanding and sharing of the original indigenous perception of these works, and their ways of recounting their history, religion, and other vital cultural knowledge, must be at the center of future digital presentations of Mesoamerican manuscripts.

3. The CITE Architecture

Our proposed solution to the problem we have outlined above is to leverage an existing digital framework to Mesoamerican manuscripts: the CITE Architecture. "CITE" is an acronym for "Collections, Indices, Texts, and Extensions" (Smith & Blackwell 2012). It is a collection of tools and techniques for organizing and working with an open-ended and diverse body of scholarly data (Blackwell & Smith 2019).

CITE was developed to support a specific project, the "Homer Multitext" (HMT), a project of the Center for Hellenic Studies of Harvard University. Its Editors are Casey Dué and Mary Ebbott. The mission of the HMT is to produce 21st Century editions of the primary source texts for Greek Epic poetry, the *Iliad* and the *Odyssey*. In contrast to the tradition of critical editing, in which the editors seek to reduce a varies manuscript tradition to a single authoritative text, the HMT aims to preserve the variation found in the transmission of Homeric epic, variants in the text found in Byzantine manuscripts and earlier papyri, as well as variants mentioned in the tens of thousands of ancient scholarly comments, the *scholia*, that date back to the writings of the earliest scholars working in the Library of Alexandria. This project, then, presented a challenge of "scholarly identity"—multiple texts that all instantiate a notional *Iliad*, in whole or in part, that are to be aligned and compared, but with no "base text" given priority.

Since 2006, the HMT has produced editions of several deluxe codices of the *Iliad* with commentary, beginning with the 10th Century Venetus A (*Marcianus Graecus* Z.454). This data is archived on GitHub and freely available.[10] In parallel with this ongoing work of editing, the HMT developed code-libraries to support the project. The humanities problems that framed these libraries were: "How can we organize and align many different versions of the same text (as critical editions have always done) but without privileging any one version

[10] The HomerMultitext Archive: https://github.com/homermultitext/hmt-archive.

(unlike what critical editions do)?" And also, "How can we allow scholars to document coherent narratives when a narrative might skip from text to text?" For example, the story of a Homeric hero, like Patroclus or Odysseus' sister, might never appear as a single "story" in the epic poetry. But from a passing mention in the *Iliad*, a particular adjective in the Odyssey, a scholarly comment on one manuscript, an intra-linear gloss in another manuscript, we can reconstruct a mythological story.

The **data model** that has emerged over twenty years of development is very straightforward: in plain-text, a series of pairings of URN-formatted identifiers with some data, whether that be a passage of text, a data-record, or metadata identifying a binary image. A complex digital library can be serialized into a single plain-text file following the CEX ("CITE Exchange") format.[11]

CITE is, at heart, mainly a scheme by which any object of scholarly study, concrete or abstract, can be identified with a unique identifier that (a) depends on no specific technology, working as well in print as in a digital environment, (b) identifies the context of the object as well as the object itself. The rest of CITE are tools that work with the data identified in this way. CITE has always complemented standards like IIIF (for images), TEI-XML (for texts), and relational database systems. The advantage of CITE is that it allows data to move freely across technologies and formats, since it is not limited to any particular technology. Over the years, the HMT's data has been in XML, RDF, RDBs, and implemented in Perl, C++, Javascript, Python, Go, XSLT, and Java. The current reference implementation is in Scala, with versions of the core libraries under development in the Julia language.

For an open-world project like editing and commenting on the Codex Xolotl, a clean separation of concerns—texts, images, comments, geo-spatial data, back-end storage, end-user applications—is most desirable. With the CITE Architecture, it should be possible to implement a rigorous separation of concerns. A Spanish translation of a seventeenth-century commentary should be just that, a text; it should exist independently of a manuscript-image (for example) while being aligned with it; the image, the text, and the alignment should all stand alone. CITE lets each kind of data exist in its own right and uses canonical citation to integrate them for either functionality or analysis or display. Users always retain the ability to go to the primary data and re-use it in novel combinations.

Large scholarly digital libraries recognize the value afforded by CITE. Brill Scholarly Editions, for example, uses the CITE Architecture for its TEI-XML based collection of edited texts.[12] Likewise, Das Deutsches Textarchiv,[13] and

---

[11] CEX format: https://cite-architecture.github.io/citedx/CEX-spec-3.0.1/.

[12] https://dh.brill.com/scholarlyeditions/about/.

[13] Berlin-Brandenburgische Akademie der Wissenschaften: http://www.deutschestextarchiv.de.

the Scaife Viewer from the Perseus Project.[14] These projects recognized that standard formats like TEI-XML, while valuable for capturing archival editions of texts, are not necessarily the only, or even the best, formats for analysis or publication. For example, scholars commonly want to quote a few sentences from a larger text, but if those sentences do not align perfectly with the structure of XML markup, the resulting quotation can cause errors by being invalid XML. Or a scholar might want to work with a small subset of a large database, without necessarily reproducing the complex relational database installation and set-up. Or, a linguistic analysis might want to count words or find patterns of words, but the editorial notes and comments embedded in a TEI-XML file would confuse such analysis. CITE provides workarounds for scholarly problems like these, while always keeping new analyses or readings aligned with the archival original.

With image-based editing, there are many formats and code-libraries available to scholars, all with their strengths. The IIIF protocol is broadly used by libraries and museums, often in conjunction with the OpenSeadragon library for making web-based, "zoomable" interfaces to high-resolution images. For offering interfaces to images without the complexities of an IIIF server, there is the DeepZoom image format.[15] Sometimes, of course, a scholar might want a simple JPG image. CITE works with all of these, allowing an image, or a part of an image, to be identified precisely so that the identification remains valid for a version of the image in an IIIF service, on a DeepZoom web-view, or on a static JPG, PNG, or TIFF file. The CITE Binary Image code library supports all of these formats.

Finally, while the universally adopted standards for scholarly data—XML, RDF, IIIF, SQL, etc.—provide structure and functionality, CITE complements these by allowing us to add validation and verification of a complex digital library. Validation (as used in CITE) is error-checking that a machine can do—"is every physical surface of the codex documented with an image?" "Is this a valid Nahuatl word?"—while verification is error checking that requires a human reader, but in which a computer can help: "Are all icons identified as the hero Xolotl actually showing that hero and not another?" Both kinds of checking require working across data-types, checking a text against a database of lexical words, or regions on images with a registry of mythological figures.

4. Distributed Editing

One of the developers of the CITE protocol, Neel Smith, has always asserted that "It is easier to aggregate than to disaggregate". This has been a guiding value for the project, and it can serve well for ongoing work on these manuscripts.

---

14 Tufts University: https://scaife.perseus.org/.

15 The International Image Interoperability Framework: https://iiif.io/.

For collaborative editing across three continents, where technological resources are necessarily limited, CITE's emphasis on plain-text, tabular data can prove helpful. Because canonical citation by URN-identifier is the only linking mechanism, even very large, very diverse digital libraries can consist of a (perhaps very long) list of, either (a) URN + Data, or (b) URN + URN.

Unlike, for example, an artifact documented using TEI-XML, whose well-formedness and validity, and any transformations to it, depend on the single document's integrity, a CITE library data is easily aggregated from different sources. A user with an inexpensive laptop running only a web-browser, with access to, *e.g.*, Google Docs, could generate commentary on an image, and by sharing a URL to that document, have their commentary integrated, with attribution, into a larger library.

Because, in the world of CITE, a commentary can be expressed simply as a collection of comments, each one associated with either a passage of text, or an object in a collection (which might be an image, or a region-of-interest on an image), the number of commentaries, and the number of commentators, can scale without limit, and there need not be any hierarchy of implied value.

It is important to distinguish between *traditional* citation and our use of *canonical* citation. Most of the texts relevant to this project have no traditional scheme of citation. To render them canonically citable, for the purposes of this work, we simply invent a citation-hierarchy that is organic to the structure of the text, independent of any particular presentation of the text (so, page numbers from one edition would not be appropriate), which (for prose texts at least) aligns across versions of the text (editions and translations) and which captures the semantics of the text. Like many texts (epic poem, biblical texts) a two-level hierarchy of Book + Section is usually sufficient.

To describe briefly how CITE would serve as the basis for an evolving body of commentary and exegesis of the *Codex Xolotl*, we can walk through some scenarios. First, a scholar might work to associate individual scenes on the Codex (clusters of figures, icons, and illustrations) with events described in Torquemada's *Monarquía Indiana*. By identifying regions-of-interest on images of the Codex, a reader can generate URN identifiers for specific graphical components (a depiction of the character Xolotl, that of an Aztec woman, that of a lake, dots representing the passage of time). The reader could identify these with individual URNs, or generate a URN to a region of interest that bounds the whole "scene", *or* identify individual scene and calculate the region of interest bounding box that includes all of them. This reader could associate these scenes with passages of text, identified by canonical URNs, in Torquemada's text, at any level of granularity, from a whole section down to a short phrase or single word. This association would simply look like a two-column text file, with URN-of-scene in one field, and URN-to-text in the associated field. The whole record would constitute a CITE "Collection" with its own URN, associated with the scholar who asserts these connections. A second reader with different ideas about how to interpret the Codex could generate a different table of associations, as a different work of scholarship. The associations of image-to-text need not be exclusive, need not be coordinated, and need no elaborate infrastructure beyond a text editor, or something like a Google spreadsheet. The "texts" that can be canonically citable in CITE need not be ancient text, nor previously published texts. Any text, including oral histories or interviews with members of the Nahuatl communities are canonically citable in CITE. The activities of commentary and exegesis can proceed in many places at once, among different communities of interested readers, without granting privileged status to any of them. Any collection of observations carries with it authorship, and as data would be cited like any scholarly source, whether it comes from people living in a community of professional scholars at a European University. Integration would merely be a matter of bringing copies of text files together for some purpose. One of the foundational principles of CITE is that it is *always easier to aggregate than to disaggregate*, and we think this principle will be especially important for a text like the *Codex Xolotl*, of interest to so many parties, and continuing to pose so many fundamental questions. A primary virtue of CITE has been its simplicity of use in collaborative study of the Codex Xolotl. By itself, the novel ability to canonically define (CITE) and present a region or regions of interest in a graphic, rather than alphabetic, manuscript facilitated communication, analysis, and commentary on Codex Xolotl among the authors of this chapter and other collaborators. Stored collections of "URNs" and images captured through CITE have so far facilitated the construction and publication of one article on it (Offner 2021b), with more to follow.

The infrastructure for this small collaborative community, along with the intellectual property rights, were, it must be noted, already in place. Investigators in the U.S. are assumed to have capable computers with robust internet connections that they can readily adapt to use of shared programs. Offner owns but will be releasing under appropriate creative commons licenses in the coming years for his multispectral Codex Xolotl images, and the BnF, under French law, does not impede non-profit publication of images of items in their collection. Indeed, it has posted visible light images of its own in an IIIF viewer for public inspection.

In a parallel example, the digital map of Cuaxicala above demonstrates what its community members can do with sufficient resources. No attempts have yet been made to introduce people there to CITE, but there is no doubt they could quickly learn to adapt it to their needs. Both computers and internet connectivity are expensive in local terms. These could be made available to community members at an educational institution, ranging from the telesecundaria within Cuaxicala to the Universidad Intercultural del Estado de Puebla (UIEP). They can easily produce a set of photos of their prized Tlalamatl Cuaxicalan and arrange to store them on a server within Mexico, perhaps also at the UIEP. From that point, community leaders could arrange for study sessions moderated by young community members instructed in CITE and data entry and storage protocols. These could easily be annotated to identify the contributing community member. The instructions and protocols could also be rendered in any of the several Indigenous languages in the region, although only Nahuatl and Spanish are now spoken in Cuaxicala. Abundant and strong motivations already exist: curiosity, civic pride, language and cultural revitalization, and the centuries-old use of their Tlalamatl Cuaxicalan as "defender of their lands."

Results could be distributed as the community sees fit. In recent years, such sharing of images of the manuscript has been open and scarcely moderated. On the one hand, the community is interested in making its by now famous manuscript better known, but on the other hand, with many images already made and distributed in regional social media and worldwide scholarly networks, it has neither funds nor ability to enforce intellectual property in any jurisdiction or to benefit commercially from images of its manuscript. In recognition of their intellectual property rights, goodwill, and expense in sharing information about themselves and their Tlalamatl, academic researchers, and especially their employers and granting agencies, should in future allocate funding for the community in any research project involving Cuaxicala and other communities similarly situated.[16] Documents are not simply "discovered" by academics with ensuing intellectual property rights and career benefits for them and their employers. Instead, such documents are, in the first instance, shared with academics by the documents' owners, and the benefits generated from this sharing should benefit all.[17] Offner and his wife Kathleen, who generate neither income nor career development from their research activities, donate to the community from time.

5. Conclusion

Because "Digital Humanities" is practiced by humanists, it is not surprising that the traditional disciplinary divisions tend to persist. European historians, doing digital work, tend to collaborate with other European historians doing digital work. Classicists with Classicists; scholars of Mesoamerica with other scholars of Mesoamerica. This is regrettable and perhaps unnecessary. One of the great advantages that computational work affords a humanist is the necessity of abstraction, of asking "what, in essence, are we looking at?" When the answer is "information-bearing surfaces, whose interpretation is in doubt," we should be able to share tools and approaches, and a distributed approach focus-

[16] There is good precedent for this approach. Cuaxicala astutely negotiated for and received substantial enhancements to electrical service and road construction and maintenance from the state of Puebla in exchange for their assent to have their manuscript published by Stresser-Péan in 1995.

[17] On IP and heritage sovereignty see also Granados García & Ashley (Chapter 9 in this volume); Okorie (Chapter 11).

ing on data, as opposed to applications or presentation, in the simplest formats might be most helpful.

Simple, readily deployable technologies such as CITE, provide opportunities to engage, and indeed, privilege, the insights and understandings of the descendants of the people who produced Mesoamerican graphic documents. The continuity of their languages and cultures across centuries is well demonstrated. There is considerable urgency to this task, as members of older generations pass away and Indigenous language use decreases. As Granados and Ashley describe elsewhere in this volume, "Digital tools offer a fluid and flexible set of resources to capture and represent … complex systems of individual and overlapping knowledge and are especially relevant in situations where knowledge is not catechised by western tropes of learning and linear process." That is, we have open questions that might admit of answers from different communities of learners, all of whose voices should be welcomed and preserved. Now is their time to be heard.

6. References

Anónimo Mexicano. (2005). Translated and edited by Richley H. Crapo and Bonnie Glass-Coffin. Logan: Utah State University Press.

Bierhorst, J. (1992a). *Codex Chimalpopoca: TheText in Nahuatl with a Glossary and Grammatical Notes.* Tucson: University of Arizona Press.

Bierhorst, J. (1992b). *History and Mythology of the Aztecs: The Codex Chimalpopoca,* translated by John Bierhorst. Tucson: University of Arizona Press.

Blackwell, C., & Smith N. (2019). The CITE Architecture: a Conceptual and Practical Overview. In Berti, M. (ed). *Digital Classical Philology: Ancient Greek and Latin in the Digital Revolution* (De Gruyter, Saur, 2019). http://dx.doi.org/10.1515/9783110599957.

Boone, E. H., & Urton, G. (Eds.) (2011). *Their way of writing : scripts, signs, and pictographies in Pre-Columbian America.* Washington, D.C. : Dumbarton Oaks Research Library and Collection.

Dibble, C. E. (1951). Códice Xolotl. México Universidad Nacional Autónoma de México.

Garrido Cruz, G., Animas Vargas, L., & Offner, J. A. (forthcoming). Landscape and Territory in ritual and visual media in Cuaxicala, Huauchinango, Puebla, Mexico.

Ixtlilxochitl, F. de A. (1975). *Obras históricas,* edited by Edmundo O'Gorman. 2 vols. Mexico City: Universidad Nacional Autónoma de México, Instituto de Investigaciones Históricas.

Mikulska, K., & Offner, J. A. (Eds.) (2019). *Indigenous Graphic Communication Systems: A Theoretical Approach.* Louisville, Colorado: University Press of Colorado.

Offner, J. A. (2010). "Un segundo vistazo al Códice de Xicotepec." *Itinerarios* 11: 55–83.

Offner, J. A. (2012). "'Production' of Indigenous Pictorial Manuscripts to the East of the Basin of Mexico" (54th International Congress of Americanists, Vienna, Austria, July 2012).

Offner, J. A. (2021a). Defender of our lands! Five centuries with the living codex of Cuaxicala, Puebla, Mexico. Keynote Lecture, The 6th Annual London Nahuatl Study Day, Institute of Archaeology, University College London, United Kingdom.

Offner, J. A. (2021b). "Empires of Xolotl." *Ethnohistory* 68(4), 455–491.

Ortiz Arroyo, J. (2021). *El Rollo de Itzcuintepec Análisis Histórico-Genealógico de un Códice del Siglo XVI* (Doctoral dissertation, Centro de Investigaciones y Estudios Superiores en Antropología Social, Mexico). Retrieved from: https://ciesas.repositorioinstitucional.mx/jspui/bitstream/1015/756/1/TE%20O.A.%202010%20Joel%20Ortiz%20Arroyo.pdf.

Oudijk, M. R. (2008). "De tradiciones y métodos: investigaciones pictográficas." *Desacatos*, no. 27 (2008), 123–138. https://lccn.loc.gov/96193735.

Oudijk, M. R. (2009). Itzcuintepec, Papeles de. In *Wiki-Filología*. Retrieved from: https://www.iifilologicas.unam.mx/wikfil/index.php/Itzcuintepec,_Papeles_de.

Smith, D. N., & Blackwell, C. (2012). Four URLs, Limitless Apps: Separation of Concerns in the Homer Multitext. In D. Elmer, D. Frame, L. Muellner, V. Bers (Eds.), *Donum natalicium digitaliter confectum Gregorio Nagy septuagenario a discipulis collegis familiaribus oblatum*. Harvard University Press. Retrieved from: https://chs.harvard.edu/d-n-smith-c-w-blackwell-four-urls-limitless-apps-separation-of-concerns-in-the-homer-multitext-architecture/.

Stresser-Péan, G. (1995). Codex de Xicotepec. Spanish *El Códice de Xicotepec : estudio e interpretación* [traducción del manuscrito original, Araceli Méndez ; dibujos, Françoise Bagot ; fotografías del códice, Georges-Yves Massart]. 1. ed. en español. México : Gobierno del Estado de Puebla : Centro Francés de Estudios Mexicanos y Centroamericanos : Fondo de Cultura Económica.

Torquemada, Fray J. de. (1969). *Monarquía Indiana*. Biblioteca Porrúa, vols. 41–43 (facsimile of 1723 edition, Madrid). Mexico City: Editorial Porrúa.

CHAPTER 7

Not the same landscape. Rediscussing digital approaches to premodern spatial knowledge systems

Chiara Palladino
Furman University

Abstract

This chapter examines the status of the digital study of premodern spatial documents understood as expressions of local knowledge systems. It investigates the tension between the prevalently Cartesian perception of the world underlying modern efforts of mapping and spatial analysis, and the contrasting multiplicity of premodern spatial epistemologies, which reveal deep, multi-layered forms of representation.

The first part summarizes the dynamics in the development of spatial knowledge and offers a gallery of examples showing the complexity of premodern spatial descriptions. The second part evaluates current trends in Digital Humanities and examines the ways in which this complexity is (or is not) addressed. The conclusion emphasizes the main issues that still affect the study of premodern spatial perception and proposes some recommendations.

How to cite this book chapter:
Palladino, C. 2023. Not the same landscape. Rediscussing digital approaches to premodern spatial knowledge systems. In: Palladino, C. and Bodard, G. (Eds.), *Can't Touch This: Digital Approaches to Materiality in Cultural Heritage*. Pp. 141–163. London: Ubiquity Press. DOI: https://doi.org/10.5334/bcv.h.

Abstract (Italiano)

Questo capitolo esamina la situazione corrente nell'ambito dei metodi digitali applicati allo studio di fonti sulla percezione dello spazio in età premoderna, intese come testimonianze di specifici 'knowledge systems'. Si analizza la tensione fra la percezione del mondo prevalentemente Cartesiana su cui si basano i metodi moderni di mappatura e analisi spaziale, e la contrastante molteplicità di epistemologie premoderne, che rivelano forme di rappresentazione complesse e sfaccettate.

La prima parte sintetizza le dinamiche di sviluppo della percezione spaziale e offre una galleria di esempi per dimostrare la complessità delle rappresentazioni premoderne. La seconda parte analizza le più recenti tendenze nelle Digital Humanities e valuta i metodi di (non) affrontare questa complessità. Nella conclusione si sottolineano le problematiche più importanti ancora rilevabili nello studio della percezione premoderna dello spazio, e si propongono alcune raccomandazioni.

1. Introduction: Not the Same Landscape

It is very difficult to imagine a world without maps.[1] The ways most of us interact with our spaces daily are almost inescapably mediated by certain predominant representational frameworks, such as the Mercator projection and the Cartesian grid, and by navigational technologies, such as GPS and Web maps.

The foundation of this system relies on a set of ideas, which originated in some European countries and expanded globally through economic and territorial colonialism. We will refer to this system as the 'Cartesian paradigm'. The word 'Cartesian' derives from the name of the French philosopher René Descartes (1596–1650), and it implies a process of representing information through a geometrical framework, the horizontal plane, defined by axes: as such, it is inherently representational and positivist, as it implies a rigid definition of what is 'mappable' and 'scientific', vs. what is 'unmappable' and 'unscientific' (Dunn 2019).

However, human societies did not always understand space in this way.[2] Throughout most of Antiquity and the Middle Ages, diagrammatic representations

---

[1] This chapter was developed from a talk given for the *Digital Humanities and Materiality Seminar Series* (University of London – Babes-Bolyai University) in 2022. Many people contributed to the thoughts expressed here: in particular, I would like to thank Valeria Vitale, Karen Allen, Julie Velásquez Runk, Ute Dieckmann and Øyvind Eide. I am also grateful to Ruth Mostern, whose inspiring and thoughtful feedback made this chapter so much better.

[2] It is unclear when a map-based navigational practice was born. It is generally assumed that by the 16th century cartography and navigational

were not the primary mediator of the human relationship with the environment. To explain why the ancient Greeks and Romans did not seem to use maps to find their way, Pietro Janni (1984) utilized the notion of 'hodological space', coined by German psychologist Kurt Levin: a pragmatic understanding expressed through narrative (rather than vision), structured as a linear sequence of features seen through an egocentric perspective, and opposed to a Euclidean, 'bird's eye' cartographic cognition. Although the two notions were never rigidly separated in practice, maps were approached with skepticism as tools to represent the material world, and this carried important implications for the development of spatial cognition: while cartography could be one way of representing the world philosophically through geometry and mathematics, other tools were used to conceptualize the human relationship with it.

The predominance of the Cartesian paradigm—a set of concepts that inevitably and somehow unconsciously frame the perception of the world for most people today—created a form of hierarchy of spatial knowledge, according to which non-cartographic representations were regarded as primitive, underdeveloped, or not sufficiently 'objective'. Cartography, interpreted as the only truly scientific means to understand space, could be used to illustrate non-cartographic information by placing it within a 'real-world' context.

In recent times, however, it has been acknowledged that Western cartography and technology are not neutral tools that can be applied to any notion of space, but carry certain epistemological implications. This process has created the conditions to deconstruct and decenter the Cartesian paradigm, and to support a more nuanced inquiry into other modes of representation. Most importantly, however, it generated a reconsideration of spatial cognition in different human groups as an organic knowledge system, where ideas, concepts and material features interact and provide autonomous and effective representations. There are ways of interpreting, or seeing (or hearing, or tasting, or touching) the spaces we inhabit, that are completely different from our own. We all look at the same space, but do not see the same landscape.[3]

The purpose of this chapter is to examine documents from societies located before or outside of the expansion of map-based culture, and to provide a per-

---

technologies were sufficiently efficient to mark that shift in a good part of the world, although European colonialism is responsible for the expansion of this practice in the Americas and the Pacific, where evidence suggests that navigational knowledge was still working through different systems.

[3] The meaning of the word "landscape" is very complex. Its use has been criticized as strongly connected with Western representational models and techniques, but there is no agreed-upon terminology to describe the same group of ideas. In the context of this discussion, the term is to be understood as the manifestation of "the world as it is known to those who dwell in it" (Ingold 2000: 193), and as the conglomerate of discourses and concepts describing the human relationship with the environment (Olwig 2019: 13–16).

spective on how they challenge the Cartesian paradigm. Then, I will examine the implications of this situation for research, particularly in the domain of Digital and Spatial Humanities, two fields literally born out of, and inextricably connected to, Western technological epistemology, but that have an unprecedented potential of simulation and reconstruction. Can digital methods provide an opportunity to go beyond the Cartesian paradigm? To what extent are they generalizable to different knowledge systems? What ethical implications lie in their application? What models, if any, could offer new ways to look at the problem?

2. Humans and the World

The starting point to understand human conceptualization of space is the idea of embodied experience (Tuan 1977): the mediation of human perception constructs meaning on the environment and turns it into something that can be represented, re-expressed, and re-encoded in different media.

The body and its interaction with the physical world are the primary mediators through which we experience our surroundings. The second crucial element is the substrate of knowledge, or navigational skillset, which informs how to recognize and engage with environmental features. Such knowledge will be different depending on culture, on the nature of the ecosystem, and even on individual experience.

The embodied experience of the environment is *multi-sensorial* and *interactive*. All our senses participate in it and convey information, and the very act of moving generates intuitive and physical input that is used to navigate across the territory: we interact with the material characteristics of the environment to gather information from it and construct an image of it.

An additional mediation is provided by culture, language, or, more broadly, the cognitive frameworks that help us process spatial information. These are sometimes referred to as mental models, cognitive representations of space that mediate between the phenomenological world and its semiotic expressions (Thiering 2014). These models, however, are not pre-constituted signifiers that humans impose on space: they are affected by the environment and the way it is experienced. So, while they work as a knowledge filter, through which a person can make sense of the world, they are constructed and modified based on that experience. This knowledge is then translated into various forms of spatial communication, in a transmedial process, through which a community fixates and reflects upon the experience, selects what to communicate and how, and transmits it in a systematic way (Figure 7.1).

However, spatial communication is not a mere description of the landscape: it is a codification of this whole process in all its complexity and, in turn, provides a frame of conceptualization for it. Spatial knowledge is the result of a 'feedback loop', where the material embodied experience informs a representation

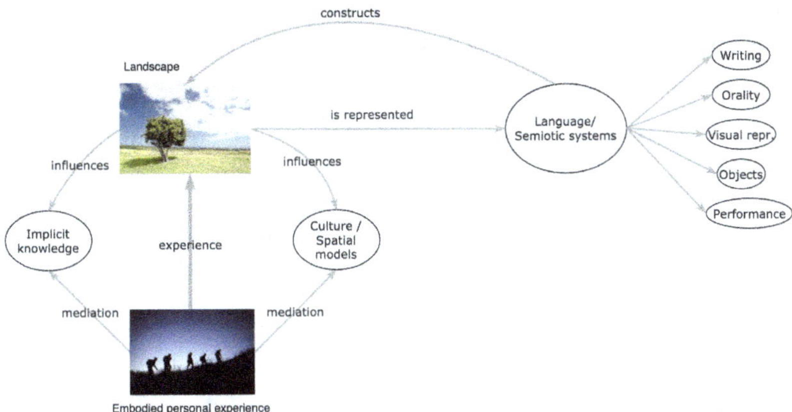

Figure 7.1: A diagram illustrating the passage from landscape to representation. Photo Credit: Jeff King and Tobias Mrzyk (Public Domain).

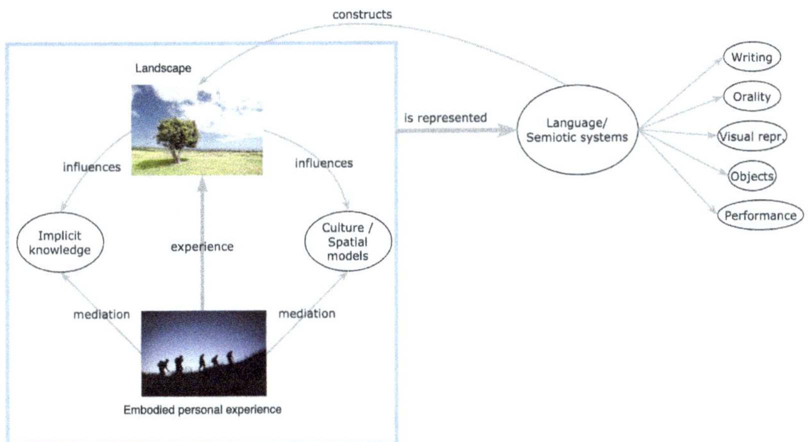

Figure 7.2: The diagram in Figure 1, modified. Photo Credit: Jeff King and Tobias Mrzyk (Public Domain).

of the world, which in turn gets codified in a new semiotic system, which then provides conceptual reference points to move through the environment (Figure 7.2). Spatial knowledge is not the result of an arbitrary set of ordering parameters imposed on a disordered sensory input, but of the dynamic interaction of body, culture and environment in the act of moving and dwelling in the world (Gibson 1979; Ingold 2000; Merleau-Ponty 1945). The product of this interaction is constituted by the material evidence of spatial communication: visual, oral, performative or written sources. These are the (inevitably fragmentary) traces we use to reconstruct an experience that is geographically, temporally and culturally distant from us.

3. The World and Premodern Civilizations: First Gallery

The material environment (whether 'natural' features or infrastructure marking human presence) can shape spatial cognition and communication in very distinctive ways. In ancient Greece, one of the most typical forms of spatial communication were the *periploi* (from περιπλέω, 'I sail around'), the conventional name for a type of sea travel description that, despite being mostly a literary product, took navigational information from real-world accounts. When describing navigation, this narrative structure is paradigmatic and hodological, articulated through a linear sequence of features on the coastal line, connected by various kinds of spatial and conceptual relations. For this reason, *periploi* sparked debate among scholars, who questioned the effectiveness of this system at providing support for navigation: some believe that a big part of the Greek navigational skillset was transmitted orally (Medas 2008), while others, combining archaeological evidence, believe that Greek seafaring was just primitive and approximate (Janni 1996). But the shape of the *periploi* is a result of the material circumstances under which navigation happened: Ancient Greek seafaring originated from coastal navigation in a closed sea during the Colonization (7th c. BCE) and from the subsequent establishment of habitual routes of communication across coastal centers (Dueck 2012: 111-ff.). Therefore, the system of spatial communication generated from it was as accurate as it needed to be, given the material environment in which it was designed to function.

Sometimes, the process would be reversed: human conceptualization of the landscape may foreground its material modifications, creating deeply integrated forms of spatial discourse. In the Roman Empire, spatial conceptualization was predominantly expressed through the appropriation and centralization of infrastructure, of which the most prominent example was the road network.

One of the structural elements of the Roman roads were the milestones (*miliaria*), epigraphic monuments placed at specific endpoints, providing the distance, mile by mile, to the beginning of the road, and intended to function as authoritative reference points for travelers (Figure 7.3). Everything about the *miliaria* is functional to spatial discourse: their physical location and shape were as important as the information they conveyed, and their linguistic component was structured topologically as a linear sequence of intervals, an obvious effect of the travel infrastructure. On the other hand, they clearly marked the landscape as Roman, functioning as ideological manifestations of power (Kolb 2016).

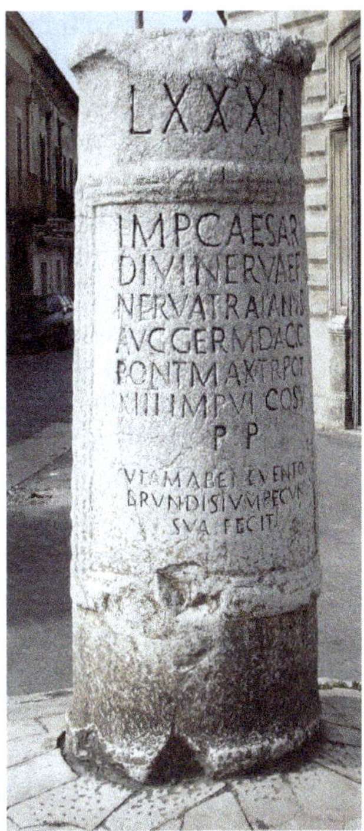

Figure 7.3: Roman milestone of the ancient Via Traiana. From Cerignola, Facciata di Palazzo Ducale. Public Domain. https://commons.wikimedia.org/w/index.php?curid=5040277.

The milestones are hardly works of art. Yet, this form of spatial discourse was so pervasive that it was replicated, both in form and language, in non-functional and artistic objects: for example, it is reproduced in monuments of propaganda like the large-scale milestone pillar called *Stadiasmus Patarensis* (45–46 BCE), or in small-scale personal objects like the Vicarello Goblets (50–150 CE), literally mini-milestones that utilized the same language to display a personal, memory space for private use.

Beyond the materiality of the landscape, spatial representation could also be framed by cosmological preoccupations, with a deeper sense of a more-than-human surrounding reality. For example, Early Chinese perception of space was based on the cosmographic tension between the primeval undifferentiated chaos and the principle of order: as the creation of the world was structured as an ordered sequential separation of things emerging from chaos, the principles of division and order were substantial to spatial understanding (Lewis 2012). Accordingly, spatial knowledge was not descriptive and representational, but prescriptive and operational (Henderson 2009): the practice of ordering the world was at the same time administrative and cosmological, reflecting the supreme goal of Chinese statecraft.

The main metaphor used to organize space was based on the same principles of order and separation: the square was the main unit of division, displayed in various arrangements, such as the grid, used to organize the territory in the Nine Provinces system (Lewis 2012). The grid, however, was also pervasive in visual and architectural arrangements:[4] a chief example was the 'Bright Hall' (*Ming Tang*), the central hall of the imperial palace described in Han texts. The Bright Hall was structured through a geometrical, grid-like arrangement: the ritual passage of the ruler across the various chambers symbolized both the annual cycle and the ordering power of the state. As such, the Bright Hall was a symbolic representation of the entire ancient Chinese cosmos and social order (Tang 2020), but it also functioned as a diagram, representing the universe through forms and patterns. The same fund of ideas that generated the Bright Hall also served as a model for personal objects with ritual and divinatory value, such as diviner's boards, TLV mirrors (Figure 7.4), and *liu bo* game boards, which used geometrical diagrams to represent the cosmos and reduced the world to an object that one could hold in the palm of the hand and allowed access to a realm of cosmological totality (Hung 2007). Immaterial space, therefore, was represented through carefully crafted material objects.

In other civilizations, local history and mythology provided a conceptual filter through which the deeper meanings of the landscape could be constructed, creating multi-dimensional narratives about space. In pre-colonial and early colonial times, Mesoamerican spatial knowledge was based on a conceptual, totalistic association between the landscape and the community, which was expressed through multi-scalar communication that manifested through depth rather than arrangement of features. Moreover, because Mesoamerican time perception was cyclical, there is no linear progression in spatial storytelling. A well-known example is offered by the Mixtec Codex Zouche-Nuttall, which merges recognizable geographic features with foundational-mythical stories, to create a deeper, culturally meaningful representation of a recognizable landscape (Mundy 1998). Even the basic spatial unit of Mexica administration, the *altepetl*, represented as pictograms enriched by toponymic glyphs, resembles multi-dimensional 'deep maps', where multiple aspects are joined together in such a way that it is impossible to make a clear demarcation. Finally, the material features of manuscripts, like color and composition, were used as spatial metaphors to reflect environmental and cultural characteristics (Murrieta-Flores, Favila-Vázquez & Flores-Morán 2022).

---

[4] It is debated at what point in time this geometrical ordering of space led to the development of the cartographic grid as a representational standard. The grid is traditionally dated back to Pei Xiu (3rd century CE), but it is unattested in maps until at least the 12th century.

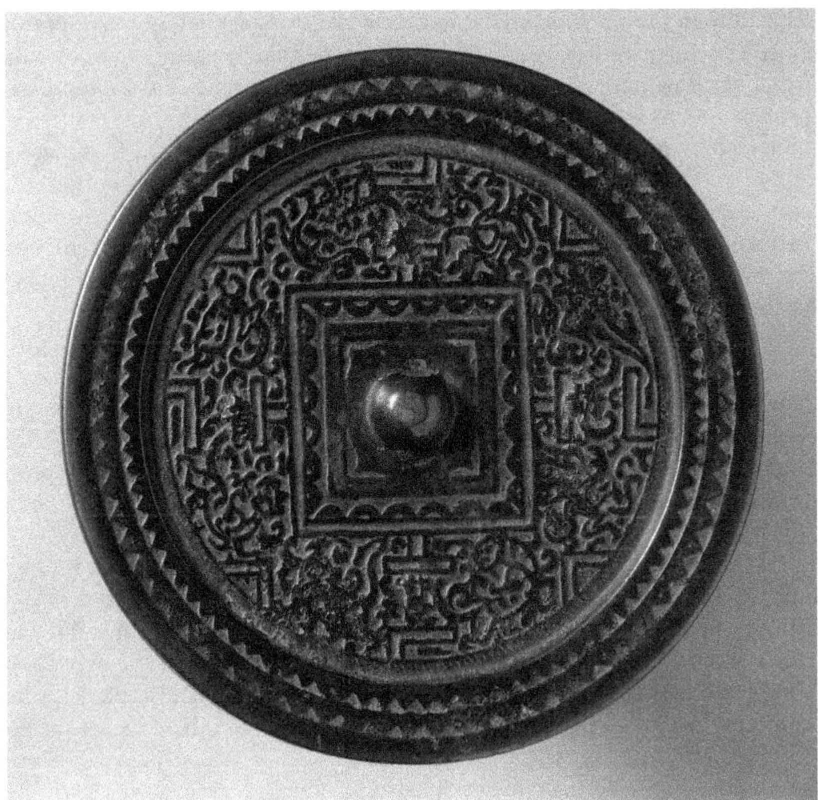

Figure 7.4: Cast bronze mirror with TLV design. China, Eastern Han dynasty, 25–220. Los Angeles County Museum of Art. Public Domain. https://commons.wikimedia.org/w/index.php?curid=27215358.

One of the most complex manifestations of a holistic perception of space is the Aboriginal Songline tradition, also called Dreaming or Dreamtime. The name, popularized by Bruce Chatwin's bestseller (1987), broadly refers to the tracks, or footprints, with which the Ancestral Beings marked the landscape while they were living in it, making it what it is today. In the Songlines, the spiritual and the material dimension of the landscape overlap exactly: they merge recognizable features of the landscape with the images and stories of the Ancestral Beings, at the same time functioning as orientation devices (Norris & Harney 2014) and as memoryscapes, where every single feature of the landscape is meaningfully connected (Turnbull & Watson 1989).

The Songlines, however, are also inextricably connected to the material circumstances of their production: they are primarily ritual songs, made to be recited in particular contexts, while their designs are transferable across media.

Especially in the Classical tradition,[5] their visual manifestations were drawn on ephemeral materials, ranging from the famous bark paintings to bowls and weapons, sometimes even to be destroyed during ceremonies. The most prominent exceptions are ancient exemplars inscribed on rocks, which are regarded as produced by the Ancestors themselves, and therefore precluded from access and reproduction (Sutton 1998). This ritual aspect underlies forms of secrecy also at the local and individual level, with profound differences across communities: a Songline and its corresponding patterns and interpretation may be regarded as personal to the individual or clan, therefore its disclosure or reproduction are forbidden.[6]

Hopefully, these examples have shown the variety and complexity of the processes considered under the notion of 'spatial knowledge'. Spatial documents reflect the complexity of the human-environment interaction, and therefore are multi-layered. This merging of dimensions happens in two ways: conceptually, through the overlapping and mixing of cosmological, religious, topographic, political and cultural categories, and transmedially, through the integration of different types of media, material and immaterial elements.

This complex system works as a framework to the landscape so that the elements that are important *conceptually* also become prominent *materially*. Spatial representations served as mnemonic devices for the community, often at times when communication was predominantly oral: through the overlap of conceptual and material features, they really created the landscape, with no clear-cut distinction between environmental features and their deeper meanings. So, a promontory placed at a certain angle, a particularly shaped stone, a mountain at the horizon, may not mean anything to a foreign navigator: in fact, it may not be distinguishable from the rest of the environment at all. However, because of its role in local knowledge, it becomes instantly visible to a member of the community.

Finally, one should consider the added complexity, specific to premodern sources, of the distance in time, space, difference in media, and various forms of secrecy and uncertainty, which inevitably affect the completeness of the evidence, while the very landscape that they were supposed to represent has drastically changed or disappeared. This is the challenge that is posed to

[5] The term 'Classical tradition', which is usually indicated in English as 'Aboriginal art', indicates the Aboriginal cultural practices at the time of the arrival of the first non-Aboriginal people in Australia: some of these still survive, while most of the current production is defined as 'post-colonial' (Sutton 1998).

[6] The research on this part has been conducted on images of Songlines that are published on the web with adequate permission and are available for anyone to see. However, since the author has not obtained direct permission for publication in this volume, no figures of Songlines or clear links to them are included here.

research, and specifically to a field that defined the investigation of spatial knowledge as its chief objective: the Spatial Humanities.

4. Challenging the Spatial Humanities

The Spatial Humanities flourished at the intersection between humanistic place and machine-actionable models of representation. The term appears for the first time in the volume *The Spatial Humanities: the Future of GIS in Humanities Scholarship* (Bodenhamer, Corrigan & Harris 2010), and it was broadly adopted to define an area of research that utilized computational methods to investigate spatial documents. The Spatial Humanities emerged during a period defined by the spatial turn, which placed a renewed emphasis on the social and cultural aspects of space.

From the start, the Spatial Humanities were clearly associated with the Cartesian paradigm: they made massive use of technologies designed to facilitate the digital representation of places, including Geographic Information Systems (GIS), Web maps (such as Google Earth or OpenStreetMap), GPS navigators, and Semantic Web standards like the Keyhole Markup Language (KML). These technologies defined the fundamental toolkit used by any scholar who wanted to apply computational methods to study spatial information.

By adopting these methods, the Spatial Humanities also inherited their tensions. The discipline placed itself at the tail end of a long tradition of critique of the Cartesian paradigm, which started within geography and cartography. By emphasizing the humanistic value of notions of place, geographers already indicated the limitations of the Cartesian paradigm to represent the complexity of spatial knowledge (Harley 1989; Kitchin & Dodge 2007; Pickles 2012; Tuan 1977). GIScience specialists pushed for a deeper understanding of the concept of 'map' as a creative/expressive project, as opposed to an always-there, always-true representational paradigm (Wilson 2017). The Cartesian paradigm, in other words, is just one of the many possible representational frameworks.

Still, the challenge is far from resolved. Scholars have emphasized how the generalized use of GIS and Web mapping systems tends to rework or even reinforce established power structures within more traditional practices (Haklay 2013; Massey 1991; Wainwright & Bryan 2009). Moreover, there are important ethical implications when researching or disseminating the geographical knowledge of indigenous populations, from ethical and epistemological standpoints (Wickens Pearce & Louis 2008), but also from the very concrete perspective of access and reproduction, which may be strongly regulated by the communities themselves, or even tied to the necessity of hiding the location of natural resources.

This issue calls into question the entire array of digital technologies and standards used to accomplish spatial analysis. The Spatial Humanities remains a discipline that applies a methodological toolkit deeply ingrained in Western epistemology, to the understanding of cultures that did not even remotely use the same tools in their own cognitive and communication processes. It is important, therefore, to ask ourselves to what extent these methods of representation are effective tools of inquiry into other knowledge systems, how we may further problematize our assumptions, and what new solutions may be attempted.

5. Spatial Knowledge and Spatial Humanities: Second Gallery

The mapping of the premodern world immediately stimulated reflection on the complexities of spatial representation. The largest gazetteer of the premodern world, Pleiades,[7] established a richer and more nuanced digital representation of 'place,' understood not just as a set of GIS coordinates, but as a bundle of associations to information of different kinds, including names, attestations, cultural heritage data, chronologies, semantic categories, and so on (Elliott & Gillies 2009).

Recently, Linked Open Data (LOD) infrastructures like Pelagios[8] introduced a framework to connect a multiplicity of resources, including text, images, place data, but also material objects and cultural heritage information, with a strong focus on places as a connecting element (Vitale et al. 2021): ideally, this would facilitate the integration of online resources for the creation of complex, multi-layered digital representations.

The Digital Periegesis[9] and ToposText,[10] although with different research goals, provide intensely annotated digital editions of ancient Greek texts and use LOD to connect place references to external information on significant sites and cultural heritage objects. In this way, Greek texts function almost as 'ancient travel guides' to the geography of the Mediterranean (and beyond), and the resulting datasets reinforce a sense of interaction between the narrative of the written document, real-world geography, and the material and cultural dimension of space (Figure 7.5).

Of course, there are limitations: somehow against the notion of a 'travel guide,' the resulting visualizations privilege a cartographic, bird's eye view, and do not allow for a hodological perspective.[11] An additional issue is the general

---

[7] Which derived nonetheless from a traditional print atlas, the *Barrington Atlas of the Greek and Roman World* (Talbert 2000).

[8] Pelagios Project: https://pelagios.org/.

[9] Digital Periegesis: https://www.periegesis.org/.

[10] ToposText: https://topostext.org/.

[11] The Digital Periegesis is experimenting with alternative visualizations: see https://gis.periegesis.org/.

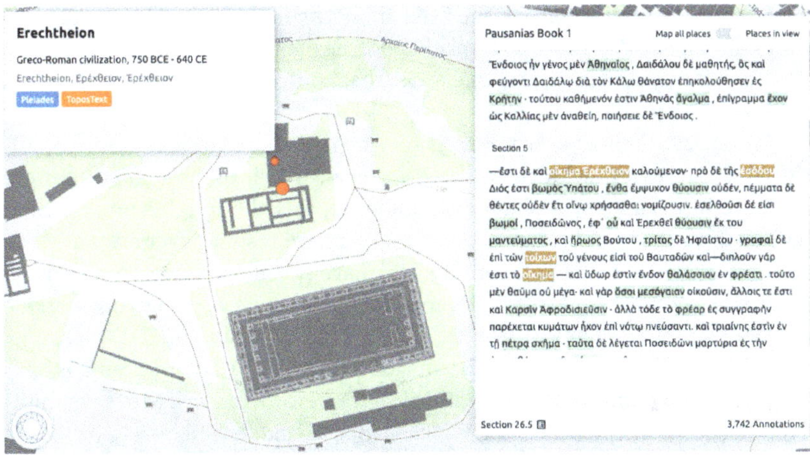

Figure 7.5: A screenshot from the Digital Periegesis illustrating various linked resources around a text mentioning the Erechtheion in Athens. Published in: Elton Barker, Early Steps in Digitally Mapping Pausanias's Description of Greece. Pelagios Blog, 2021. URL: https://medium.com/pelagios/early-steps-in-digitally-mapping-pausaniass-description-of-greece-548301b2a54d. Reproduced with permission of the Author.

inability of current technologies to visualize narrative and topographical distortion, such as the non-linear juxtaposition of stories belonging to different periods, or the alterations used to assign prominence to locations with specific mythistorical characteristics (for example, in Pausanias: Hutton 2005).

Another big issue is the lack of strategies to represent semantic depth of spatial information. Despite the enormous flexibility of semantic annotation, one of the most successful methods for the collection of data from narrative sources, two main elements are missing: generalizable ontologies and standards to encode semantic information, and suitable workflows to represent the overlap of different conceptual dimensions (culture, religion, mythology, poetry and geography) that is characteristic of spatial documents (Foka et al. 2021). As we will see, these two problems are common.

Another LOD-based project, Digging into Early Colonial Mexico (DECM),[12] uses a similar workflow to analyze the complex stratification of the *Relaciones Geográficas de la Nueva España*, a 16th-century corpus documenting Mexican precolonial and early colonial spatial knowledge. The corpus was georeferenced and annotated with large-scale computer-assisted methods, enriching place data through supervised text mining and machine learning to show various

[12] DECM Project. Digging into Early Colonial Mexico: https://www.lancaster.ac.uk/digging-ecm/.

types of contextual information. Even though still within a GIS framework, annotation provides a certain level of depth, as the spaces described are associated to cultural and semantic categories that contribute to define their role in local knowledge.

The biggest challenge, however, is to integrate the maps (or, more broadly, visual documents) included in the *Relaciones*, which provide important evidence to indigenous spatial understanding, expressed through a multi-dimensional narrative where environmental and cultural realities overlap, and where features like arrangement, color and style have specific meaning. Such images cannot be annotated automatically and are also extremely challenging to model as data (Murrieta-Flores, Favila-Vásquez & Flores-Morán 2022). Even though there is no lack of technologies for image annotation,[13] what is missing is, once again, the operational and methodological framework to work with such multi-layered spatial manifestations: it is a challenge to understand how to collect the information from the source and how to represent—and differentiate across—its various constituents. Therefore, the creation of a comprehensive digital representation of Mexican spatial knowledge is still very much a work in progress.

The most intense experimentation in new data models has happened precisely in the digitization of cultural and mythological sources: semantic annotation, applied with increasingly philological rigor, is often combined with ad-hoc ontologies that are created from the data, rather than imposed top-down. The Norse World gazetteer,[14] which models spatial information from manuscript sources of Medieval Sweden and Denmark, combines a philological approach of manual annotation and data entry with a tailored database structure and uses GIS as a management and exchange tool, rather than for visualization (Petrulevich 2023).

The Manto project[15] is an original attempt to model ancient Greek mythologies through their references to places and people, creating a 'map' that combines LOD and relational databases. Even though the purpose of this project is not to investigate space, but rather mythology as a knowledge system, it is a useful point of comparison. The project places itself within a longstanding history of relational models, such as graphs and networks, for the representation of space (Barker, Isaksen & Ogden 2016). In this framework, spatial knowledge is fundamentally understood as a conglomerate of relations (Palladino 2021): between features, concepts, or even words. Relational models provide a way to

[13] The IIIF standard provides an important starting point within the LOD framework, as Baba indicates (Chapter 3 in this volume). An alternative approach is proposed by Woodward, Offner & Blackwell (Chapter 6 in this volume), using the CITE infrastructure already adopted in the Homer Multitext.

[14] Norse World: https://norseworld.nordiska.uu.se/.

[15] Manto: https://www.manto-myth.org/.

complement traditional GIS maps and at the same time empower research beyond the map's constraints. They are, therefore, particularly suitable for projects that deal with non-Cartesian notions of space: mythological places, in this case, are obviously not easily mappable according to Cartesian criteria. Therefore, they are considered as nodes in a network rather than georeferenced locations, and their relations are of multiple kinds: spatial, but also cultural, familial, narrative, religious, temporal, and conceptual. The resulting ontology, represented through a relational database, is created through a careful and well-documented bottom-up process of annotation and data modeling. What is still missing in this large and multi-layered network is the integration with non-textual data, such as annotated depictions of mythological characters in cultural heritage objects (even though artifacts are included in the database as sources), or information about archaeological sites, which could potentially be integrated through the underlying Linked Data structure.

The success of Linked Open Data shows that data exchange can improve our understanding of spatial documents. Yet, this potential does not seem to be fully exploited: even though the interlinked structure facilitates the exploration across datasets, very few projects actively engage in this process.

On the other hand, in Archaeology there are numerous efforts to model spatial knowledge and practice through the interaction of different media. For example, various combinations of agent-based modeling, 3D and Virtual Reality simulations are used to place humans in virtual spaces and analyze their interaction with the environment, to study how different material circumstances could alter the perception and use of certain places in the ancient world: this is the case of the Virtual Pompeii Project (Frederick & Vennarucci 2021)[16] and of the 3D Babylon model (Pedersén 2021).[17] The BEMA project simulates the experience of attending Athenian assemblies on the Pnyx, measuring reactions to various environmental changes, such as the number of assembly men, perspective of the viewer, or sound changes (Kyungyoon et al. 2015). In their experiment of digital reconstruction of funeral processions at the Roman Forum, Favro and Johnason (2010) show an application of 3D digital immersive models by testing various reconstructions of the forum, and by including human variables in each scenario, showing how digital models can contribute different perspectives to the study of spatial perception. Finally, Collar and Eve (2020) recently illustrated a very powerful combination of AR technologies and sensory input in the reconstruction of the route to access Mount Kasios, a very important site in Neolithic, Hittite and Ancient Greek cultures. The reconstruction was deployed to test user behavior in the simulation of various spatial

---

[16] Virtual Pompeii: http://tesseract.uark.edu/virtual-pompeii/.

[17] Digital Model of Babylon: https://www.lingfil.uu.se/research/assyriology/babylon/.

scenarios, suggesting emotional responses through the change of atmosphere, movement, and arrangement of features.

These kinds of immersive experiences have many advantages: they recreate spaces that would be impossible to access otherwise, and significantly expand access to cultural heritage sites. However, they often suggest a phenomenological approach, which maintains that experiencing place through embodiment can reveal insights into the spatial cognition of other civilizations. In so doing, they make certain assumptions on the nature of that experience, which can be problematic (Barrett & Ko 2009), as they must blur the boundary between the documentary evidence used and the inevitable reconstruction of data that is not there. Elsewhere in this volume, Vitale[18] warns against a conceptualization of 3D reconstructions as representations of the 'real' ancient artifact, and recommends instead considering them as representations of the reception, or localized knowledge of it. In other words, reconstructive models are needed, that are conceived to leave more space to conflicting interpretation, alternative reconstruction and diversity of scenarios.

A separate class of methods use popular gaming platforms to recreate parts of ancient spaces and experiences. These tools often have significantly lower access barriers than expensive Virtual Reality platforms and, differently from these, allow for conflictual interpretations through multi-user engagement, rather than imposing one view for the sake of realistic reconstruction. Moreover, depending on context, many of these platforms (such as The Sims and Minecraft) are not chiefly preoccupied with verisimilitude or accuracy, but rather with recreating spatial dynamics embedded in the material conditions of living (Morgan 2009).

Walking simulators have recently emerged for their powerful integration of storytelling and immersive reality: in these types of games, a story is developed alongside an immersive environment that allows the user to follow and interact directly with both the narrative and the place where things happen, through first-person navigation, exploration, and an interactive environment that triggers specific physical and emotional inputs (Whistance-Smith 2021). A very similar principle is employed by Danelon & Zielinski (2023), who propose a non-photorealistic reconstruction of the ancient site of Memphis through a combination of 3D landscape reconstruction and 2D maps, integrated with a VR experience where the user can explore hotspots and at the same time read excerpts of original source texts that talk about them. This project, a novel effort in Digital Egyptology,[19] attempts an original integration of material experience, spatial simulation, and cultural understanding through primary sources (Figure 7.6).

A question that remains is the potential of simulation models to represent spaces that are 'beyond the material.' Current simulation systems are primarily based on the reconstruction of visible features, but spatial knowledge integrates

[18] See Chapter 1 in this volume.

[19] See also Lucarelli (Chapter 8 in this volume).

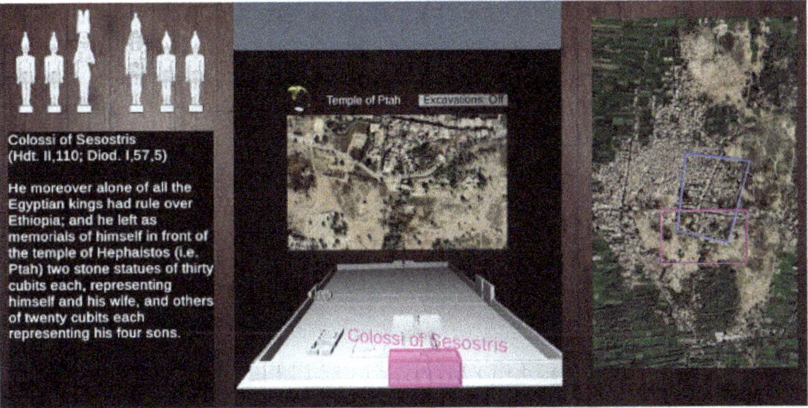

Figure 7.6: An overview of the Memphis App in Oculus Go. In the center, a schematic model of the temple of Ptah, with satellite view showing the modern area at the southern entrance. On the left, Herodotus' description of the colossi of Ramses II that could be found here. Published in Danelon & Zielinski (2023). Reproduced with permission of the Authors.

the visible with the non-visible, non-human, into the landscape. Moreover, spatial knowledge and storytelling can alter the physical aspect of the landscape to emphasize cultural or conceptual importance of certain features. While gaming engines and 3D show a lot of potential for non-realistic simulations, so far there have been no attempts to engage with these questions.

6. Conclusion

In the past few years, there has been much emphasis on the hermeneutic value of digitization practices, where the study of a document in the digital space is seen more as an exploratory way to engage with it, rather than as a representation (Krämer 2023). This is reflected in a prevalent heuristic approach to spatial analysis, where the production of GIS maps and other visualizations is often presented as the starting point to ask new questions, rather than the final product (Barker, Isaksen & Ogden 2016). At the core of Digital Humanities research there is a necessary transformation of the object of investigation through the lenses of technology: this process implies an exploratory mode where the outputs are revised iteratively, and the methodologies rediscussed, until the result is deemed somehow satisfactory.

However, representation and exploration are not the same thing. While digital models certainly help us understand our sources in different ways, they are, nonetheless, representations that we put out in the world, which have implications for how these sources exist in the digital space, and for what types of things are emphasized or hidden about them (Drucker 2011).

Technologies like Linked Open Data prioritize interoperability across datasets and mappability according to existing authorities. Interoperability and mappability, however, do not come without drawbacks: as Kahn and Simon have shown elsewhere in this volume, mass-digitized repositories may include artifacts or sites that were meant to have certain access barriers. Moreover, the *operational* step of mapping to an authority determines an almost automatic *epistemological* shift, where it becomes necessary to make preliminary distinctions between what is 'mappable' and what is not. Consequently, the following questions gravitate around the problem of perceived outliers: is Hyperborea a 'real place?' (Foka et al. 2021), where 'real place' is already a predetermined category.

Then, there is the problem of structure. There is, currently, no codified standard to digitally represent and model knowledge systems with the same stability and flexibility that there is in other domains.[20] The results are a set of recurring issues, such as the lack of integration with other media and the scarcity of semantic depth in available technologies. Cartesian representations, while being convenient for groundtruthing and data management, do not provide that structure, and are not meant to. We seem to be going in a direction where no general models are provided, but many different structures are created to accommodate different types of datasets.

This means that, when it comes to premodern spatial knowledge, interoperability and generalization may be more limited. However, this should not discourage multidisciplinary approaches. The projects described above offer a glimpse into what could be achieved with a combination of material and textual approaches, that goes beyond data exchange but prioritizes *methodological* integration. Virtual reconstructions can overcome some limitations of Cartesian mapping by providing a space for distortions, alternative perspectives and immersion; at the same time, a more conscious integration with primary sources may contribute better context, emphasizing cultural and immaterial aspects that can only be expressed through narrative.

In light of these tendencies, the first recommendation is unsurprising: when adopting certain standards of representation, extremely careful documentation must be a priority.[21] Documentation should actively engage with the epistemological side of the models adopted, emphasizing how technology imposes a certain way of conceiving and talking about the data. In the same vein, perceived outliers must be treated not as exceptions but as evidence of existing technological limitations.

A second recommendation, however, is less banal. Many scholars from multiple backgrounds have recently advocated for more inclusive approaches to digital representation and for a deeper engagement with local bodies of knowledge (Hacıgüzeller, Taylor & Perry 2021; Sletto 2009; Wickens Pearce & Louis

[20] See also Filosa, Gad & Bodard (Chapter 3 in this volume).

[21] See also Vitale (Chapter 1 in this volume), Filosa, Gad & Bodard (Chapter 3), and Elagina (Chapter 5).

2008).[22] This process may help uncover ethical and political implications in our models, providing the tools to enact a productive tension and challenge our own assumptions. In other words, it can help us uncover the inner workings and ideas behind our technologies.

Engaging with local epistemologies could also be an opportunity to actively enrich, or even reverse, our approaches. Elsewhere in this volume, Okorie[23] advocates for an active involvement of local communities in the processes of restitution of the Nigerian cultural heritage, to better understand how the local perception of artifacts, their preservation, access and reproduction may guide efforts in digitization. This is a necessary decolonization practice: rather than just be used as tools to deconstruct our own systems, local epistemologies could provide *the operational starting point* to develop new ones. What would a digital project look like, that started from the question of how a spatial document represented the landscape, rather than how technology may represent the document? What if instead of mapping onto an existing model, local knowledge became the starting point to imagine new ways of representation?

It is certainly important to be transparent about the implications of digital technologies. However, integrated approaches are not just useful to uncover inner tensions. The world is more than a Web map: despite its omnipresence and undeniable impact, the Cartesian paradigm is not the only way modern humans conceptualize the world. Prioritizing local spatial knowledge as a system may help reconfigure existing dynamics of spatial understanding and recover different ways of seeing the world. In other words, it can create the conditions for a multiplicity of imaginations (Massey 2005).

7. References

Barker, E., Isaksen, L., & Ogden, J. (2016). Telling Stories with Maps: Digital Experiments with Herodotean Geography. In E. Barker, L. Isaksen, S. Bouzarovski, & C. Pelling (Eds.), *New Worlds from Old Texts: Revisiting Ancient Space and Place* (pp. 181–224). Oxford: Oxford University Press. DOI: https://doi.org/10.1093/acprof:oso/9780199664139.001.0001.

Barrett, J. C., & Ko, I. (2009). A Phenomenology of Landscape: A Crisis in British Landscape Archaeology? *Journal of Social Archaeology, 9*(3), 275–94. DOI: https://doi.org/10.1177/1469605309338422.

Bodenhamer, D. J., Corrigan, J., & Harris, T. M. (Eds.). (2010). The Spatial Humanities: GIS and the Future of Humanities Scholarship. Bloomington & Indianapolis: Indiana University Press.

Chatwin, B. (1987). The Songlines. London: Jonathan Cape.

Collar, A. C. F., & Eve, S. J. (2020). Fire for Zeus: Using Virtual Reality to Explore Meaning and Experience at Mount Kasios. *World Archaeology, 52*(3) 530–47. DOI: https://doi.org/10.1080/00438243.2021.1920458.

[22] See also Bianchini (Chapter 4 in this volume).

[23] See Chapter 11 in this volume.

Danelon, N., & Zielinski, D. J. (2023). Mythological Landscapes and Real Places: Using Virtual Reality to Investigate the Perception of Sacred Space in the Ancient City of Memphis. In R. Lucarelli, J. A. Robertson, & S. Vinson (Eds.), *Ancient Egypt, New Technology. The Present and Future of Computer Visualization, Virtual Reality and Other Digital Humanities in Egyptology* (pp. 85–117). Leiden-Boston: Brill. DOI: https://doi.org/10.1163/9789004501294_005.

Drucker, J. (2011). Humanities Approaches to Graphical Display. *Digital Humanities Quarterly, 5*(1). Retrieved from: http://www.digitalhumanities.org/dhq/vol/5/1/000091/000091.html.

Dueck, D. (2012). Geography in Classical Antiquity. Cambridge: University Press. DOI: https://doi.org/10.1017/CBO9781139027014.

Dunn, S. E. (2019). A History of Place in the Digital Age. London-New York: Routledge.

Elliott, T., & Gillies, S. (2009). Digital Geography and Classics. *Digital Humanities Quarterly, 3*(1). Retrieved from: http://www.digitalhumanities.org/dhq/vol/3/1/000031/000031.html.

Favro, D., & Johanson, C. (2010). Death in Motion: Funeral Processions in the Roman Forum. *Journal of the Society of Architectural Historians, 69*(1), 12–37. DOI: https://doi.org/10.1525/jsah.2010.69.1.12.

Foka, A., McMeekin, D. A., Konstantinidou, K., Mostofian, N., Barker, E., Demiroglu, O. C., Chiew, E., Kiesling, B., & Talatas, L. (2021). Mapping Ancient Heritage Narratives with Digital Tools. In E. M. Champion (Ed.), *Virtual Heritage: A Guide*. London: Ubiquity Press. DOI: https://doi.org/10.5334/bck.f.

Fredrick, D., & Vennarucci, R. G. (2020). Putting Space Syntax to the Test: Digital Embodiment and Phenomenology in the Roman House. *Studies in Digital Heritage, 4*(2), 185–224. DOI: https://doi.org/10.14434/sdh.v4i2.31521.

Gibson, J. J. (1979). The Ecological Approach to Visual Perception: Classic Edition. Boston: Houghton Mifflin.

Hacıgüzeller, P., Taylor, J. S., & Perry, S. (2021). On the Emerging Supremacy of Structured Digital Data in Archaeology: A Preliminary Assessment of Information, Knowledge and Wisdom Left Behind. *Open Archaeology, 7*(1), 1709–1730. DOI: https://doi.org/10.1515/OPAR-2020-0220.

Haklay, M. (2013). Neogeography and the Delusion of Democratisation. *Environment and Planning A: Economy and Space, 45*(1), 55–69. DOI: https://doi.org/10.1068/a45184.

Harley, J. B. (1989). Deconstructing the Map. *Cartographica: The International Journal for Geographic Information and Geovisualization, 26*(2), 1–20. DOI: https://doi.org/10.3138/E635-7827-1757-9T53.

Henderson, J. B. (2009). Nonary Cosmography in Ancient China. In K. A. Raaflaub & R. J. A. Talbert (Eds.), *Geography and Ethnography: Perceptions of the World in Pre-Modern Societies* (pp. 64–73). Oxford: Blackwell Ltd. DOI: https://doi.org/10.1002/9781444315653.ch5.

Hung, W. (2007). Picturing or Diagramming the Universe. In F. Bray, V. Dorofeeva-Lichtmann, & G. Métailié (Eds.), *Graphics and Text in the Production of Technical Knowledge in China* (pp. 191–214). Leiden-Boston: Brill. DOI: https://doi.org/10.1163/ej.9789004160637.i-772.31.

Hutton, W. (2005). Describing Greece. Landscape and Literature in the Periegesis of Pausanias. Cambridge: Cambridge University Press.

Ingold, T. (2000). The Perception of the Environment: Essays on Livelihood, Dwelling and Skill. London-New York: Routledge.

Janni, P. (1984). La Mappa e il Periplo: Cartografia Antica e Spazio Odologico. Roma: G. Bretschneider.

Janni, P. (1996). Il Mare Degli Antichi. Bari: Edizioni Dedalo.

Kitchin, R., & Dodge, M. (2007). Rethinking Maps. *Progress in Human Geography, 31*(3), 331–344. DOI: https://doi.org/10.1177/0309132507077082.

Kolb, A. (2016). The Romans and the World's Measure. In S. Bianchetti, M. R. Cataudella, & H.-J. Gehrke (Eds.), *Brill's Companion to Ancient Geography. The Inhabited World in Greek and Roman Tradition* (pp. 223–238). Leiden-Boston: Brill. DOI: https://doi.org/10.1163/9789004284715_014.

Krämer, S. (2022). Should We Really 'Hermeneutise' the Digital Humanities? A Plea for the Epistemic Productivity of a 'Cultural Technique of Flattening' in the Humanities. *Journal of Cultural Analytics, 7*(4), 1–22. DOI: https://doi.org/10.22148/001c.55592.

Kyungyoon, K., Jackson, B., Karamouzas, I., Adeagbo, M., Guy, S. J., Graff, R., & Keefe, D. F. (2015). *Bema: A Multimodal Interface for Expert Experiential Analysis of Political Assemblies at the Pnyx in Ancient Greece.* Paper presented at the *2015 IEEE Symposium on 3D User Interfaces (3DUI)*, Arles, France. DOI: https://doi.org/10.1109/3DUI.2015.7131720.

Lewis, M. E. (2012). The Construction of Space in Early China. Albany: State University of New York Press.

Massey, D. (1991). A Global Sense of Place. *Marxism Today.*

Massey, D. (2005). For Space. London-Thousand Oaks-New Delhi: SAGE Publications.

Medas, S. (2008). La Navigazione Antica Lungo le Coste Atlantiche dell'Africa e verso le Isole Canarie. Analisi della Componente Nautica a Confronto con le Esperienze Medievali. In R. González Antón, F. López Pardo, & V. Peña Romo (Eds.), *Los Fenicios y El Atlántico* (pp. 143–215). Madrid: Centro de Estudios Fenicio y Púnicos.

Merleau-Ponty, M. (1945). Phénoménologie de La Perception. Paris: Gallimard.

Morgan, C. L. (2009). (Re)Building Çatalhöyük: Changing Virtual Reality in Archaeology. *Archaeologies, 5*(3), 468–487. DOI: https://doi.org/10.1007/s11759-009-9113-0.

Mundy, B. E. (1998). Mesoamerican Cartography. In D. Woodward & M. G. Lewis (Eds.), *Cartography in the Traditional African, American, Arctic, Australian, and Pacific Societies*, Vol. 2.3 (pp. 183–256). Chicago-London: University of Chicago Press.

Murrieta-Flores, P., Favila-Vázquez, M., & Flores-Morán, A. (2022). Indigenous Deep Mapping. A Conceptual and Representational Analysis of Space in Mesoamerica and New Spain. In D. J. Bodenhamer, J. Corrigan, & T. M. Harris (Eds.), *Making Deep Maps: Foundations, Approaches, and Methods*, (pp. 78–111). London-New York: Routledge. DOI: https://doi.org/10.4324/9780367743840-6.

Norris, R. P., & Harney, B. Y. (2014). Songlines and Navigation in Wardaman and Other Australian Aboriginal Cultures. *Journal of Astronomical History and Heritage, 17*(2), 141–148.

Olwig, K. R. (2019). The Meanings of Landscape: Essays on Place, Space, Environment and Justice. London-New York: Routledge.

Palladino, C. (2021). Mapping the Unmapped: Transmedial Representations of Premodern Geographies. *Berichte. Geographie und Landeskunde, 94*(2), 139–160. DOI: https://doi.org/10.25162/bgl-2021-0008.

Pedersén, O. (2021). Babylon. The Great City. Münster: Zaphon.

Petrulevich, A., & Boeck, S. S. (2023). Norse World from Plan to Action: Building a Digital Gazetteer of East Norse Medieval Literature Step by Step. In A. Petrulevich & S. S. Boeck (Eds.), *Digital Spatial Infrastructures and Worldviews in Pre-modern Societies* (pp. 91–114). Leeds: Arc Humanities Press.

Pickles, J. (2012). A History of Spaces: Cartographic Reason, Mapping and the Geo-Coded World. London-New York: Routledge.

Sletto, B. (2009). 'Indigenous People Don't Have Boundaries': Reborderings, Fire Management, and Productions of Authenticities in Indigenous Landscapes. *Cultural Geographies, 16*(2), 253–77. DOI: https://doi.org/10.1177/1474474008101519.

Sutton, P. (1998). Icons of Country: Topographic Representations in Classical Aboriginal Traditions. In D. Woodward & M. G. Lewis (Eds.), *Cartography in the Traditional African, American, Arctic, Australian, and Pacific Societies*, Vol. 2.3 (pp. 353–386). Chicago-London: University of Chicago Press.

Talbert, R. J. A. (Ed.) (2000). Barrington Atlas of the Greek and Roman World. Princeton-Oxford: Princeton University Press.

Tang, Q. (2020). Between the Sacred and the Profane: On the Spatial Narrative of Places in the Hall of Distinction. In Tang, Q. (Ed.), *Ritual Civilization and Mythological Coding: Cultural Interpretation of Li Ji* (pp. 165–201). Singapore: Springer. DOI: https://doi.org/10.1007/978-981-15-4393-7_3.

Thiering, M. (2014). Implicit Knowledge Structures as Mental Models in Common Sense Geography. In K. Geus & M. Thiering (Eds.), *Features of Common Sense Geography. Implicit Knowledge Structures in Ancient Geographical Texts* (pp. 265–317). Wien-Berlin: Lit Verlag.

Tuan, Y. (1977). Space and Place: The Perspective of Experience. Minneapolis: University of Minnesota Press.

Turnbull, D., & Watson, H. (1989). Maps are Territories: Science is an Atlas: A Portfolio of Exhibits. Chicago: University of Chicago Press.

Vitale, V., de Soto, P., Simon, R., Barker, E., Isaksen, L., & Kahn, R. (2021). Pelagios – Connecting Histories of Place. Part I: Methods and Tools. *International Journal of Humanities and Arts Computing, 15*(1–2), 5–32. DOI: https://doi.org/10.3366/ijhac.2021.0260.

Wainwright, J., & Bryan, J. (2009). Cartography, Territory, Property: Postcolonial Reflections on Indigenous Counter-Mapping in Nicaragua and Belize. *Cultural Geographies, 16*(2), 153–78. DOI: https://doi.org/10.1177/1474474008101515.

Whistance-Smith, G. (2021). Virtual Wanderings: Embodied Spatial Narrativity in 'Walking Simulators'. In D. Punday (Ed.), *Digital Narrative Spaces: An Interdisciplinary Examination* (pp. 49–69). London-New York: Routledge.

Wickens Pearce, M., & Louis, R. P. (2008). Mapping Indigenous Depth of Place. *American Indian Culture & Research Journal. Special Issue, "Mainstreaming Indigenous Geographies", 32*(3), 107–126.

Wilson, M. W. (2017). New Lines: Critical GIS and the Trouble of the Map. Minneapolis-London: University of Minnesota Press.

CHAPTER 8

From Virtual Reality to virtual restitution: How 3D-Egyptology can contribute to decolonizing the field and the question of digital copies vs the original

Rita Lucarelli
University of California Berkeley

Abstract

3D digital and printed replicas of various ancient Egyptian antiquities, from statues and busts to coffins, stelas and other magical objects, are becoming increasingly popular on the web as well as in museums, but some issues and challenges related to replicas and copies in the study and fruition of the ancient Egyptian heritage remain, which include difficult questions of intellectual property rights and accessibility of the virtual platforms where the replicas are shared. The 3D models of the ancient Egyptian coffins produced for the "Book of the Dead in 3D" project housed at the University of California, Berkeley, will be taken as a case-study to analyze and discuss those issues. Given the importance of annotations on 3D models of an inscribed artifact such as an ancient Egyptian coffin, this article will also discuss the materiality of the text and its

How to cite this book chapter:
Lucarelli, R. 2023. From Virtual Reality to virtual restitution: How 3D-Egyptology can contribute to decolonizing the field and the question of digital copies vs the original. In: Palladino, C. and Bodard, G. (Eds.), *Can't Touch This: Digital Approaches to Materiality in Cultural Heritage*. Pp. 165–181. London: Ubiquity Press. DOI: https://doi.org/10.5334/bcv.i.

digital reproduction, and how the metadata of a historical object and its text decoration need to be produced "responsibly" and according to museum ethics, to ensure sustainability and access in the language of origin of the artifact.

The issue of "decolonization" will be analyzed in relation to the use of Virtual and Augmented Reality in the digital reconstructions of archaeological sites, monuments, and artifacts in Egypt, through examples of VR apps such as "From the Museum to the Tomb", a joint project of UC Berkeley and UC Santa Cruz, where a 26th Dynasty's stone sarcophagus is virtually replaced in his tomb and analyzed in its original ritual space.

الملخص

مما لا شك فيه أن النسخ المقلدة الرقمية والمطبوعة ثلاثية الأبعاد للعديد من الآثار المصرية القديمة قد أصبحت شائعة بشكل متزايد على شبكة الإنترنت وكذلك في المتاحف، سواء كان ذلك للتماثيل والتماثيل النصفية أو للتوابيت واللوحات والقطع الأخرى ذات الطابع السحري، ولكن تظل هناك بعض المشاكل والتحديات المتعلقة بالمستنسخات والنسخ المقلدة خلال دراسة التراث المصري القديم. هذه التحديات تتضمن مسائل صعبة تتعلق بحقوق الملكية الفكرية وكذلك إمكانية الوصول إلى المنصات الافتراضية حيث يتم عرض النسخ المقلدة. فى هذا البحث ستتم دراسة النماذج ثلاثية الأبعاد للتوابيت المصرية القديمة التي تم إنتاجها فى إطار مشروع "كتاب الموتى ثلاثي الأبعاد" في جامعة كاليفورنيا فى بركلي ، كدراسة حالة لتحليل هذه المسائل ومناقشتها. ونظرًا لأهمية الملاحظات التوضيحية على النماذج ثلاثية الأبعاد للقطع الأثرية المنقوشة مثل التوابيت على سبيل المثال، ستناقش هذه المقالة أيضًا الأهمية المادية للنص واستنساخه الرقمي، والحاجة الملحة أن يتم إنتاج البيانات الوصفية للقطع التاريخية والزخارف النصية "بمسؤولية" ووفقًا لأخلاقيات المتاحف، وتحقيق الاستدامة وكذلك الوصول لأصل القطعة.

بالإضافة إلى ذلك، سيتم تحليل مسألة "إنهاء الاستعمار" فيما يتعلق باستخدام الواقع الافتراضي والمعزز في إعادة البناء الرقمي للمواقع الأثرية والآثار الثابتة والقطع الأثرية في مصر، من خلال أمثلة لتطبيقات الواقع الافتراضي مثل تطبيق "من المتحف إلى المقبرة" ، وهو عبارة عن مشروع مشترك لجامعة كاليفورنيا في بيركلي وجامعة كاليفورنيا في سانتا كروز ، حيث تم من خلاله استبدال تابوت حجري يرجع للأسرة السادسة والعشرين افتراضيًا في المقبرة التى تم العثور عليه فيها، وتحليله في نطاقه الطقسي الأصلي.

1. Introduction: (3D) replicas vs the originals

There is a general and widespread agreement, today, about the very useful role that 3D models and prints play for educational and research purposes in museums, universities and research institutions, but also on an individual level, for a more private, "one to one" relationship between the viewer/museum visitor/digital user, the replica, and the original.[1]

[1] I wish to dedicate this article to the memory of Marcello Barbanera, whose book *Originale e copia nell'arte antica* (2011) has been of inspiration for my

Techniques of digital capture are in fact closely connected to the issue of copies vs. originals and their fruition in a discourse on cultural heritage preservation, restitution and knowledge production (Di Giuseppantonio Di Franco 2014).

3D visualizations, both digital or printed ones, directly relate to the crucial issue of identity, authenticity, and uniqueness of each artifact (Di Giuseppantonio Di Franco, Galeazzi & Vassallo 2018). A 3D replica, a computer-generated image, could be considered as an avatar of the object in question, in close interrelationship to its original since it conveys information and perception of the latter (Nowak & Rauh 2006). The original, on the other hand, becomes the prototype of a replica, to which one needs to refer in order to justify the creation of the digital replica itself.[2] Such an intimate interrelationship between the original and its copy has been discussed widely within the study of Antiquity and, more recently, according to an anthropological approach (Forberg & Stockhammer 2017). If it is true that 3D replicas are useful in the dissemination of cultural heritage that it is too often not accessible if not to an elite of museum visitors, scholars and students, we should also reflect on the patterns and methods of production,[3] storage and dissemination of those replicas. Questions such as the function and use of copies within academia need to be tackled as well, since they involve issues of copyrights and "knowledge society", namely based on the control of those copyrights (Ribeiro 2017).

The recent growth in 3D visualizations of monuments and artifacts from ancient Egypt provides good evidence for the study of the issues presented above. The art of producing models and replicas has a long history in ancient Egypt itself. We could even claim that the first 3D models were produced in ancient Egypt itself, where tomb and temple models and reproductions of daily activities are well attested. Within a funerary context, these models had a ritual and magical function, aiming at re-activating the life power of the deceased in the tomb and benefit her or him in the afterlife.[4] In temples, scaled models of buildings could have been used also to show how the final architectural work would have looked; these are the so-called *maquette*-projects, namely mini-sculpture projects. As suggested by Davoli (2017), these *ante litteram* 3D models may have also functioned as votive offering at the end of the

---

own study of this topic. I also wish to thank Ghada Mohamed for her help with the Arabic version of the abstract of this article.

2 However, digital replicas can be perceived and recognized as craft objects on their own, because of their agency, especially within a museum context: see Cooper (2019).

3 On the production of 3D visualizations and the importance of the secondary sources used as references, see Vitale (Chapter 1 in this volume).

4 This is the case of the 3D reproduction of daily activities for food production found in the tombs of the Middle Kingdom, as well as the so-called "soul houses", namely tomb models of the same period (Tooley 1995).

construction process of the real building or in rituals of temple foundation.[5] The latter includes a scene attested in the temples of the Greco-Roman period in Upper Egypt, where the Pharaoh is delivering a miniature model of the temple to the god after having gone through a purification ritual (Martzolff 2011). In this case, the scaled replica acts as ritual substitute of the original building.

The production of copies relates not only to the world of art but also to written and literary cultures; scribal professionals in different historical periods and geographical areas are skilled in the art of copying, and those copies of literary, historical, and religious texts ensured the continuation of a cultural tradition and had their own identity, occasionally as "variants" of a text (Cerquiglini 1999), connected but at the same time distinguished from their archetype, the handwritten manuscript or the rare book that they copy from. Those copyists did not have to worry about copyright-protected material, but what they were reproducing was rather considered a gift from the gods/God, "...the material manifestation of a divinely-ordered universe. They cried out to be copied in order to bring this manifestation into the world; in this sense, the work of copying was a revered craft" (Beier-de Hann 2010).

In his book *The Culture of the Copy*, Schwartz (1996) discusses the replicability vs the authenticity of the world and how replicas may transcend originals and present ethical issues about the way they are used.[6] Ethical issues are also important to consider when dealing with digital replicas of artifacts that perfectly replicate a prototype and therefore may be considered "real copies" rather than "creative imitations" like those of the so-called *Idealplastik*, "ideal sculpture", namely Roman statues that are Greek in form and content although not replicating a specific prototype (Marvin 2008; Francis 2004).

In Egyptology, there is still some confusion in the use of the terminology surrounding fake and real objects. Only recently the question has been raised, thanks to new studies that analyze terms such as 'fake', 'forgery', 'replica', 'reproduction', or 'facsimile', in order not to use them as synonyms or in such a vague way that forgeries may be taken as "copies" and forgers could use juridical terminology to avoid accusations of any crime (Smith 2018).[7]

Art was a copying process in ancient Egypt anyway, as proved by the large number of artifacts and monuments inspired by archaism; the authority of

---

[5] An example of a temple model has been found at Soknopaiou Nesos.

[6] When a digital copy transcends its original artifact, which is dismissed and replaced by the former, we could even think of "digital escapism", as coined and discussed in Stobiecka (2019).

[7] The definition of "forgery" and related terminology is being discussed also in papyrology and manuscript studies and it was a focus of the recently concluded project "Forging Antiquity": https://researchers.mq.edu.au/en/projects/forging-antiquity-authenticity-forgery-and-fake-papyri/fingerprints/. On forgeries of ancient Egyptian papyri, see Choat and Lucarelli (2023).

tradition gave much importance to the copies of statues, monuments and texts from the past (Silverman, Simpson & Wegner 1994; Manuelian 1994, in particular in the Middle Kingdom and in the Saite Period).

When confronting the conception and function of copies in the past with the contemporary digital copies and 3D visualizations of artifacts, the main difference is in the appreciation of a copy as a new original (as for the Saite copies of earlier sculpture in Egypt (Manuelian 1983) or as a sort of avatar of a human or divine figure (in the case of digitally printed copies). The function of such an avatar in the form of a 3D print recalls that of earlier plaster casts: they can duplicate and present the object in places where the original cannot be exhibited. The range of educational and pedagogical uses that can be made by these copies (casts and 3D prints) is vast and also implies some ethical choices on where and how to present a copy, especially when related to an artifact that has been acquired illegally and displaced through colonial extraction (Durgun 2021). Moreover, what a copy makes possible is the tactile experience that museum and heritage sites visitors have loved since Antiquity. Today, 3D prints and reproductions for tactile galleries allow vision-impaired visitors to experience the artifacts (Segalovich 2022). The human need for tactile feeling but also of an immersive experience replicating the sensation of "being there" is in fact a form of understanding and "seeing" more deeply an object or monument; it is what made 3D printed and digital replicas as well as the whole experience of Virtual and Augmented Reality, and more recently of the Metaverse (CUSEUM 2022), so attractive in educational and museum environments. In these environments, standing in front of an original ancient artifact, with its "magic of the past" and the sense of wonder pervading it, is certainly a unique experience. However, generally museum objects cannot be touched or moved around and only a high-resolution set of photographs or even better a 3D replica can help to examine it properly and eventually read the inscriptions on its full surface.

2. Ancient Egyptian coffins and their 3D visualizations

When dealing with heavy and large objects, 3D digital replicas and visualizations are especially useful, as in the case of the ancient Egyptian stone sarcophagi and wooden coffins produced during the Pharaonic and Greco-Roman periods of ancient Egyptian history. These are among the most important sources for our understanding of the ancient Egyptian funerary religion, art and ritual practices connected to beliefs in life after death. Wooden coffins and stone sarcophagi have been inscribed with magical texts and decorated with ritual scenes of protections throughout the millennia; their typological, material, and textual study is central within Egyptology (Taylor & Vandenbeusch 2018).

Because of their large dimensions, coffins often lie in storage rooms due to the lack of gallery space, especially in smaller museums, while if exhibited, they are rarely mounted in a way that makes it possible to observe their tridimensional architecture, both on the exterior and in the interior. When anthropoid in form, they are often exhibited while standing, not considering that when placed in the tomb to keep and protect the mummified body of a deceased, they were resting in a horizontal position.[8]

They are also among the most digitized ancient Egyptian objects; an increasing number of 3D models of coffins kept in museums around the world are becoming available on Sketchfab.[9] Although most of those models are built with high resolution photographs and provide an incredibly detailed digital reproduction of the artifact, when shared through commercial platforms like Sketchfab, they cannot be complemented by a comprehensive set of metadata in order to allow the viewer also to historically contextualize the coffin and learn about his decoration. Sketchfab only allows a limited number of annotations, whose function is instead essential to fully experience the 3D model.[10]

The Book of the Dead in 3D Project aims at providing high resolution 3D models of ancient Egyptian wooden coffins and stone sarcophagi, which are complemented by a complete set of annotations that inform the user about the historical context, owner, decorative and textual program of each coffin (Figure 8.1).[11] The annotations provided for each coffin are user-friendly and intuitive in order to provide an easy and immediate access to the information on the artifacts and so that the annotated 3D model can function as a scholarly publication, at the same time being accessible to a wider and non-specialized audience on the web, where each user can choose what kind of metadata to look at (geographical location and place of origin, prosopography, text translation, iconographic description). Special attention has been given to the annotations related to the text digitization and its translation, which could serve as basis for future electronic or printed text editions.[12] A section providing "Technical Documents" provides paradata explaining the editing and processing of the models and their rendering on the current Javascript Model Viewer.[13]

---

8 See for instance the gallery # 126 at the Metropolitan Museum (NYC): https://maps.metmuseum.org/?screenmode=base&floor=1&feature=LTczLjk2MjE5ODYsNDAuNzgwMDg3NUBsbUAxMDMyOTgzMTY0MzYy#hash=18.53/40.7800875/-73.9621986/-61 (last accessed May 2023).

9 https://sketchfab.com/search?q=egyptian+coffins (last accessed May 2023).

10 For an example of 3D annotations on ancient Egyptian coffins, see Lucarelli (2021).

11 Book of the Dead in 3D: https://3dcoffins.berkeley.edu/.

12 On digital editions of text-bearing objects, see Filosa, Gad & Bodard (Chapter 3 in this volume).

13 On the importance of paradata for 3D reconstructions, see Vitale (Chapter 1 in this volume).

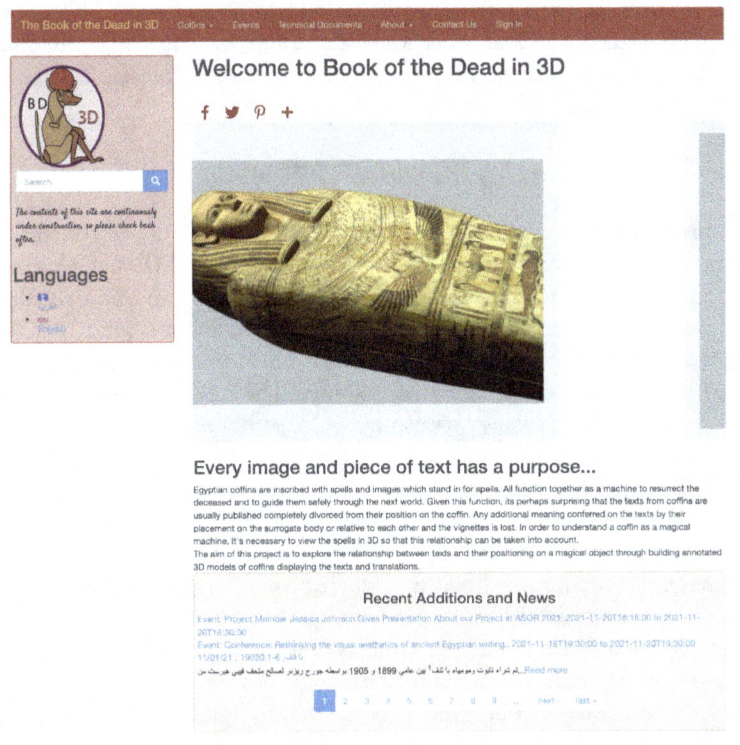

Figure 8.1: Opening page of the Book of the Dead in 3D website.

3. 3D replicas in museum environments

In museums, exhibitions where 3D replicas—printed and digital—play a main role are becoming increasing popular; from the exhibition *Replica Knowledge – An Archeology of the Multiple Past*, held in Berlin in 2018, exploring the use and function of copies of archaeological finds and their worldwide distribution, to the most recent exhibition on the tomb of Tutankhamun made exclusively of replicas of the tomb's funerary equipment within a virtual tomb reconstruction (Malek 2009), "history is continually being constructed; between the fragmentary originals and (re)construction, between truth and myth" (Simandraki-Grimshaw & Sattler 2017–2018).[14] In other words, replicas create new narratives on the originals, for which they become new media; they play a role in

[14] https://www.interdisciplinary-laboratory.hu-berlin.de/en/content/repliken-wissen-eine-archaologie-vervielfaltigter-vergangenheit_2/index.html (last accessed April 2022).

forming scientific narratives in museum and collection contexts. They are composites of 'original' and additional knowledge, and this knowledge can often be embedded in their materiality (Sattler & Simandiraki-Grimshaw 2018).

4. Digital Egyptomania

The possibility of digitally (re)constructing the past has been increasingly fascinating Egyptologists and Egyptophiles who apply Digital Humanities methodologies and tools to the study of ancient Egypt and of archeological sites, monuments, and material culture. Such a fascination for a new digital Egypt can be interpreted as a new form of Egyptomania, which feeds itself on 3D models on the web, VR and AR apps that make ancient sites accessible from home as well as Egypt-inspired videogames on the model of *Assassin Creed. The Origins*, where the user gets a glimpse of life in Ptolemaic Egypt, while on a hyperreal quest for vengeance and victory over a series of inimical encounters on the way (Casey 2021). Digital Egyptomania generally follows the same tropes traceable in traditional Western Egyptomania: ancient Egypt becomes a sort of timeless dimension where pharaohs, queens, warriors, mummies, priests, and jackal-headed powerful gods live in a hyperreal dimension, in between a landscape made of temples and tombs mainly, with only a few glimpses on ordinary people and households. Those digital reconstructions are easily accessible through the web and gaming platforms, therefore being able to reach a wide audience that values playing as a learning experience. The value of archaeogaming (Rassalle 2021) and storytelling techniques for engaging the user to learn about history and archaeology has been widely recognized by the scholarly community (Reinhard 2018)[15] and should be taken into consideration when building new scholarly digital projects.

5. Virtual restitutions

Against an unhistorical "digital Egyptomania," Digital Humanities, 3D, VR and AR technologies can be used to create a counternarrative that presents historically sound replicas within a reconstructed archaeological context that could virtually bring back an artifact to its place of origin. Peter der Manuelian was a pioneer in this field at the Harvard Museum of the Ancient Near East: the replica of the so-called Dream Stela at the Harvard Museum is an example of how replicas are an optimal pedagogical and educational tool. The original artifact lies in between the paws of the Great Sphinx of Giza and tells the story of Pharaoh Thutmosis V before his coronation, when the young prince fell asleep at the feet of the Sphinx and had a divine encounter with the god Harmachis in a dream,

[15] Archaeogaming Blog: https://archaeogaming.com/.

telling him that he would become a king after restoring the Sphinx to new life by uncovering it from the sand (lines 8–13; Szpakowska 2003). The Dream Stela actually dates back to 1401 BCE, a millennium after the time when the Great Sphinx was erected and it is an important example of prophetic literature from ancient Egypt, beside showing how pharaohs respected the monuments of the past. The replica at the Harvard Museum has been created by a student team based on a cast that dates to the 1840s; the work is now on display on the museum's second floor (Kinnaer 2014). As already mentioned, it shows how casts can be considered as a sort of predecessors of the current 3D replicas and how they create a new ontology of objects with their own digital narratives (Durgun 2021). Particularly useful, in the case of the replica of the Dream Stele, is the augmented-reality app "Dreaming the Sphinx",[16] which allows the visitors of the museum to learn about the Great Sphinx and the way it changed through history, interacting with the replica as well as reading the text of the Dream Stela in English translation (Figure 8.2) (Radsken 2018). The whole process of building the replica has been described in the *Harvard Magazine*, including the

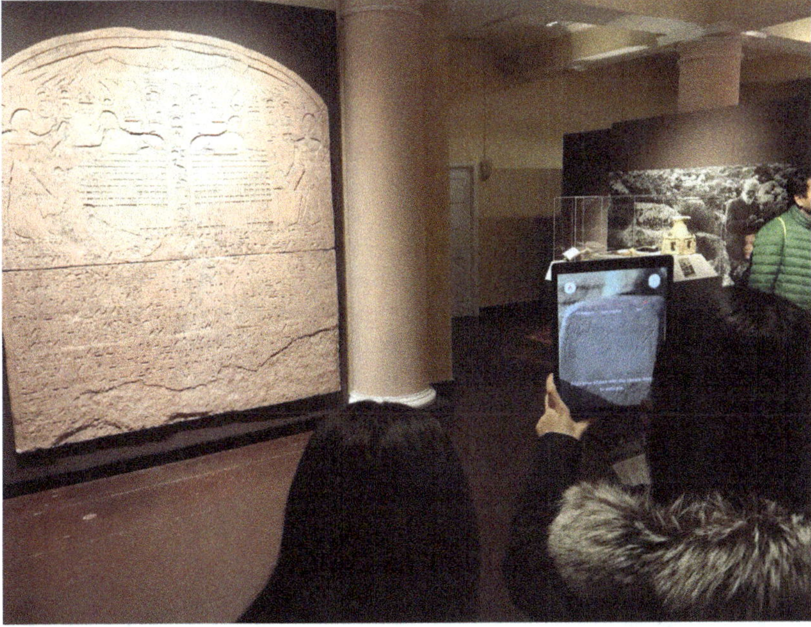

Figure 8.2: Looking at the replica of the "Dream Stele" at the Harvard Museum of the ancient Near East through the "Dreaming the Sphinx" VR App (courtesy of Peter Der Manuelian).

[16] https://play.google.com/store/apps/details?id=edu.harvard.fas.semiticmuseum.sphinx&hl=en&gl=US.

story of the casts of the museum, which were bought at the beginning of 1900 from major museums such as the Metropolitan Museum of Art in NYC and the Museum of Fine Arts in Boston (Nguyen 2017).

The AR app built for the Dream Stela is one of the very few VR and AR apps that have been created by Egyptologists to contextualize artifacts kept in museums. Another example of the potential of VR apps as educational tools is the reconstruction of the burial context of a 26th Dynasty sarcophagus kept at the Phoebe A. Hearst Museum of Anthropology of the University of California, Berkeley, entitled "Return to the Tomb". This project is a cooperation of the author of this article with the digital Egyptologist Elaine Sullivan of UC Santa Cruz, with the collaboration of Digital Cultural Heritage scholar Eiman Elgewely and a team of other IT specialists, librarians and students (Lucarelli & Sullivan 2021).[17] The aim of the project is to create a cultural context for immersive visualization of the user who is brought into the ancient Egyptian necropolis of Saqqara and successively into the tomb of Psamtek, the High Official who lived in Memphis around the second half of the First Millennium BCE and whose tomb contained the empty sarcophagus (the body of Psamtek never reached its final resting place) whose inscribed lid is now at the Hearst Museum in Berkeley (Figure 8.3).[18] Through this app, landscape reconstruction, study of the funerary culture and its sacred spaces are combined into an immersive experience, currently accessible on the HTC Vive Cosmos and Oculus VR headsets, that allows the visitor to experience the dimension of death in ancient Egypt through a new medium: the 3D model of the sarcophagus lid, virtually returned to its tomb in Egypt (Figure 8.4).

In the study of the ancient world and of ancient Egypt in particular, immersive visualization technologies such as those employed for the "Return to the Tomb" and the "Dreaming the Sphinx" apps are designed according to a main aim: making "real" (Forte 2010) ancient Egypt accessible to a wider audience and decolonizing our view of ancient Egypt, whose heritage preservation and restitution are still too often discussed according to the same eurocentric view that dominated at the time of the first archaeological expeditions following the "rediscovery" of ancient Egypt from the West after the Napoleonic campaign (Reid 2003). Such a "rediscovery" has been implicitly hiding the ancient Egyptian people, the diversity and unicity of their human

---

[17] The project has been supported by a seed grant offered by CITRIS and the Banatao Institute of the University of California, Berkeley (https://citris-uc.org/).

[18] The sarcophagus lid has been also the first case-study of the Book of the Dead in 3D project and its 3D annotated model is available on the project's website: www.3dcoffins.edu. An article with a more complete text edition of this sarcophagus lid is in course of preparation by the author.

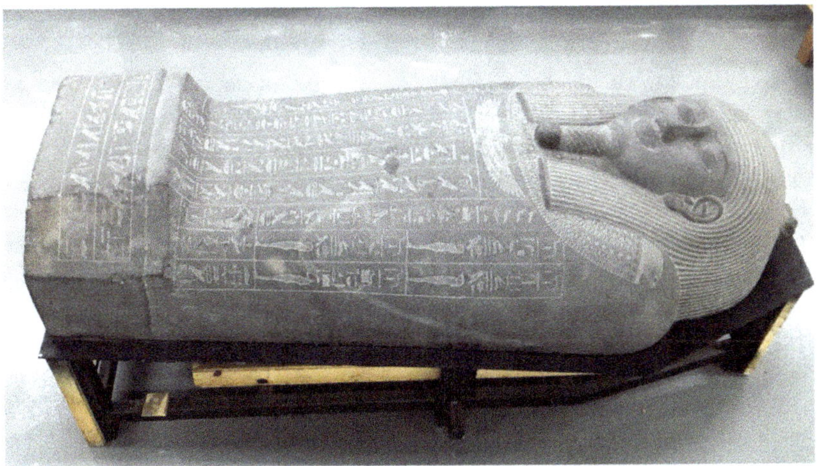

Figure 8.3: The sarcophagus of Psamtek (PAHMA 5-522).

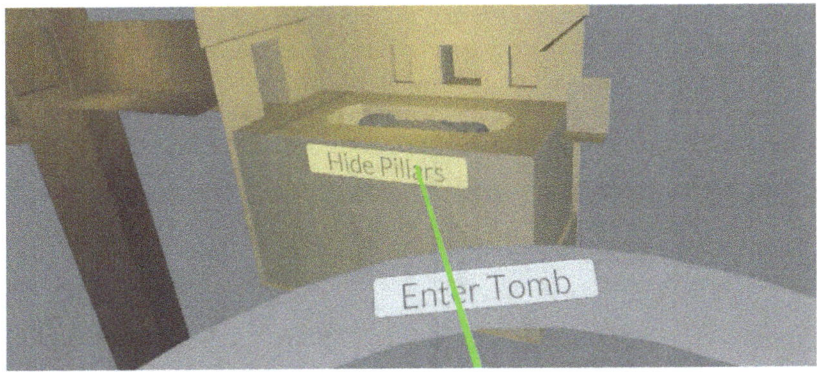

Figure 8.4: Visualization of the interior of Psamtek's tomb from outside through the VR app "Return to the Tomb".

cultural experience because of the exclusive focus on elite culture and the "wondrous curiosities" that were given major exhibition spaces in museums in Europe (Moser 2006).

3D and VR technologies today provide instead a tool for disseminating Egyptological content to the public and for museum visitors to engage in meaningful ways with content that promotes scholarly research, at the same time visualizing and describing it in an easily accessible and jargon-free way. VR and AR techniques are in fact powerful tools for reproducing not only a "potential past" (Forte 2010) but also for re-enacting an emic perspective of the monuments and their spatial context according to the way the ancient Egyptians viewed and experienced their sacred spaces.

6. Conclusions

The kind of knowledge that a 3D replica generates in the viewer/user creates a new "epistemology of the copy", related to but distinguished from the original artifact, influencing the perception of the latter and its function, and the ways to reconstruct it or restore it. The 3D replica becomes a new medium with its own life and adapted to the role its creator wanted it to play, from educational tool to protest symbol, as in the case of the controversial "Nefertiti Hack" or "the other Nefertiti", as the digital artists (Nora Al-Badri and Jan Nikolai Nelles) who created it call the 3D replica of the famous bust of queen Nefertiti (Figure 8.5).[19] The aim of this 3D replica, which after a digital exhibition has been printed and buried in the sands of the desert, is clearly stated on its artists' website: "*Nefertiti is returning to the place where it was found. For the first time since the sculpture was excavated and stolen over 100 years ago, the iconic artefact will be shown in Cairo.*"[20] This performance, which was made possible through a data leak of the photos of the bust owned by Neues Museum in Berlin, where the bust is kept since 1923, becoming a cultural symbol of the city,[21] was intended as part of the counter narrative used to "*activate the artefact, to inspire a critical re-assessment of today's conditions and to overcome the colonial notion of possession in Germany*".[22]

3D and VR can therefore become powerful tools for cultural activism and digital repatriation against notions of colonial possession, orientalism and Western fetishization of the past. These 3D copies also raise the important

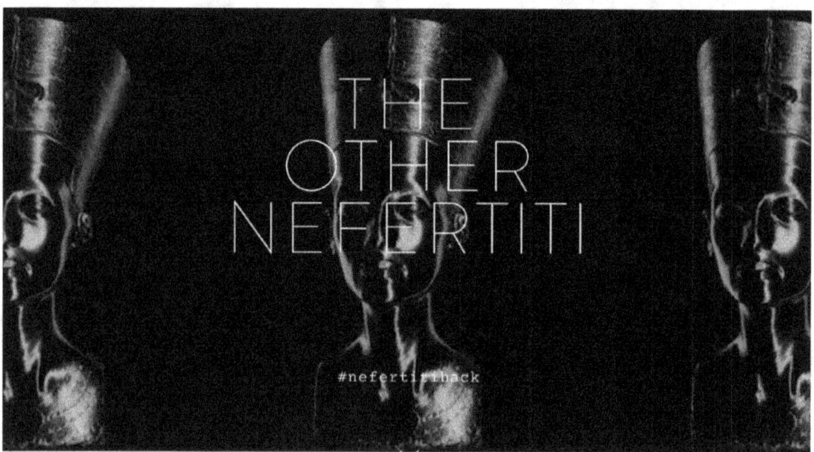

Figure 8.5: The digital replica of the bust of Nefertiti on the website of the authors (https://alloversky.com/puzzlepieces/the-other-nefertiti).

[19] The Other Nefertiti: https://alloversky.com/puzzlepieces/the-other-nefertiti.

[20] Nefertiti Hack: https://nefertitihack.alloversky.com/.

[21] See Siehr (2006), particularly on the afterlife of the bust of Nefertiti and its role in the Age of Imperialism and later in Germany and Europe.

[22] https://aksioma.org/the.other.nefertiti.

issue of who owns the objects of the past, how accessible its data should be and whom to attribute the copyrights for a replica. In the digital 3D modeling communities, such as among the 3D creators posting daily on Sketchfab, sharing and making the files available to all for download, in addition to details about the scanning and photogrammetry techniques used, is becoming common practice (Pavis & Wallace 2019; Magnani, Guttorm & Magnani 2018).

The scholarly and museum communities can learn from the work of today's digital artists about accessibility and shareability of those digital replicas that too often are instead kept inaccessible to the public, its value as artwork becoming as relevant as that of the original artifact.

"Why worship the original, while we have all the beautiful remixes as of today?" (Voon 2016).[23] The aura of authenticity[24] *vs* the awe of the replica is becoming an unavoidable issue to deal with for museum curators and scholars in the age of the metaverse. When creating narratives around digital replicas, one becomes responsible for recreating authenticity within a replica knowledge and heritage discourse (Jones, Jeffrey, Maxwell et al. 2018).

Building biographies of these digital replicas helps to better understand the original objects they come from and their historical context; to do that, we need to negotiate our traditional concept of authenticity: "replicas can work for us if we let them" (Foster and Jones 2019).[25]

Objects on display give viewers "a perception of power over the object" (Riggs 2014), which is at the basis of the colonial perception of the ancient Egyptian heritage exhibited in museums around the world. Digital replicas can instead be used to educate viewers/users to engage with those objects by analyzing their materiality in a new, non-invasive way, experiencing a previously unthinkable sense of authenticity.

7. References

Barbanera, M. (2011). *Originale e copia nell'arte antica. Origine, sviluppo e prospettive di un paradigma interpretative.* Mantova: Edizioni Tre Lune.

Beier-de Hann, R. (2010). You can always get what you want. History, the original and the endless opportunity of the copy. In: *Original, Copy, Fake, On the significance of the object in History and Archaeology Museums,*

[23] The "other Nefertiti" is still available for download on Sketchfab: https://sketchfab.com/3d-models/what-is-the-genuine-nefertiti-1295e14c5e634465aa2438004bb8886c.

[24] On the "aura" of the original and its "authenticity" see the pivotal essay of Benjamin (1935) (also available online: https://www.marxists.org/reference/subject/philosophy/works/ge/benjamin.htm).

[25] An example of a beautifully made replica re-contextualized in a museum setting is the one of the famous gilded throne of Tutankhamon, currently being prepared for exhibition at the Harvard Museum of the Ancient Near East by Peter der Manuelian (Simon 2022).

Proceedings of the 22nd ICOM General Conference in Shangai, China, 1–12th November 2010.

Benjamin, W. (1935). The Work of Art in the Age of Mechanical Reproduction. In Arendt, H. (Ed.) 1969. *Illuminations*. New York: Shocken.

Casey, C. (2021). "Assassin's Creed Origins. Video Games as Time Machines". *Near Eastern Archaeology 84*(1), 71–78.

Cerquiglini, B. (1999). *In Praise of the Variant: A Critical History of Philology*. Baltimore: Johns Hopkins University Press.

Choat, M., & Lucarelli, R. (2023). Forgeries in the Book of the Dead. In: Lucarelli, R. and M. Stadler (Eds.), *Oxford Handbook of the Ancient Egyptian Book of the Dead*. New York/Oxford: Oxford University Press.

Cooper, C. (2019). You Can Handle It: 3D Printing for Museums. *Advances in Archaeological Practice*: 1–5.

CUSEUM. (2022, March 9). Will Museums & Cultural Institutions Find a Place in the Metaverse?. In: *CUSEUM.com*. Retrieved from: https://cuseum.com/blog/2022/3/7/will-museums-cultural-institutions-find-a-place-in-the-metaverse#.

Davoli, P. (2017). Il tempio e il suo modello: nuovi rinvenimenti a Soknopaiou Nesos. M. Betrò, M., De Martino, S., Miniaci, G. and Pinnock, F. (Eds.) *Egitto e Vicino Oriente antichi: tra passato e futuro. Studi e ricerche sull'Egitto e il Vicino Oriente antico*. Pisa: 135–148.

Di Giuseppantonio Di Franco, P. (2014). *Talking about Things: A Cognitive Approach to Digital Heritage and Material Culture Studies in Archaeology* (M. S. Aldenderfer & K. L. Hull (Eds.) [University of California, Merced]. Retrieved from: https://search.proquest.com/docview/1559194482 [last accessed May 2023].

Di Giuseppantonio Di Franco, P., Galeazzi, F., & Vassallo, V. (2018). *Authenticity and cultural heritage in the age of 3D digital reproductions*. Apollo – University of Cambridge Repository.

Durgun, P. (2021). Before 3D Prints There Were Plaster Copies, *Hyperallergic*, October 3: Retrieved from: https://hyperallergic.com/681211/before-3d-prints-there-were-plaster-copies/?fbclid=IwAR0Mo6bEErUxA0Wi8p6mBY0Q8Vlkj9q1wbhasXhJYyjvLkcBNUdMklx5XBk [last accessed May 2023].

Forberg, C., & Stockhammer, P. W. (Eds.) (2017). *The Transformative Power of the Copy. A Transcultural and Interdisciplinary Approach*. Heidelberg: Heidelberg Studies on Transculturality 2.

Forte, M. (2010). *Cyber-archaeology*, London: BAR International Series.

Foster, S. M., & Jones, S. (2019). Concrete and non-concrete: exploring the contemporary authenticity of historic replicas through an ethnographic study of the St John's Cross replica, Iona, *International Journal of Heritage Studies*, Vol. 25, No. 11: 1169–1188.

Francis, J. (2004). The Modern Problem of Roman "Copies". *Mouseion: Journal of the Classical Association of Canada*, vol. 4 no. 3: 345–364.

Jones, J., Maxwell, M., Hale, A., & Jones, C. (2018). 3D heritage visualisation and the negotiation of authenticity: the ACCORD project. *International Journal of Heritage Studies*, Vol 24, No 4: 333–353. https://www.tandfonline.com/doi/full/10.1080/13527258.2017.1378905.

Kinnaer, J. (2014, November 9). Dream Stela. Introduction. *The Ancient Egypt Site*. Retrieved from: http://www.ancient-egypt.org/language/anthology/fiction/dream-stela/dream-stela---introduction.html.

Lucarelli, R. (2021). Annotating Texts on 3D (Coffin) Models, in: Gracia Zamacona, C., & J. Ortiz-Garcia (2021). *Handbook of Digital Egyptology: Texts*. Monografías de Oriente Antiguo 1. Alcalá de Henares: Editorial Universidad de Alcalá: 55–68.

Lucarelli, R., & Sullivan, E. (2021). From the museum back to the tomb. The virtual rejoining of a Twenty-sixth Dynasty sarcophagus and its burial at Saqqara, in: Krejčí, J. (Ed.). *Abusir and Saqqara in the year 2020*. Prague: 371–379.

Malek, J. (2009, January 31). Some thoughts inspired by a current exhibition: 'Tutankhamun: His Tomb and Treasures'. The Griffith Institute Archive. Retrieved from: http://www.griffith.ox.ac.uk/gri/4semmel.html.

Magnani, M., Guttorm, A., & Magnani, N. (2018). Three-dimensional, community-based heritage management of indigenous museum collections: Archaeological ethnography revitalization and repatriation at the Sámi Museum Siida. *Journal of Cultural Heritage* 31: 162–169.

Manuelian, Der P. (1983). Prolegomena zur Untersuchung saitischer 'Kopien'. *Studien zur Altägyptischen Kultur* 10: 221-245.

Manuelian, Der P. (1994). *Living in the Past. Studies in Archaism of the EgyptianTwenty-sixth Dynasty*, London: Kegan Paul International (Studies in Egyptology).

Martzolff, L. (2011). La scène de remise du temple au dieu (rdỉ(.t) pr n=bf) dans le rituel de fondation des temples égyptiens aux époques ptolémaïque et romaine. *Die Welt des Orients*, Bd. 41, H. 1: 1–26.

Marvin, M. (2008). *The language of the muses: The dialogue between Roman and Greek sculpture*. Los Angeles: J. Paul Getty Museum.

Moser, S. (2006). *Wondrous curiosities. Ancient Egypt at the British Museum*. The University of Chicago Press: Chicago.

Nguyen, S. (2017, November 8). A New Cast for the Semitic Museum. *Harvard Magazine*. Retrieved from: https://www.harvardmagazine.com/2017/11/harvard-semitic-museum-new-dream-stela.

Nowak, K. L., & Rauh, C. (2006). The Influence of the Avatar on Online Perceptions of Anthropomorphism, Androgyny, Credibility, Homophily, and Attraction. *Journal of Computer-Mediated Communication* 11: 153–178.

Pavis, M., & Wallace, A. (2019). Response to the 2018 Sarr-Savoy Report: Statement on Intellectual Property Rights and Open Access relevant to the digitization and restitution of African Cultural Heritage and associated materials. Zenodo. DOI: https://doi.org/10.5281/zenodo.2620597 (last accessed December 2022).

Radsken, J. (2018, June 8). A Cast Fit for an Egyptian King. In *The Harvard Gazette*. Retrieved from: https://news.harvard.edu/gazette/story/2018/06/dream-stela-of-ancient-egypt-re-created-by-harvard-students/.

Rassalle, T. (2021). Archeogaming. When Archaeology and Video Games come together. *Near Eastern Archaeology* 84.1: 4–11.

Reid, D. M. (2003). *Whose Pharaohs? Archaeology, Museums, and Egyptian National Identity from Napoleon to World War I.* University of California Press: Berkeley.

Reinhard, A. (2018). *Archaeogaming: An Introduction to Archaeology in and of Video Games.* Berghahn: New York.

Ribeiro, G. L. (2017). 'What's in a Copy?', in: Forberg and Stockhammer 2017: 21–36.

Riggs, C. (2014). Ancient Egypt in the Museum: Concepts and Constructions. In: A. Lloyd (Ed.). *A companion to Ancient Egypt.* Blackwell: 1129–1153.

Sattler, F., & Simandiraki-Grimshaw. (2018). "Replica knowledge. Travelling thrones", in: Brenna, B., Christensen, H.D. and Hamran, O. 2018. *Museums as Cultures of Copies. The Crafting of Artefacts and Authenticity.* Oxfordshire: Routledge.

Schwartz, H. (1996). *The Culture of the Copy: Striking Likenesses, Unreasonable Facsimilies*, New York: Zone Books.

Segalovich, I. (2022). 15 Things Museums Do That Piss Me Off, *Hyperallergic*, March 15, 2022. Retrieved from: https://hyperallergic.com/700164/15-things-museums-do-that-piss-me-off/?fbclid=IwAR0yY0GxhWAQpDRGhnIwikMr5mmqUyHoM2e1mr-kniQUgBj1Q3Hbm62CpV0 (last accessed May 2022).

Siehr, K. G. (2006). The Beautiful One has come – to Return. In: Merryman, J. H. (Ed.). *Imperialism, Art and Restitution.* Cambridge University Press: Cambridge.

Silverman, D. P., Simpson, W. K., & Wegner, J. (Eds.) (2009). *Archaism and Innovation: Studies in the Culture of Middle Kingdom Egypt*, Philadelphia: University of Pennsylvania.

Simandraki-Grimshaw, A., & Sattler, F. (2017–2018). *Replica Knowledge. An Archaeology of the Multiple Past.* Tieranatomisches Theater der Humboldt-Universität zu Berlin. September 16, 2017 – March 31, 2018.

Simon, C. (2022, October 19). The Boy King's Throne. *The Harvard Gazette.* Retrieved from: https://news.harvard.edu/gazette/story/2022/10/replica-of-king-tuts-throne-comes-to-harvard/.

Smith, M. (2018, March). *The Concept of Fake in Egyptology.* Paper presented at Fake and Real in Ancient and Modern Societies – Objects, Places, Practices. Leiden, Netherlands.

Stobiecka, M. (2019). Digital Escapism: How Objects Become Deprived of Matter. *JCAH Perspectives. Joint Commission on Accreditation of Hospitals, 5*(2), 194–212.

Szpakowska, K. (2003). *Behind Closed Eyes: Dreams and Nightmares in Ancient Egypt*. Swansea: The Classical Press of Wales, 2003: 12–14.

Taylor, J., & Vandenbeusch, M. (2018). *Ancient Egyptian Coffins. Craft Traditions and Functionality*. Leuven: Peeters.

Tooley, A. (1995). *Egyptian models and scenes*. Oxford: Shire Publications.

Voon, C. (2016, March 9). Could the Nefertiti Scan be a Hoax - and does that Matter?. *Hyperallergic*. Retrieved from: https://hyperallergic.com/281739/could-the-nefertiti-scan-be-a-hoax-and-does-that-matter/.

CHAPTER 9

Preserving the intangible: The challenges and responsibilities of documenting material knowledge practices and skills through digital media

Paula Loreto Granados García
British Museum
Ceri Ashley
British Museum & Nottingham Trent University

Abstract

The role of digital archiving in the preservation of intangible heritage is considered in this paper, using the case study of the British Museum's Endangered Material Knowledge Programme. Concerned with the documentation of the skills, understanding, experience and embodied knowledge required to make and shape material worlds, this case study sits at the junction between the material and immaterial and the tangible/intangible, as the influence of everything from the availability of raw materials to cosmology are implicated

How to cite this book chapter:
Granados García, P. L. and Ashley, C. 2023. Preserving the intangible: The challenges and responsibilities of documenting material knowledge practices and skills through digital media. In: Palladino, C. and Bodard, G. (Eds.), *Can't Touch This: Digital Approaches to Materiality in Cultural Heritage*. Pp. 183–203. London: Ubiquity Press. DOI: https://doi.org/10.5334/bcv.j.

in material decisions. Working across the globe, but with a strong focus on documenting knowledge systems in the global south that are under extreme threat of change, EMKP supports projects, researchers, and communities to record the details of material practice before they disappear. Digital tools offer a fluid and flexible set of resources to capture and represent these complex systems of individual and overlapping knowledge and are especially relevant in situations where knowledge is not catechised by western tropes of learning and linear process. Digital technology is also increasingly accessible and offers a chance to destabilise traditional heritage hierarchies, as the ability to carry out the documentation is decentred away from researchers to include communities and practitioners themselves. Nevertheless, challenges remain, notably how to collect such alternative ontologies, and how to manage and disseminate the results appropriately, protecting the rights of the original knowledge holders. In this paper we explore how EMKP has been working during its development phase to create a digital environment that is responsive to the particularities of material knowledge, recognising its fragility and urgent need to be preserved, but also sensitive to, and respectful of, the environment in which this knowledge emerged and grew.

Resumen

El papel del archivado digital en la preservación del patrimonio intangible se analiza en este artículo, utilizando el caso de estudio del Programa de Conocimiento Material en Peligro del Museo Británico. Este programa se centra en la documentación de las habilidades, la comprensión, la experiencia y el conocimiento necesarios para crear y dar forma a los mundos materiales, y se sitúa en la confluencia entre lo material y lo inmaterial, lo tangible y lo intangible, ya que la influencia de todo, desde la disponibilidad de materias primas hasta la cosmología, tiene un papel en las decisiones sobre lo material. Trabajando en todo el mundo, pero con un fuerte enfoque en la documentación de los sistemas de conocimiento en el sur global que están bajo una amenaza extrema de cambio, EMKP apoya proyectos, investigadores y comunidades para registrar los detalles de la práctica material antes de que desaparezcan. Las herramientas digitales ofrecen un conjunto fluído y flexible de recursos para capturar y representar estos complejos sistemas de conocimientos individuales y superpuestos, y son especialmente relevantes en situaciones en las que el conocimiento no está catequizado por tropos occidentales de aprendizaje y proceso lineal. La tecnología digital también es cada vez más accesible y ofrece la oportunidad de desestabilizar las jerarquías tradicionales del patrimonio, ya que la capacidad de llevar a cabo la documentación se descentra de los investigadores para incluir a las comunidades y a los propios artesanos. Sin embargo, siguen existiendo retos, en particular cómo recopilar esas ontologías alternativas y cómo gestionar y difundir los resultados de forma adecuada, protegiendo los derechos de las cominidades originarias del conocimiento. En este artículo exploramos cómo el programa EMKP ha trabajado durante su fase de desarrollo para crear un entorno digital que responda a las particularidades del conocimiento material, reconociendo su fragilidad y su urgente necesidad de ser preservado, pero también de forma sensible y respetuosa con el entorno en el que este conocimiento surge y se desarrolla.

1. Background

Intangible heritage is now rightly recognised as an integral part of the heritage spectrum, with its status enshrined in global structures of valorisation and protection within the 2003 UNESCO Convention for the Safeguarding of Intangible Heritage. Defining Intangible Heritage as:

> "[T]he practices, representations, expressions, knowledge, skills—as well as the instruments, objects, artefacts and cultural spaces associated therewith—that communities, groups and, in some cases, individuals recognize as part of their cultural heritage."
>
> (Article 2.1, UNESCO 2003 Convention for the Safeguarding of the Intangible Cultural Heritage 2020 Edition)

The 2003 convention marks a shift in values from material preservationist approaches to ones where lived heritage experiences are celebrated. Within this definition, intangible heritage can include oral histories, performing arts, unique social practice(s), rituals and festivals, cosmologies and understanding of nature, as well as crafts and material practices (Article 2.2). The focus is therefore clearly on the richness of living knowledge and can be seen as a shift to a more inclusive form of heritage. In particular, this re-orientation has been welcomed as a redress that celebrates the values of indigenous communities and traditional knowledge, empowering non-western heritage voices and decolonising heritage practice (Alivizatou 2012; Smith & Akagawa 2006: 2).

The impetus for such safeguarding measures came from the recognition that while intangible heritage is integral to notions of identity and culture, threats to such heritage are severe and increasing. Intangible heritage is fragile and locked in the lifestyles, actions, and ways of being of individuals, groups and societies who can move, change or simply cease to exist. Threats to intangible heritage are multi-scalar, from the effects of globalisation and urbanisation that alter the fabric of social life, to localised trauma, be it environmental, societal, political, or economic. Threats can be slow and insidious like the urban drain of younger generations no longer interested in learning crafts, or the catastrophic effects of localised actions from war and conflict to the loss of homes through environmental crisis such as flooding and deforestation.[1] The urgency of preserving intangible heritage is often then acute.

While the future of traditional knowledge systems and practice is uncertain, the world of digital heritage superficially may seem to offer easy and accessible solutions. In particular, the advancement and democratisation of digital technologies in recent decades has triggered a number of digital documentation systems that enable users without a digital background to generate and manage born-digital content with a minimum of additional training (see Zuanni 2020 for the difference between digitised and born-digital objects). Increasingly accessible, egalitarian and dynamic, digital heritage is also not reliant on the large and costly infrastructures of traditional heritage institutions. Digital heritage is also accessible in ways that traditional object or site-based heritage is not; it is mobile. Digital heritage can be widely shared and consumed, even if it is still hosted in a traditional memory institution. It is also amenable to living memory projects because of the means by which knowledge can be captured usurps traditional material or literature-based preservation, and directly supports the collection of visual, spoken, performed, and practiced knowledge that may better reflect non-western ontologies. Digital curation and preservation therefore seem initially to provide a ready solution to tackle some of the challenges facing intangible heritage documentation.

However, despite these promising shifts, digitally preserving intangible heritage is not without its challenges. First and foremost, for heritage embedded in the experiences and memories of living communities, is the responsibility to protect and safeguard the rights of the knowledge holders themselves. Knowledge and practice held in communal or individual memory might be linked to economic value and skill (creation of specialist objects or designs) or related to protected or restricted knowledge that should not be indiscriminately shared, as for example in the case of ritual knowledge, or access to knowledge related to gender, social status or age. The issue of access and sharing of knowledge, which may seem simple and axiomatic in a world that lauds 'open access', is fraught with ethical tensions when dealing with intangible heritage and living memories. Moreover, notwithstanding the advantages of digital initiatives in recording intangible heritage, it is no simple panacea either; digital collections can be as vulnerable and complex as analogue ones and are similarly weighed down by power struggles played out in ownership, hosting and curation narratives.

In this chapter we discuss the complexities of preserving a particular set of intangible heritage—related to material knowledge—in a digital format, and making it available under open access licenses, while still safeguarding the source community conventions, rights, and ownership. Drawing on the

---

1 On threats to intangible heritage, see UNESCO's Living Heritage and threats platform available at https://ich.unesco.org/dive/threat/?language=en.

experiences of the Endangered Material Knowledge Programme at the British Museum, we will focus on the concept of material knowledge, its preservation and the varied challenges that emerge when attempting to digitally store and preserve the intangible.

2. Material Knowledge: what and why?

EMKP defines material knowledge as 'the understanding of the resources, skills, technologies and social values necessary to create and maintain the material world' encompassing the 'knowledge systems associated with the making, use, repair and re-purposing of material objects, spaces, architecture, performances and environments' (www.emkp.org). Material knowledge then is the layers of interconnected systems of practice, skills, and value that shape how individuals and communities make and structure their worlds—from how food is prepared and presented to the making of costumes for festivals of celebration and occasion. Material knowledge is embedded in, and draws from, a plethora of shared social, economic, ecological, and technical spheres of knowledge, and is thus vitally important to cultural identity and heritage, but also straddles the tangible/intangible worlds. This porous tangible/intangible relationship is well exemplified by the recognition that knowledge of the material world is not restricted to externalised systems of specialist knowledge—be it technical, mechanical, symbolic, or ecological—but is also embodied, that is, it lies within the actions, impulses, and movement of the maker to manipulate, respond to, and interact with the material in hand. This emphasis on experiential and tacit knowledge further erodes any notion of a divide between intangible and tangible, but also challenges researchers in how to document a knowledge system that resides within an individual. It also offers a compelling reminder that traditional ontologies of knowledge need to be re-thought in a world where knowledge is expressed through fluid movement, gesture, and action, not verbalised instruction. The potential for visual media to represent embodied knowledge is well demonstrated by a video from Sam Lunn-Rockcliffe's EMKP project 'Histories of Honey: Material Practices of Beekeeping in the Cherangani Hills, Kenya', which shows practitioners, experienced and inexperienced, preparing a log for use as a beehive in the Kenyan Rift Valley. Through the course of the video the easy expertise and effectiveness of the first axeman is highlighted through contrast to the missed cuts and imbalanced swings of the apprentices; what initially appears easy becomes a masterclass in refined and practiced action and movement (Lunn-Rockliffe, Sam; Cheptorus, Joseph Kimutai (2022): Stripping bark. The British Museum. Media. https://doi.org/10.25420/britishmuseum.19935878.v1). See below (Figure 9.1 to 9.4) of the process documented in the video.

A focus on material knowledge also has the virtue of democratising heritage values through its emphasis on, and celebration of, everyday material heritage as well as the exceptional. This range is well demonstrated by a review of grants

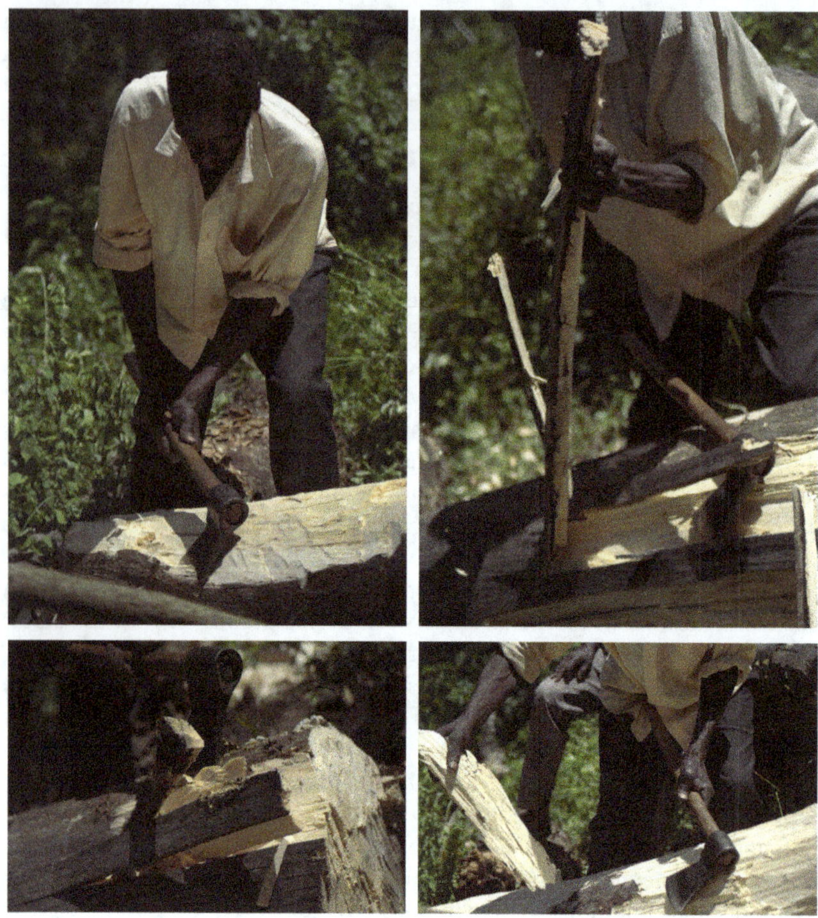

Figs. 9.1– 9.4: Lunn-Rockliffe, Sam; Cheptorus, Joseph Kimutai (2022): Stripping bark. The British Museum. Figure. Shared under a CC BY-NC-SA 4.0 license. https://doi.org/10.25420/britishmuseum.19948205.v1; https://doi.org/10.25420/britishmuseum.19948196.v1; https://doi.org/10.25420/britishmuseum.19948193.v1; https://doi.org/10.25420/britishmuseum.19948202.v1.

awarded over the last five years, which range from the everyday, mundane worlds of garden fencing, shoe making and pottery, to the exceptional, events charged with spiritual, ceremonial or celebratory significance. In the first year of EMKP, grants were awarded to support two projects—one in Ghana, documenting the making of gold ornaments for Asante royalty,[2] the other in Malaysia,

[2] For further reference, see the project's page on the EMKP website (https://www.emkp.org/research-and-digitization-of-indigenous-gold-forging-in-ghana/).

recording Batek hunter-gatherer material culture, including sleeping mats, spears, digging sticks and hair ornamentation, most of which are organic and never intended to be preserved.[3] Heritage values here are not restricted by the 'authorised' notions of significance, or criteria of universal global merit; material heritage's importance is refracted through a local lens of meaning and value. As Alice Rudge, PI of the project with the Batek, recounts "Making these items, and the sonic, visual, and olfactory experiences of doing so, are imbued with cosmological, personal, and ecological significance" (https://www.emkp.org/material-culture-of-batek-hunter-gatherers-in-pahang-state-malaysia/). It is also arguable that the commensality of many material practices places them at extreme and higher risk than the more celebrated and special event activities (although as the case-study from Ghana demonstrates, even a practice as well known and globally celebrated as Asante goldwork is not immune). The everyday worlds are what anchor many societies and help structure and express worldview and social organisation.

Material knowledge then can be a vehicle to explore larger social life and more, and is also a facet of lived heritage with real potential to diversify and democratise what is celebrated as meaningful. For this reason, the Endangered Material Knowledge Programme (EMKP) was launched at the British Museum in 2018. EMKP is a 10-year programme to provide grants globally to scholars, practitioners and communities to digitally document material practices that are in danger of disappearing as a result of changing lifestyles and worlds (www.emkp.org). Anthropologists have long recognised the precarity of social and material worlds, and the speed at which these could change. From the mid-nineteenth century, there was an increasing sense of urgency, driven by the impact of global European expansion and industrialisation among other, which prompted early attempts to salvage the practices and knowledge of in-danger communities through recording, documentation and collection (Gruber 1970; see also Redman 2021). This impetus continued, and included museums, who increasingly engaged in collecting the ethnographic present as well. As Sir Charles Hercules Read, Keeper of British and Mediaeval Antiquities and Ethnography[4] at the British Museum, wrote in his 1910 *Handbook to the Ethnographic Collections*,

> Meanwhile civilization is spreading over the earth, and the beliefs, customs, and products of practically all aboriginal peoples are becoming obsolete under new conditions … In proportion as the value of

[3] For further reference, see the project's page on the EMKP website (https://www.emkp.org/material-culture-of-batek-hunter-gatherers-in-pahang-state-malaysia/).

[4] EMKP is based in the current Department of Africa, Oceania and the Americas, and which has developed from earlier iterations, including the Department of British and Mediaeval Antiquities and Ethnography.

> Anthropology is appreciated at its true worth, the material for anthropological study diminishes; in many cases native beliefs and institutions described in the book have already become obsolete … Such facts alone enforce the necessity for energetic action before it is too late.
>
> (Read 1935:vi, cited in Gruber 1970:1296)

Approaches and methods have changed significantly since 1910, but there remains a linking thread that urges action, in 1910 towards collecting artefacts, in the contemporary context, to document the knowledge systems behind these objects.

With a strong emphasis on facilitating rather than directing research, within EMKP the aim is to support the global community of practitioners to carry out their work in the most appropriate and relevant ways for the local situation. Successful EMKP project grantees, who can be based globally, carry out documentation work over one or two years, producing a detailed corpus of records which can be in almost all possible digital formats (e.g. video recording, audio, text, photos, maps, 3D models, VR etc.). These records are hosted in an open access repository by the British Museum using a CC BY-NC-SA license.[5] EMKP currently supports research in Africa, Oceania, Caribbean and Latin America, Asia and Europe (https://www.emkp.org/supported-projects/), working to document knowledge held across national boundaries, within specific communities and even held solely by a handful of individuals. The programme offers training and advice, but never delineates how projects should happen or methods to be used. Much of the focus for the early years of programme establishment was on creating a digital platform that would support such diverse projects and dynamic records. The challenge therefore has been to mould a resource that is practical, accessible, and suitably robust to ensure long-term preservation of these important records but is also sufficiently flexible and resilient enough to accommodate the diversity of records, formats, ontologies, needs and rights of specific projects and communities. In the following discussion, we reflect on the development of the EMKP repository and the process of envisioning and implementing a robust but reflexive platform.

[5] This license specifies that download and reuse of EMKP's assets must be under the following requirements: a) give appropriate credit to the researcher; b) the material cannot be used for commercial purposes; and c) any copies, remixes, or material that uses the researcher's contributions will have to be shared under the same license.

3. Documentation and access

At the heart of EMKP's endeavour is the recognition that living material knowledge is endangered, and it is the responsibility of the programme to support its documentation and dissemination via digital means.[6] EMKP and the British Museum host the final records and documentation in a digital repository currently provided by Figshare (https://drs.britishmuseum.org/EMKP). Within the repository, users can navigate, download, and play the different images, videos, and audios available. The search interface enables users to search the collection by different concepts and themes such as type of content (e.g. project, collection, or asset), type of item (e.g., dataset, media, figure etc) or category (e.g., musicology and ethnomusicology, anthropology etc) (see Figure 9.5).

High emphasis is placed on records that are visual and try to capture the actions and interactions of the individuals involved, as well as the materials and processes. In contrast to 'how-to' style manuals, it is not just the hands of the maker who are documented; body position, movement, emotion as well as the background and context in which the actions are taking place are equally important. See for example Fig 9.6. from a project led by Tracy Peter Samat to document Sarawak native blades. In the image, two participants are collecting Artocarpus integer wood from a farmland at Kampung Sorak Dayak, for making hilts and sheaths. As well as capturing how the raw material is collected, the image shows the two participants' position, movement, and expression as they stand in front of a clump of tall, lush trees in a heavy and wet environment.

In the second example below, Figure 9.7, Catherine Grant and team document the making of the Cambodian mouth harp 'Angkuoch'. In the wide shot, the camera captures practitioner Bin SONG crafting the angkuoch daek, as his wife, other project participants and villagers sit around him to watch the process. We can also see the project team and the recording equipment on the right. The context here is also about self-reflection on the research process, and awareness of its impact.

Sound is also a valuable tool in capturing a sense of environment and place; off screen noises from cockerels crowing, children playing and rain falling all help build a textured picture of the context. Also from Catherine Grant's

---

[6] EMKP operates within the parameters of 'endangerment' as set by the programme funder, but we acknowledge that the conception of heritage 'under threat' is not without its complexities, and has, in some contexts, been contested or thought to not adequately convey the multifaceted challenges that heritage faces. Recognising the complexity of cultural legacy in all its manifestations, and the intricate relationships that exist between heritage, communities and the environment is at the core of the EMKP.

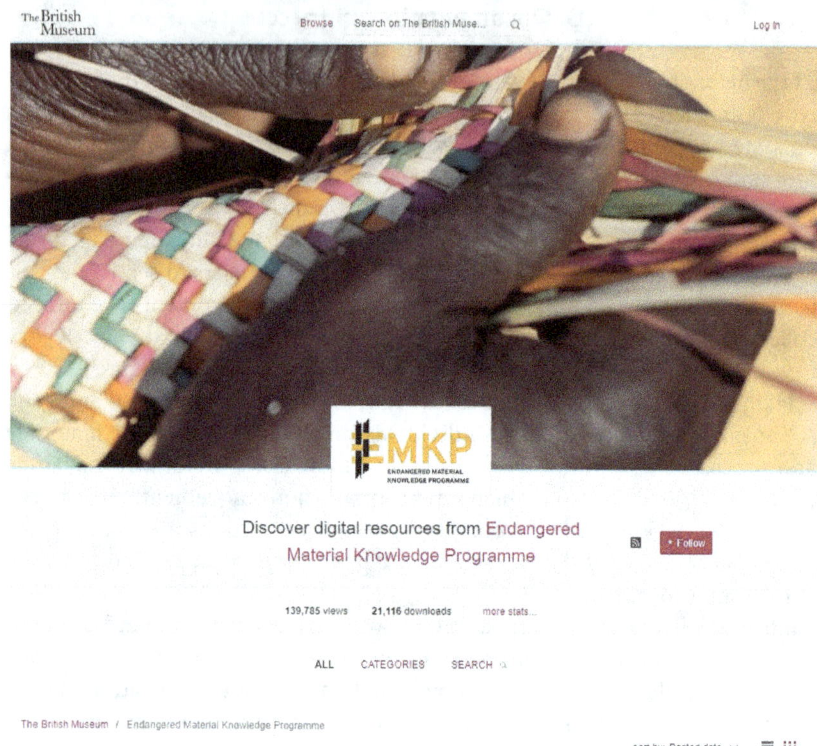

Figure 9.5: Screenshot of EMKP repository homepage and statistics.

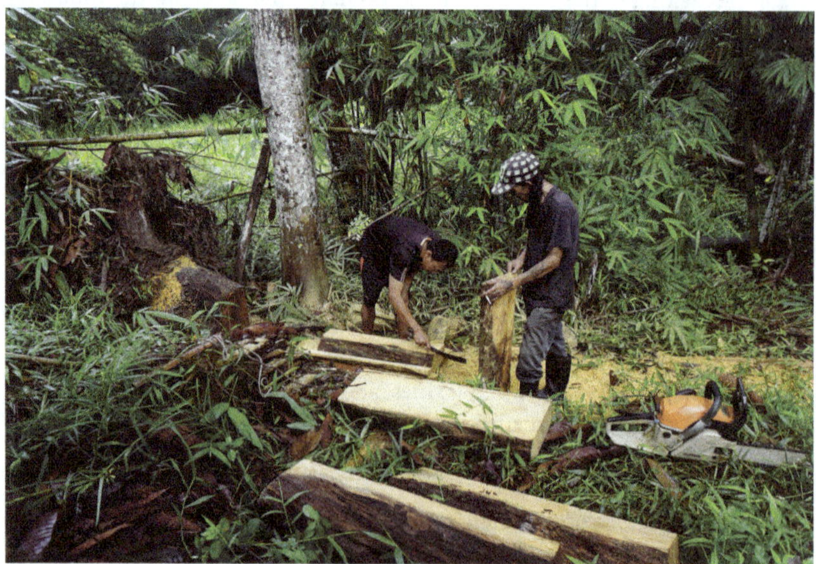

Figure 9.6: Peter Samat, Tracy (2023): Collecting wood—MIA and PAN. The British Museum. Figure. Shared under a CC BY-NC-SA 4.0 license. https://doi.org/10.25420/britishmuseum.21770567.v1.

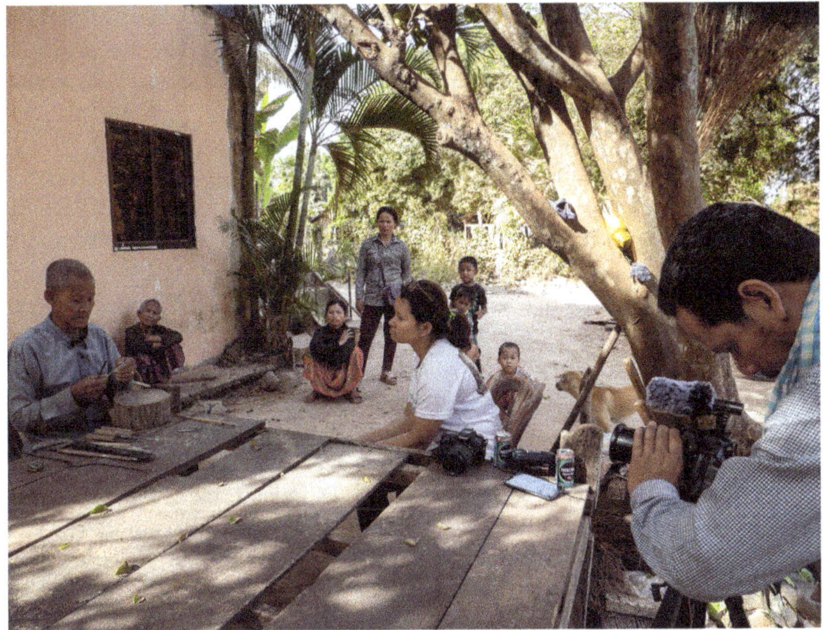

Figure 9.7: GRANT, Catherine (2021): Making angkuoch—Bin Song makes angkuoch daek while the team records it. The British Museum. Figure. Shared under a CC BY-NC-SA 4.0 license. https://doi.org/10.25420/britishmuseum.14958627.v1.

project, this video documentary beautifully captures the environment and sounds in which the Angkuoch is produced (https://doi.org/10.25420/britishmuseum.14981148.v1). In the first 40 seconds of the film, the characteristic sound of crowing cockerels gives way to the sound of leaves moving in the wind in the background, contrasting with the metallic resonance of the mouth harp played by its maker.

As these examples demonstrate, the ability to support diverse knowledge systems, often including non-verbal and/or embodied knowledge, is central to the conceptualisation of EMKP and the repository. Although still a new programme, it is evident that projects are actively using the range of digital media to create experiences of material knowledge, practice and space that go beyond a traditional descriptive experience.

4. Supporting Material Knowledge Ontologies

Central to the repository is therefore the desire to foster and support diverse archiving practices and knowledge preservation. However, there is a danger in unconditionally supporting diversity and unique expression, as the repository would soon lose coherence, manageability, and resilience. Therefore, underpinning the push for flexibility, is a robust metadata schema that ties together the disparate assets and stories. Metadata broadly defined as "data about data", in the context of EMKP, is what allows the research teams to collect key information about the assets (when, where, what, how, why) and enables the internal architecture of the repository in terms of information pursuit and retrieval.

With the aim to deploy a schema that allows flexible categories and terminologies while also providing a fixed and robust structure, EMKP developed and implemented the Material Culture Ethnography Metadata Schema (MCEMS) for the recording of information about projects. The MCEMS is a new ad hoc metadata schema created by Nik Petek-Sargeant that lays out the skeleton of the data structure and has been tailor-made for EMKP projects' needs. The schema is explained and documented by an ontology that provides the formal definition of the metadata elements and the schema structure (Petek-Sargeant 2020).

Together with more standard metadata categories to record time, location or authorship, the architecture of the MCEMS also includes a full unit to document socio-cultural context, including categories for defining the cultural space in which activities are taking place (e.g., home, forest, workshop) as well as intent, a category that explicitly aims to interrogate the motivation and decision making behind the action being performed. Another active decision was made to include a mixture of controlled and unrestricted vocabularies, so that project participants have the leeway and flexibility to describe situations more freely (see Figure 9.8, for unrestricted vocabulary categories). All categories within the socio-cultural context field for example have un-restricted vocabularies.

Similarly, another important aspect of its development has been the ontology's flexibility in terms of multilingualism and representation of alternative vocabularies and voices. The yellow-coded fields (i.e., alternative title, description, materials, etc.; see Fig. 9.8) enable the recording of specialised information in multiple languages, incorporating local languages for asset documentation and navigation, enabling free text searches in other languages, (see for example Fig. 9.9, for a search in Khmer 'ការធ្វើឧបករណ៍អង្កួច-ប.ស' of the English translation 'Making angkuoch').

Finally, the schema also enables the introduction of additional or alternative terms or authorities to those fields in which a controlled vocabulary may not suffice to represent the details of practice or social context. For example, the MCEMS uses the British Museum's taxonomy of controlled vocabularies for materials (cotton, plastic, iron), and techniques (carved, bleached, coiled) but also offers the opportunity to add alternative terms that can reflect the specific cultural name of a certain technique or type of material being used. This blend allows the use of the controlled vocabularies of the British Museum thesauri (grey coded in Figure 9.8) enabling interoperability and future reconciliations

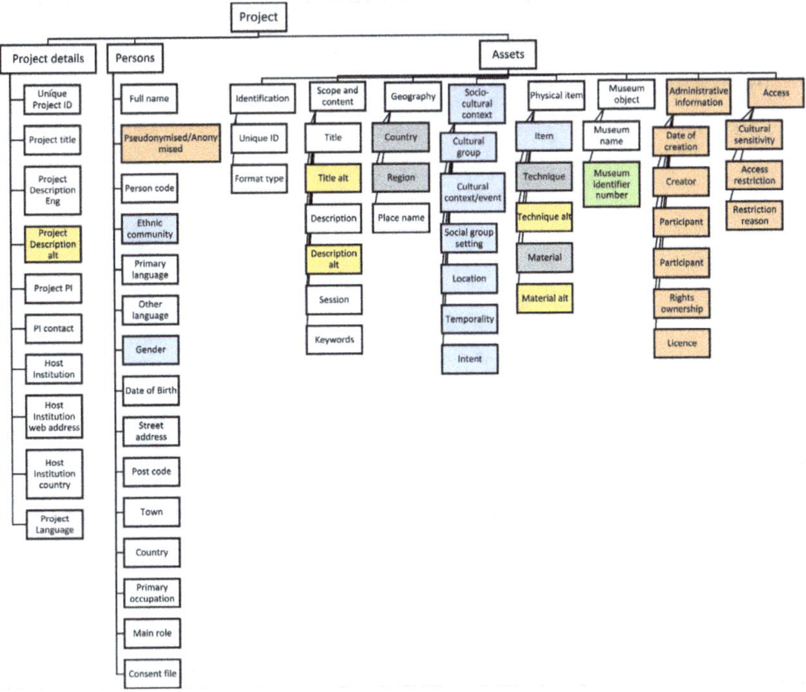

Figure 9.8: MCEMS metadata schema elements overview, based on Nik-Petek Sargeant (2020) with colour coding (yellow: multilingual fields; red: rights and access; blue: un-restricted vocabulary; grey: restricted vocabulary—British Museum thesauri- and green: links to other museum objects in collections online).

with the museum collection, to be set beside autochthonous names and conventions that more appropriately represent locally used terminology and ontology.

5. Rights protection

The emphasis on capturing alternative and representative ontologies in the metadata and repository architecture is about fostering new ways of thinking about, and representing, intangible heritage in the form of material practice. However, these initiatives are also about knowledge holders' rights and the responsibilities of the EMKP to support and valorise these voices through appropriate taxonomic representation. This is just one very small part of rights protection efforts that must be at the heart of any responsible repository, and particularly one with such a direct and close relationship with living contributors and communities of knowledge.

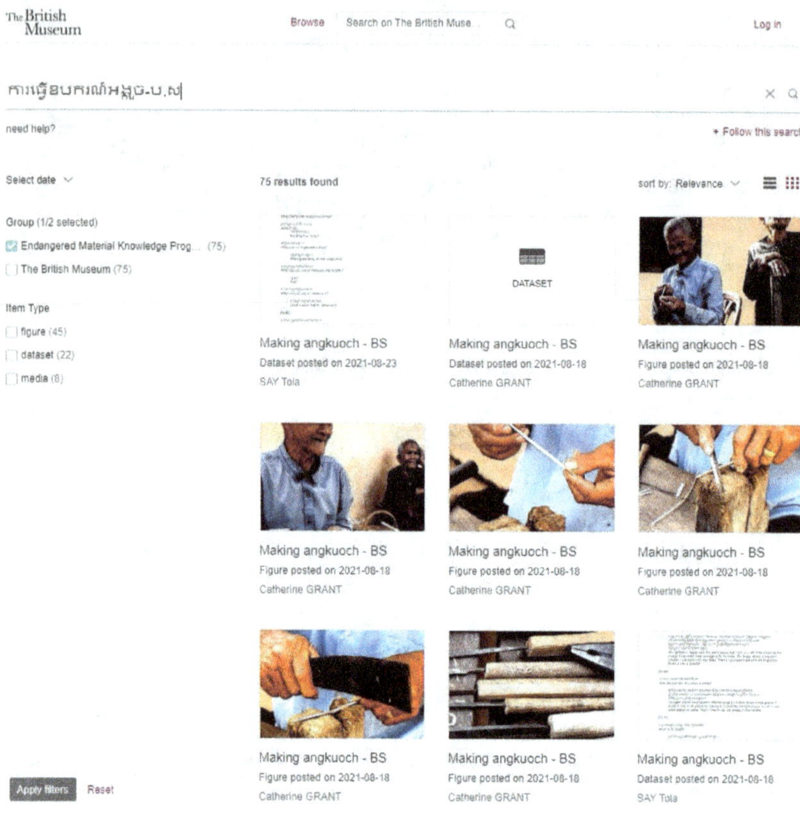

Figure 9.9: Screenshot of EMKP repository, search interface (with free text search in Khmer).

In this regard, it is encouraging to see other digital heritage initiatives globally that are actively working to put community rights at the centre of repository work. In Australia, from 1994, the Ara Irititja project[7] was developed as a response to the need from Anangu communities in Australia to preserve and provide access to their cultural heritage. The initiative adopts a community-based approach to compile and disseminate materials of cultural and historical significance through the interactive multimedia software known as Keeping Culture KMS. The aim was to build a computer archive constructed specifically to hold these materials and where indigenous protocols are embedded into the platform's architecture to replace legacy schemes. In this case, the project provides a glossary of the terms used by the community and makes a differentiation between different types of material available: "open" for publicly available items, "restricted" for materials accessible only by specific groups (e.g., by

[7] https://irititja.com/archive/the-ara-irititja-approach/.

gender, age, initiation etc), "sensitive" for material considered embarrassing, offensive, or disturbing by the community, and "sorrow" referring to material depicting recently deceased community members.

Other projects in North America, such as the Mukurtu[8] knowledge management system, have been designed in collaboration with indigenous communities to ensure culturally appropriate dissemination by the insertion of indigenous protocols and "labels" into the platform architecture to help communities manage and share their heritage in culturally relevant and ethically minded ways. The Traditional Knowledge (TK) Labels applied have evolved into a different initiative named Local Contexts founded by Jane Anderson and Kim Christen in 2010.[9] Local Contexts generates and encourages the use of TK Labels for sensitive use, sharing and circulation of information. The labels are classified into provenance (e.g., TK Attribution), protocol (e.g., TK Verified) and permission (e.g., Tk Non-commercial) and have been translated into Spanish, French and Māori. The idea is to provide a tool to increase indigenous involvement in data governance through the integration of indigenous values into data systems.

The release of data originating from indigenous communities under open access licenses remains a challenge and should always be framed in relation to questions of ownership, intellectual property rights, and control over the information and its material expressions. Countries approach the issue of data protection in different ways and in most cases the challenge starts from the lack of legal definitions for concepts like "traditional" and "indigenous" knowledge (Bell & Shier 2011). EMKP acknowledges that Open Access is a Western concept that can be challenging for indigenous communities that seek to maintain control over their knowledge or the ways in which it will be accessed in the future. Indigenous groups often experience the tension between protecting indigenous rights and ethics over the data and supporting the principles of FAIR data sharing (Carroll et al. 2020). In this context, various international initiatives have emerged in recent years to approach the issue of Intellectual Property in Cultural Heritage from the outset, and help communities and bodies understand their rights and responsibilities. Some good examples for this are the now finished IPinCH (Intellectual Property Issues in Cultural Heritage) project[10] and the most recent CARE principles initiative developed by

---

8 http://mukurtu.org.

9 https://localcontexts.org/.

10 This was a seven-year project based at Simon Fraser University in British Columbia and funded by Canada's Social Sciences and Humanities Research council. The project co-developed by Prof. George Nicholas, Julie Hollowell (Indiana University) and Kelly Bannister (University of Victoria) to explore the rights, values and responsibilities of material culture, cultural knowledge and heritage research (https://www.sfu.ca/ipinch/about/project-description/, last accessed March 2023).

the Global Indigenous data alliance in 2019 and discussed below as one of the frameworks adopted in the development of the EMKP schema.

Unlike many of the programmes and initiatives outlined above which are region or community specific and developed in response to needs, EMKP supports a world-wide network of partners working across the globe with different communities, knowledge systems and ways of being. Hence, it was essential to develop a uniform standard framework with a strong data protection policy that was also adaptable enough to accommodate different requirements in terms of data access and protection coming from the different communities and groups that the programme showcases. At a very basic level, issues around rights are considered from the outset, and begin with the programme and grantees appropriately recognising and attributing the knowledge holders as owners, and ensuring they are acknowledged within the records and metadata. For this purpose, MCEMS enables the recording of rights ownership, licensing and attribution data. This is all collected in the red-coded fields within the model diagram in Figure 9.8. These fields enable the collection of administrative information about the assets, (i.e., the creator, the rights owner, the licenses for distribution) to protect and safeguard the rights of the knowledge holders themselves. In this sense, it is worth emphasising that the rights ownership over the assets produced by EMKP projects does not reside with the British Museum but is rather designated by the research team and the community and specified via the red-coded fields.

Another crucial area in which rights are concerned is with the publishing of assets to an open access repository. Following Arcadia's open access and digital preservation policy[11] all outputs published in the EMKP repository must be open access, therefore freely available online for copying, re-use and distribution with as few restrictions as possible. In the case of EMKP the decision was made to use the CC-BY-NC-SA 4.0 license to try and reconcile the need for accessibility with the need to duly acknowledge and recognise the knowledge holders. This license ensures that the assets are properly attributed to the community and the team in charge of the documentation project and that they cannot be used for commercial purposes. In addition, all data uploaded must be in accordance with FAIR and CARE principles. The FAIR principles (Findable, Accessible, Interoperable, Reusable)[12] ensure the accessibility and reutilisation of data to increase its interoperability across databases and projects. These principles establish a framework to enable the access of computer systems to academic research data and therefore ensure its reuse and sustainability in the long term. EMKP complies

[11] For more information about the policy see https://www.arcadiafund.org.uk/open-access-digital-preservation-policy.

[12] The FAIR principles (https://www.go-fair.org/fair-principles/) emerge from the Open access movement and were published in 2016 to provide guidelines on data sharing and accessibility. They have grown in recent years among academic outputs in Europe and North America and their emphasis is on increasing the access of computer systems to data.

with FAIR principles by making the data and materials generated by the projects available under an open access license with unique permanent identifiers that can be linked and de-referenced. The assets are enriched by publicly available metadata produced following a public vocabulary and domain ontology and deposited in a public digital repository that is computationally accessible via an Application Programming Interface (API) provided by Figshare.[13] Finally, the assets are also enriched with additional documentation and protocols describing the process of acquisition licensing and provenance which is publicly available on the programme website and repository.

Despite the FAIR principles aim to ensure the shareability and interoperability of the information, they were conceived for scientific research and computer accessibility and therefore in some cases neglect the "human" element of EMKP projects and teams. For this purpose, the programme also complies to the greatest extent possible with the CARE principles for Indigenous Data Governance (Collective Benefit, Authority to Control, Responsibility and Ethics).[14] These principles complement the existing FAIR values and encourage open access data movements to consider both people and purpose, and to engage with indigenous people's rights and interests. CARE principles encourage indigenous groups to re-assert their ownership and control over their knowledge and data and ensure their right to engage in decision making processes responding to collective interests and values. EMKP follows CARE principles by recognising indigenous/traditional authorship of the information, as well as implementing responsive archiving practices that enable their participation in its stewarding. The programme encourages the generation of data in local languages to represent community epistemologies and worldviews and enabling searchability and accessibility in said languages. EMKP also provides digital and documentation training, to ensure ethical research by minimising harm, ensuring respect to indigenous rights and responsible representation. The digital training also builds digital literacy in the research teams, encouraging responsible use of the information as well as local stewarding, fostering reciprocal relationships between the programme, the research teams, and the communities.

As part of the FAIR and CARE protocol, the digital workflow of the programme controls the ingest, auditing, processing, and upload of the assets to the repository. Although it can be seen as supplementary, it is actually the key element that keeps all the gears together (see Figure 9.10). Among its different parts, the data auditing process is perhaps the most fundamental, since it is what allows the team to ensure that all the requirements that make the data FAIR and CARE have been properly followed from the point of creation to

13 https://docs.figshare.com/.

14 The CARE principles (https://www.gida-global.org/care) stem as a reaction to FAIR principles to address power inequalities that FAIR cannot regarding the source communities' access and control over their data and knowledge and emphasising their right to engage in the decision-making process in accordance with indigenous values and interests.

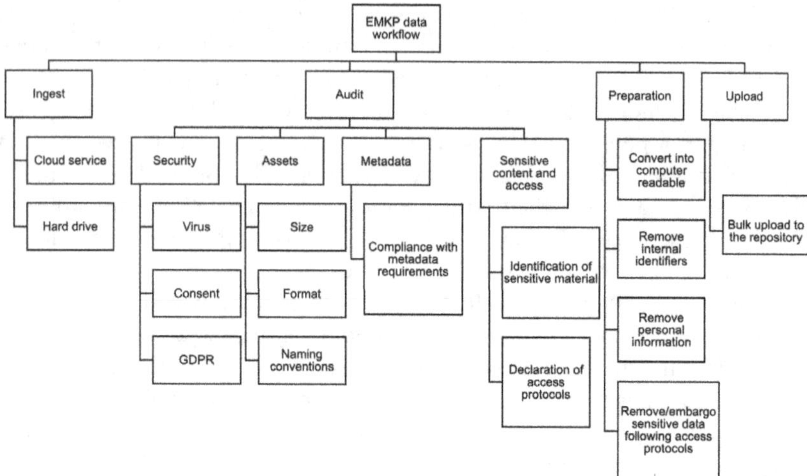

Figure 9.10: EMKP data upload workflow diagram.

the point of publication and that all the data complies with regulations such as GDPR and issues related to access and cultural sensitivity.

The method can be compared to a peer review process in traditional academic contexts in which all assets are properly audited and processed to ensure their compliance with the programme's standards, that they are of sufficient quality, that the research is ethically grounded, and to spot any sensitive materials that have not been previously marked. After the assets have been deposited, the auditing process is carried out by the EMKP team, and it involves four main steps. Firstly, the assets are checked for consent and security issues including the checking of consent release forms (it is required that all participants in the project have provided consent prior to any documentation taking place) and issues of personal information processing (for example participants or groups that have decided to be anonymised or pseudorandomised). This examination is followed by the assets check to make sure that all assets have been recorded in the approved formats, including size, quality, and file naming conventions. Simultaneously the metadata checking takes place to make sure all the assets have been properly recorded and documented in the metadata schema and that no compulsory fields have been left empty. Finally, in the last stage of the process the assets are checked to identify any potential sensitive material that should be considered before publication as well as any materials marked as restricted knowledge to ensure that relevant protocols will be applied at the time of publication.

Even with these safeguards in place, sometimes knowledge remains too sensitive to be published. This sensitivity can be varied and is often guided by cultural norms and requirements that may be at odds with the underlying ethos of open access. As with the examples noted above from Australia and North America, knowledge may be culturally restricted and not suitable for wide consumption. Material practices are often gendered for example, meaning knowledge should be restricted to the participating gender. Other factors might include ritual or spiritual knowledge, as well as secret knowledge associated with specialist material practices that is only shared within tightly defined knowledge transmission situations. While EMKP asks grantees to try and avoid projects that have extensive knowledge restrictions, we acknowledge and recognise that sometimes some material must be embargoed and not made publicly available. The programme can therefore put partial or definite embargoes on the materials, so that they can still be preserved but not necessarily publicly displayed. EMKP also recognise that knowledge rights and restrictions are dynamic; situations change, which might demand new embargoes or changing restrictions on access.

6. Discussion and conclusions

Global initiatives for the valorisation, research, and protection of Intangible Cultural Heritage have increased dramatically since the 2003 UNESCO Convention for the Safeguarding of Intangible Heritage. Especially in recent decades, the focus has shifted from individualising tangible and intangible heritage to emphasising the fluidity of this relationship and the inseparability of both in the deeply intertwined hybrid, complex, and evolving components of living culture. In this sense, material knowledge offers an excellent example of the deep interconnection between the material and immaterial worlds. In this paper we have offered an insight into how EMKP has been developed to try and capture and represent this complex richness via digital media and made accessible in its open access digital repository. However, we have also demonstrated how despite the potential of digital to provide new ways to present and preserve intangible heritage, it comes with as many issues and challenges as traditional analogue archives.

Here we reflect on how EMKP has tried to build a robust system that will be resilient into the future, ensuring the long-term preservation of this fragile heritage, while maintaining a flexibility of use that allows contributors to define and demarcate their narratives according to the specifics of the particular cultural context and ontology. In this, EMKP has tried to foreground the ethics of rights, access, and ways of representing knowledge in the design of our digital workflows, from a custom-built metadata schema to a structure to protect and embargo knowledge in the public domain. EMKP is a new programme, and these conversations will continue as new ethical challenges and needs arise in the digital record.

7. References

Alivizatou, M. (2012). Intangible Heritage and the Museum: New Perspectives on Cultural Preservation (1st ed.). Routledge. DOI: https://doi.org/10.4324/9781315426372.

Andrews, C., Viejo-Rose, D., Baillie, B., & Morris, B. (2006). Conference Report: Tangible-Intangible Cultural Heritage: A Sustainable Dichotomy? the 7th Annual Cambridge Heritage Seminar.

Bell, C., & Shier, C. (2011). Control of information originating from Aboriginal communities: Legal and ethical contexts. Études/Inuit/Studies, 35(1–2), 35–56. DOI: https://doi.org/10.7202/1012834ar.

Bertacchini, E., & Morando, F. (2013). The future of museums in the digital age: New models for access to and use of digital collections. *International Journal of Arts Management* (15.2), 60–72.

Bialogorski, M., & Fischman, F. (2002). Una aproximación crítica a la dicotomía tangible/intangible en el abordaje del patrimonio cultural desde las nuevas perspectivas del folklore. *Cuadernos de la Facultad de Humanidades y Ciencias Sociales. Universidad Nacional de Jujuy*, (18), 233–240.

Brügger, N. (2016). Digital Humanities in the 21st Century: Digital Material as a Driving Force, *Digital Humanities Quarterly, 10*(3).

Carroll, S. R., Garba, I., Figueroa-Rodríguez, O. L., Holbrook, J., Lovett, R., Materechera, S., & Hudson, M. (2020). The CARE principles for indigenous data governance.

Chapagain, N. K. (2016). Blurring boundaries and moving beyond tangible/intangible and the natural/cultural classifications of heritage: cases from Nepal. In Silva, K., & Sinha, A. (Eds.), *Cultural Landscapes of South Asia* (pp. 44–58). London: Routledge. DOI: https://doi.org/10.4324/9781315670041.

Gruber, J. W. (1970). Ethnographic salvage and the shaping of anthropology. *American Anthropologist, 72*(6), pp. 1289–1299.

Hennessy, K., Lyons, N., Loring, S., Arnold, C., Joe, M., Elias, A., & Pokiak, J. (2013). The Inuvialuit living history project: Digital return as the forging of relationships between institutions, people, and data. *Museum Anthropology Review, 7*(1–2), 44–73.

Lunn-Rockliffe, S., & Cheptorus, J. K. (2022): Stripping bark. Media. British Museum. DOI: https://doi.org/10.25420/britishmuseum.19935878.v1.

Lusenet, Y. (2007). Tending the Garden or Harvesting the Fields: Digital Preservation and the UNESCO Charter on the Preservation of the Digital Heritage. *Library Trends, 56*(1), 164–182. DOI: https://doi.org/10.1353/lib.2007.0053.

Petek-Sargeant, N. (2020). Material Culture Ethnography Metadata Schema – Ontology. The British Museum. DOI: https://doi.org/10.25420/britishmuseum.13238090.v1.

Redman, S. J. (2021). Prophets and Ghosts: the story of salvage anthropology. Harvard University Press.

Schorlemer, S. (2020). UNESCO and the Challenge of Preserving the Digital Cultural Heritage. *Santander Art and Culture L. Rev., 2*(6), 33–64. Retrieved from: https://www.ejournals.eu/pliki/art/18632/.

Smith, L., & Akagawa, N. (Eds.). (2009). *Intangible heritage* (p.1). London: Routledge.

UNESCO. (2003). Charter on the Preservation of Digital Heritage.

UNESCO. (2003). Convention for the Safeguarding of the Intangible Cultural Heritage.

Zuanni, C. (2020). Theorizing Born Digital Objects: Museums and Contemporary Materialities. *Museum and Society, 19*(2), 184–198. Retrieved from: https://journals.le.ac.uk/ojs1/index.php/mas/article/view/3790.

CHAPTER 10

Skulls, skin and names: The ethics of managing heritage collections data online

Rebecca Kahn
University of Vienna
Rainer Simon
Rainersimon.io

Abstract

The care, preservation and display of sensitive cultural heritage materials in museum collections is a well-studied and highly regulated aspect of museum practice. Institutional, national and international guidelines exist to help museums treat these objects with discretion, sensitivity and respect, and ongoing discussions around decolonisation have resulted in growing numbers of these objects being repatriated to the communities from which they originated. However, although there is emerging practice at institutional, local and national levels no such broadly accepted guidelines exist for managing the digital surrogates of these objects which reside in databases around the world. This chapter explores the complexity of managing sensitive data in large repositories, and highlights the need for guidance specifically tailored to the emerging digital spaces.

How to cite this book chapter:
Kahn, R. and Simon, R. 2023. Skulls, skin and names: The ethics of managing heritage collections data online. In: Palladino, C. and Bodard, G. (Eds.), *Can't Touch This: Digital Approaches to Materiality in Cultural Heritage*. Pp. 205–224. London: Ubiquity Press. DOI: https://doi.org/10.5334/bcv.k. License: CC BY 4.0

Through a qualitative analysis of open museum data harvested from the European heritage portal Europeana, we show that the proportion of this type of material is small. It could be argued that this makes managing such data even more difficult: what degrees of openness are appropriate? What are the implications for managing a relatively small number of sensitive objects in massive collections retrospectively, once they have been released openly online?

It is important to highlight that this paper is not intended as a critique of Europeana itself. The questions we are asking apply across repositories and portals of museums and other heritage data. Indeed, Europeana provides us with an ideal opportunity to think critically about ethical, legal, and policy issues associated with managing large-scale heritage collections online under increasingly ubiquitous regimes of openness in a way that few other projects do.

Zusammenfassung

Die Pflege, Bewahrung und Ausstellung von sensiblen Objekten in Museumssammlungen ist ein gut untersuchter und stark regulierter Aspekt der Museumspraxis. Institutionelle, nationale und internationale Richtlinien helfen Museen dabei, sensible Objekte mit Diskretion und Respekt zu behandeln. Die laufende Diskussion um Dekolonisation hat zudem dazu geführt, dass immer mehr Objekte an ihre Herkunftsgesellschaften zurückgegeben werden. Für den Umgang mit den digitalen Surrogaten solcher Objekte, die sich in Datenbanken auf der ganzen Welt befinden, fehlen solche Richtlinien jedoch. Dieses Kapitel diskutiert die Herausforderungen, die im Zusammenhang mit der Verwaltung von sensiblen Daten entstehen, und argumentiert für die Notwendigkeit von Leitlinien, die den digitalen Räumen gerecht werden.

Anhand einer qualitativen Analyse offener Daten aus dem europäischen Kulturerbe-Portal Europeana zeigen wir, dass der Anteil dieser Art von Material gering ist. Man könnte aber argumentieren, dass gerade dies die Verwaltung solcher Daten noch schwieriger macht: Welcher Grad an Offenheit ist angemessen? Welche Herausforderungen entstehen bei der Verwaltung einer relativ kleinen Anzahl sensibler Objekte in umfangreichen Sammlungen, insbesondere nachdem sie bereits online veröffentlicht worden sind?

Es ist wichtig zu betonen, dass dieses Kapitel nicht als Kritik an Europeana selbst zu verstehen ist. Im Gegenteil: Die Fragen, die wir stellen, gelten für alle Repositorien und Portale von Museen und Kulturerbe-Organisationen. Vielmehr bietet uns Europeana, wie nur wenige andere Projekte, eine geradezu ideale Gelegenheit, um kritisch über ethische, rechtliche und regulatorische Fragen nachzudenken, die sich aus der zunehmenden Digitalisierung von Kulturgütern, und der wachsenden Forderung nach Offenheit ergeben.

1. Introduction

The care, preservation and display of sensitive cultural heritage materials in museum collections is a well-studied and highly regulated aspect of museum practice. Institutional, national and international guidelines exist to help museums treat these objects and the communities from which they originated with discretion, sensitivity and respect, and the ongoing discussions around decolonisation have resulted in growing numbers of these objects being repatriated to their communities of origin. However, no such broadly accepted guidelines exist for managing the digital surrogates of these objects which reside in databases around the world. And even less guidance is available for how to deal with these digital surrogates when they are mapped into Linked Data repositories, and released 'into the wild' via the Web. This absence is also glaring with respect to copyright and intellectual property issues.[1] In this chapter, we will explore the complexity of managing data in large, converged repositories, as well as highlighting the need for guidance specifically tailored to the emerging digital spaces.

Through a harvest of openly available museum data from the European heritage portal Europeana, and subsequent qualitative analysis of the results, we show that the proportion of this type of material is actually very small. It could be argued that this makes it even more difficult to manage such data retrospectively, once it has been ingested into the system, and made available online. The degree of openness required to leverage the power of linked data is also one of the difficulties that have to be considered when sharing heritage collections within these infrastructures—are these levels of access appropriate for the types of data being shared?[2] And if not, what are the implications for managing a relatively small number of objects in massive collections of data?

Although we have used Europeana as our test case for this exploration, we think it is important to highlight that the questions we are asking apply across the web, to large scale repositories and portals, as well as to linked data databases of museums and other heritage data. This paper is not intended as a critique of Europeana itself, or of the progress it has made in making heritage materials from across Europe available online. But Europeana provides us with an ideal opportunity to think critically about the ethical issues associated with managing large-scale linked data heritage collections online, in a way that few other projects do. As an example of a large, complex linked data project, it offers the chance to look at technical and legal issues, such as underlying data models, minimal standards for interoperability and copyright policies, which

[1] See Okorie (Chapter 11 in this volume).

[2] Filosa, Gad & Bodard (Chapter 3 in this volume) also consider openness and its limits.

have a bearing on how sensitive material is accessed and shared online.[3] At the same time, Europeana also represents the digital embodiment of European cultural policy, a policy which has its own ethics and principles, and which need to be measured and assessed in relation to the materials available via the portal. It also provides an opportunity to assess the challenges presented by technological development which moves faster than the established ways of doing things, and how to consider the implications of the increasingly ubiquitous regimes of openness.

2. Europeana: Background and context

Europeana was launched in 2008, a flagship project of the European Commission with the stated purpose of creating a digital cultural heritage portal for Europe. It was, at the time, seen by many observers as a counter-response to Google Books' mass digitisation of libraries around the world, both in terms of its public nature (in contrast to the anxieties around privatisation of cultural heritage that Google Books represented) and its pan-European focus (again, in contrast to the perception that Google Books represented a risk of American colonisation of European culture). As Thylstrup (2018) and Capurro and Plets (2021) point out, Europeana should be understood as more than a digital service, but also as a space where political, cultural, economic, and technological forces combine to into a standalone cultural product in and of itself, shaped by the processes and politics of mass digitisation and an overt manifesto of an imagined, shared European identity.

In fact, it is the mass nature of the data in Europeana that is key to the argument we present in this chapter. Dahlström, Hansson and Kjellman (2012) distinguish between what they describe as mass digitisation and critical digitisation processes and their results. They argue that critical digitisation processes are essentially qualitative in nature, primarily manual, critically recognise the distortion to data which can take place during digitisation and are designed to maximise interpretation in metadata—resulting in digital collection that can be noted for their depth. They characterise mass digitisation, on the other hand, as primarily automated, designed to treat digitisation as a cloning process, minimise interpretation of metadata and result in digital collections that are notable for their scale (p.436). Neither approach is perfect, and both have their benefits and drawbacks, depending on the initial intentions behind the digitisation in the first place. But what is worth noting, and which Dahlström et al point out, is that each approach risks falling for the fallacy

[3] Okorie (Chapter 11 in this volume) discusses how copyright law can both contribute to and help address problems with digitisation of and access to heritage materials.

of exhaustiveness. At one end of the spectrum, mass digitisation approaches conjure up the image of the all-encompassing portal or encyclopaedic library, while critical digitisation processes create the false illusion of definitiveness, if only it were possible to digitise all the detail of an object, supplemented with the most complete and complex metadata possible (p.464). Of course, neither are possible, and as this chapter will show, pragmatism and interoperability are often the deciding factors when it comes to creating digitised resources that sit between these two poles.

In this chapter, we are not going to examine the processes by which the original digital objects were created in the various institutions which aggregate and/or supply content to Europeana. However, we will examine the process by which digital heritage content is ingested into Europeana, and the affordances (and compromises) that have been made to manage this influx of complex, heterogenous, multilingual data, in the service of creating an accessible, interoperable and useful heritage infrastructure.[4]

It is important to remember that Europeana is not, in and of itself, a repository of cultural heritage materials. Rather, it has always considered its role as that of an aggregator of digital surrogates, which are ultimately owned by the providing institutions themselves (Purday 2009). At the most basic level, the institutions provide Europeana with the descriptive metadata of the object, an image of it (originally thumbnails, although increased use of the IIIF protocol has made it easier to provide high-resolution images) and a link to the object itself (Europeana 2017; see also the Europeana Data Exchange Agreement).[5] This implies that the responsibility for managing the ethical treatment of sensitive objects in their collections should remain with the providing intuitions. As Capurro and Plets (2021) point out, this decision had a pragmatic advantage for Europeana and their partner institutions by enabling the portal to overcome the issue of the diversity of digital resources' file formats, while enabling the providing institution to retain copyright over their materials, and benefit from the increased traffic to their own sites from Europeana (p.173). This is certainly a pragmatic approach to the governance of a huge volume of materials which originate from different national jurisdictions and exist in different forms. However, it is also worth noting that the quality of metadata supplied by the partner institutions varies widely, as does the appropriateness of the copyright applied to some of these objects. As we will show in the findings section, this somewhat hands-off approach means that in some cases, high-resolution images of culturally sensitive materials, which are licensed under Creative Commons licences which actively encourage reuse and sharing, are

4 Okorie (Chapter 11 in this volume) also discusses the issue of control over heritage objects and digitisation.

5 Europeana Data Exchange Agreement: https://pro.europeana.eu/page/the-data-exchange-agreement.

able to enter the linked data stream, with little allowance made for their particularities. Users who wish to download these images are able to do so from the Europeana pages directly, and since the metadata is not always complete, or, as we will show, there may be a discrepancy between the metadata available on the two sites. contextualising information may be lost, if it is even available in the first place. It also means that any warning screens which may be accessible on the providing institutions site, which alert users to the sensitive nature of the materials they might encounter, are bypassed by the direct URL linking the item into Europeana.

Institutions wishing to add their data into Europeana are required to map it to the Europeana Data Model (EDM). The EDM grew out of the Europeana Semantic Model (ESE) which defined a lowest common denominator of descriptive information required to describe an object, across domains, formats and disciplines (Isaac & Clayphan 2013). The EDM, on the other hand, was designed to be more complex, and is not built on any one particular standard. Rather, it makes use of what Europeana refer to as 'an open, cross-domain Semantic Web-based framework that can accommodate the range and richness of particular community standards (Isaac & Clayphan 2013: 5), making it appropriate for ingesting data from a range of different museum, archival or library sources. What this means is that while the model can include any element, class or property which is found in the content provider's description (Europeana 2017), practically, it is preferable that enough metadata to create a link between the surrogate and the original digital resource on the home institution's site be provided, in order to facilitate inclusion. This holds for images, but is not mandatory for text, video, sound or 3D digital objects. All metadata in Europeana are licensed as CC0, meaning it can be reused by anyone, without requiring attribution. This is in keeping with general European Commission policy on sharing cultural heritage data. However, as Capurro and Plets (2021) highlight, this approach has been problematic for many institutions. Their survey showed that many museums consider the creation of metadata as part of their intellectual work, and were reluctant to share all of this work without any institutional attribution. As a result, many provided only a restricted amount of their data in CC0, while retaining the balance in their own institutional repositories, using the reasoning that any Europeana user can simply follow the links back to the providing institution's records. This has resulted in a stripped-down subset being available in the EDM, and consequently, data of inconsistent depth being available on the platform (pp. 178–179). For sensitive heritage materials, such as human remains, where the contextualising data around an object is crucial to understanding how, when and where they were collected and preserved, and under what consequences, the absence of this data can be critical. It leaves the objects unmoored, without the biography that elevates them from being read as curiosities and serves to remind the viewer that they were once human beings, and therefore more than the sum of their parts.

3. The Ethics of Human Remains in Museums

One aspect of museum collections which illustrates these difficulties and complexities is the case of digital surrogates of human remains, both as records and images. Human remains, from mummies to fragments of bone, pieces of hair to complete organs preserved in alcohol are kept in museums around the world. Some are part of the collections of museums of natural history, others are kept in medical museums (often attached to hospitals or universities) or ethnographic museums. Some are preserved in museum stores, away from public view, others are used as the basis for ongoing research into topics as diverse as disease and human nutrition. In some institutions they are displayed in galleries as illustrations of the development of societies or religious practices. Since the 1970s, however, there has been a growing discussion and debate among museum professionals, academics and Indigenous groups from around the world as to the right for museums to hold these collections of human remains, particularly those which may be considered to have sacred significance (Förster & Fründt 2017). The result of these discussions has been the emergence of a regulatory framework for the collection, preservation and display of human remains which is conducted and implemented at the institutional, national and international levels by a range of statues and bodies.

Most museums which have human remains in their collections will have explicit policies, often guided by national policies, as to the storage of human remains. For example, in the United Kingdom, the Human Tissue Act of 2004 and the Department for Media, Culture and Sport's *Guidance for the Care of Human Remains in Museums* set the legal framework and the best practice baselines for how institutions should handle, conserve and display human remains, including defining which institutions are allowed to deaccession human remains under special licences, the conditions under which museums may acquire new materials containing human remains, (particularly those which are less than 100 years old) the legal and technical requirements for the storage of these collections, and the best practice for labelling and display of these materials (DCMS 2005). Individual institutions are also able to make their own decisions about these types of materials – for example, the University of Oxford's Pitt Rivers Museum, which holds a substantial number of human remains, as one would expect of a museum that grew out of an Anthropology department, recently decided to remove 120 objects from their public galleries, including South American *tsantsas* (commonly known as 'shrunken heads'), South Asian Naga Trophy heads and the Egyptian mummy of a child (Kendall Adams 2020). In Germany, similar guidance is laid out by the Deutsche Museums Bund (German Museums Association) who include detailed guidance on how to manage materials whose provenance is unclear, and give specific details on the process for managing materials that originated during the period of National Socialism (Deutsche Museums Bund 2021). In the United States, the

Native American Graves Protection and Repatriation Act (NAGPRA) provides the legal and ethical framework for the retention, management and, crucially, restitution of any human remains, funerary objects, sacred objects, and objects of cultural patrimony held by federal institutions in the US, including museums, university collections and local governments.[6]

Internationally, the International Council of Museums (ICOM) sets the standard for the acquisition, research, exhibition, and removal from exhibition of human remains in their *Code of Ethics* (ICOM, 2017). This text has been critiqued for being overly cautious (Lenk, 2021) but could also be read as being drafted in such a way that acknowledges the case-by-case specificities of these types of collections, and encourages innovation and active engagement at the level of local institutions, as illustrated by the example of the Pitt Rivers Museum.

What we see then, is a comprehensive set of guidance, legal requirements and best practice designed to help museum staff and the public navigate the (sometimes fraught, often emotional) topic of human remains in their collections. What is glaring in its absence, however, is a similar set of guidelines, regulations and best practices for managing the digital surrogates of these objects, once they have been created. This is described in detail by Pavis and Wallace (2019) in their discussion on the need for legal frameworks to facilitate the return of cultural heritage materials. As digital objects, they consist of a set of different components—images, textual data, metadata, and their corresponding underlying data models. As such, they are stored differently, shared differently, and accessed differently from their analogue progenitors. As more institutions digitised their collections and their records, many more of these objects are becoming accessible, via individual institutional websites, integrated research infrastructures and cross-institutional search tools. Data from these institutions is being remodelled and opened up to linked data and semantic web search functionality, making access increasingly ubiquitous. But how should museum staff, researchers, and digital humanities scholars who use these materials approach the ethical and intellectual property law questions attached to them? Do the same rules apply to the digital surrogate as to their analogue originals? Or do we need to reconsider these guidelines, in the context of these new information storage and sharing realities? In reality, there is not much to go on. The *ICOM Code of Conduct* mentions the term 'data' four times in the text, in the context of data security, data privacy, and the academic and scientific responsibilities that ICOM members have to promote investigation, preservation and use of information in their collections, and the need to keep such scientific data safe. Nowhere does it mention how to manage sensitive collections data.

[6] Facilitating Respectful Return, https://www.nps.gov/subjects/nagpra/index.htm.

4. Human Remains in Digitised Museums

Perhaps the most telling illustration of this lack of guidance is in the myriad different ways museums around the world approach the display of and access to human remains in their digitised databases and online exhibitions. In some museums, cultural sensitivity warnings are displayed when trying to access a catalogue or exhibition online. These warnings highlight the fact that historical terminology used in databases might be outdated or offensive, or that the databases might contain information on and photographs of, objects associated with certain rituals, which might bring with it certain cultural restrictions on who should have access to them, on the grounds of gender, age, or status of the viewer.[7]

In our exploration of human remains in museum collections around Europe, we encountered a range of different messaging on this subject, no direct limits to access (apart from expired or dead URLs) and some inconsistencies in what was available. As illustrative examples, these are the messages we encountered from three of the museums whose collections we investigated:

The Wellcome Collection in London (which will be discussed in detail later on) collects artefacts related to medicine and health. The Wellcome publishes over 92,000 items from their collection to Europeana, and we identified 201 of these as being human remains. The Wellcome includes a 'statement of intent regarding culturally sensitive items' on their Collections pages[8] and a Care of Human Remains policy, which includes a commitment to considering how to 'prepare visitors to view remains in exhibitions put on by Wellcome Collection, and to warn those who may not wish to see them.'[9] However no mention is made specifically of digital objects, or of these items are handled in the online database. When accessing human remains in the Wellcome directly, either via their collections database search tool, or through the source link in Europeana, these statements are bypassed entirely.

Similarly, in the database of the Horniman Museum and Gardens in London, which houses a collections of anthropological materials, natural history specimens and musical instruments, and who provide around 22,000 objects to Europeana, we identified 15 objects as being human in origin, ranging from decorated ceremonial skulls from Indonesia to mummified human remains from Peru. These can be searched for in the database by descrip-

---

7 Pitt Rivers Museum Terms of Use for Pitt Rivers Museum Database of Object Collections: https://prm.web.ox.ac.uk/terms-use-pitt-rivers-museum-database-object-collections.

8 Wellcome Collection statement of Intent: https://wellcomecollection.org/pages/YJkM-REAACMABEhW.

9 See Wellcome Collection https://wellcomecollection.org/pages/WyjY_SgAACoALCmH.

tion or object number with no access restrictions, and can be shared using permanent URIs.

The Swedish Museum of Ethnography in Stockholm provides about 264,000 objects to Europeana, and our harvest only located four of these as being human remains. When linking back to the original record for one of these objects—two human femurs, bound together and inscribed with text and collected in British Columbia, Canada in the late 1890s (inventory number 1904.19.0086), there is no restriction to accessing multiple images of the object, and all the metadata associated with it. However, as we will show later, some images of human remains in the collection have been removed and no images can be accessed.

A critical digitisation or ingestion process would allow for items such as these to be considered on a case by case basis, but in the massive data dumps of hundreds of thousands of items, which characterise the ingestion process for Europeana, these items, often relatively small in overall number, slip through the cracks. This is, to a certain extent, a practical problem: how to manage a small number of highly specific objects, when working at scale, is not a question that can easily be answered. It is also a conceptual problem. As scholars working with historical sources have pointed out (Bailey et al 2021) the Linked Data triple model has limited capacity for presenting the additional types of data needed to conduct humanistic deductions, such as assertions and attestations. In this context, we would argue, the same can be said for museum data models, which require additional contextual and historical data to present objects and their backstories in complete, and sometimes ethically sound ways. This poses a significant challenge for systems that are designed to be interoperable at both the technical (or Linked Data) and legal (specifically, copyright) levels.

At this point it is sensible to take a look at how we conducted our data harvest, and how we decided what to include, and what to exclude.

5. The Data Harvest

To inform our investigation, we used the publicly available Europeana Search API to retrieve records of potentially sensitive material.[10] Based on manual searches we had experimented with initially, we compiled a list of queries (including searches such as "human remains" or "human bone") that we knew would return a significant number of sensitive collection records. We also used the Europeana query translation service to translate the queries in our list into the languages that Europeana provided as options in the search interface.[11]

[10] Europeana Search API, https://pro.europeana.eu/page/search.

[11] Europeana Search API, query translation, https://pro.europeana.eu/page/search#translation.

Because the query translation service is, to the best of our knowledge, based on matching queries against Wikipedia page titles, it is rather conservative in its results. Many queries do not yield translations at all, resulting in a situation where a lower number of higher-quality translations is favoured over a larger number of (potentially ambiguous) ones.

The combined multilingual query we used in the harvest consisted of 15 query terms, either in English, or in one of 11 other languages for which the Europeana query translation service had returned results. The harvest itself was automated through a script, implemented as a Google Colab notebook, which i) sequentially collected EDM search result pages; ii) aggregated them to a single result set; and iii) crosswalked some of the essential EDM fields we were interested in into a more readable spreadsheet format. These fields included: each object's unique ID, in order to be sure we were not harvesting any duplicates; the title, description and type of the object, which would allow us to capture all the free text and descriptive metadata of the object. Including the edm:Concept allowed us to see the controlled vocabularies and conceptual classifications used for each object—this was particularly useful when it came to eliminating anatomical paintings, drawings and etchings from the final result, as they shared the same type ('image') as the photographs of actual remains. The last two fields included were 'Europeana_link' which provided us with the definitive URLs for each object, and 'edm:IsShownAt' which provided the link to the original record on the providing institution's site (although not 100% of these links were live at the time of the harvest, and some returned error messages). We then used OpenRefine to dig deeper into the textual data, and sort and cluster records which shared similar characteristics, such as source, type, descriptions of certain body parts, or IconClasses.

6. Results and Findings

In total, the harvest returned 1494 records, which works out to roughly 0.002% of the over 51 million objects in Europeana. Of course it is necessary to make allowance for the fact that there may well be objects which have been described using terms that we did not include, or languages that our translations did not cover. However, for the qualitative purposes of this chapter, many of the objects we did find represent some of the more contentious and problematic examples of human remains kept in heritage collections, and are illustrative of the general difficulties of managing materials such as this at the scale of a repository such as Europeana. In fact, the relative smallness of our dataset enabled us to work manually and check almost all of the links by hand, one after another, in the browser—a reality which, on reflection, shows that such a small amount of material would require a dedicated manual effort from a team of individuals to continually check, update and deal with such material—a reality that is unlikely in many heritage organisations, let along an infrastructure as large as Europeana. In that sense at least, this project can be seen as a microcosm of how to approach the ease of access to such materials.

In the following section, we describe three objects (or sets of objects) which we identified out of the 1494 records. Each has a different set of particularities which make them useful for exploring the ethical and technical challenges we have outlined above. The first should not be visible or accessible, but is. The second were collected under ethically dubious circumstances, and the third are the products of colonial looting, which is only glancingly alluded to in their documentation.

6.1 Toi Moko or Mokomokai

Perhaps the most striking example of the kinds of materials which we found in our exploration of Europeana is an item from the collection of the Musées royaux d'Art et d'Histoire (Royal Museums of Art and History) in Brussels. Described in the metadata as a 'Chopped off head with tattoos ("mokamokai") *[sic]*', (Accession number ET.38.15.1). This is in fact an example of a *toi moko* (also known as mokomokai)—the preserved head of a Māori man whose skin had been intricately tattooed and carved, so that deep grooves and geometric patterns can be seen on his cheeks, forehead and across his nose. This practice, known as *Ta moko*, was not just a process of body decoration—it was deeply embedded in the social, political and religious life of the Māori people. Moko contained information about a person's status, lineage, social rank and past exploits, as well as their divine status (Palmer and Tano, 2004). Traditionally toi moko were created as part of Māori funeral rituals, kept by the families of the deceased, and treated as objects to be revered. They were also made from the heads of enemies, taken as trophies and used as symbols of military strength. In both cases, access to them and their display was tightly controlled and strict protocols had to be adhered to (Procter, 2020); the practices were *tapu*—something sacred, and restricted, to be removed from the sphere of the profane and put into the sphere of the sacred. Tapu was used as a way to control how people behaved towards each other and the environment, placing restrictions upon society to ensure that society flourished.[12] However, after Captain James Cook's voyages to the Pacific in the 1700s, European interest in toi moko quickly grew, as did the demand for these objects. Sales of toi moko to European collectors took place openly until the 1830s, and their social and economic value shifted from being intimate and personal,

[12] Te Ara Encyclopedia of New Zealand: https://teara.govt.nz/en.

to commercial and market-driven, particularly when it became possible to trade them for high value objects such as weapons. A secondary source of toi moko emerged, as local people, reluctant to part with their sacred objects, took to tattooing the faces of prisoners or captives with less significant symbols, and then selling their preserved heads to collectors (Gilbert, 2000; Palmer and Tano). Although this practice was legally repressed, toi moko continued to be traded until the 1980s. Records at the Te Papa Tongarewa Museum of New Zealand show one being displayed for auction in 1988 for between £6,000 and £10,000.

It is impossible to know how many toi moko were transported to European museums, let alone how many were in private collections and may have been damaged or destroyed over the years. What we can do is look at the repatriation claims for toi moki that have been made over the years as a guide to the number of those which have, at least, been returned to Aotearoa New Zealand. Te Papa Tongarewa has been mandated by the New Zealand government to lead these claims, and since 2003 has received over 400 of these objects from museums in Europe, the US and Australia.[13] It is impossible to know the origins of the toi moko we found, when or under what circumstances it was created, and how it came to be in the collection. None of this information is provided in the accompanying metadata.

After finding this object in the initial data harvest, we conducted a manual follow-up search in Europeana, to see if any other toi moko could be found in the collection. The search yielded four other results. All of these were described as 'mokomokai', and made no mention, in the description, of any of the search terms we had defined, which explains why they were not part of the initial results. Of these four, only one contains an image—this is an additional toi moko which is also part of the collection of the Royal Museums of Art and History in Brussels. Of the three other results, two records point to the same object in the Ethnographic collection in the Staatlichen Museen zu Berlin (Berlin State Museums). However, neither of these records have a corresponding image—rather they show a generic outline of a vase, in grey, with the words '*Aus ethischen Gründen nicht gezeigt/ Not shown for ethical reasons*'. The final record links to an object from the Ethnographic Museum of Sweden. The accompanying image in both Europeana and on the museum's own site is a grey block, with the words '*Ritual Object: picture has been blocked*'. The description of the object makes it clear that it has been repatriated, although the full record is still accessible in the museum's catalogue.

[13] The repatriation of Māori and Moriori remains: https://www.tepapa.govt.nz/about/repatriation/repatriation-maori-and-moriori-remains.

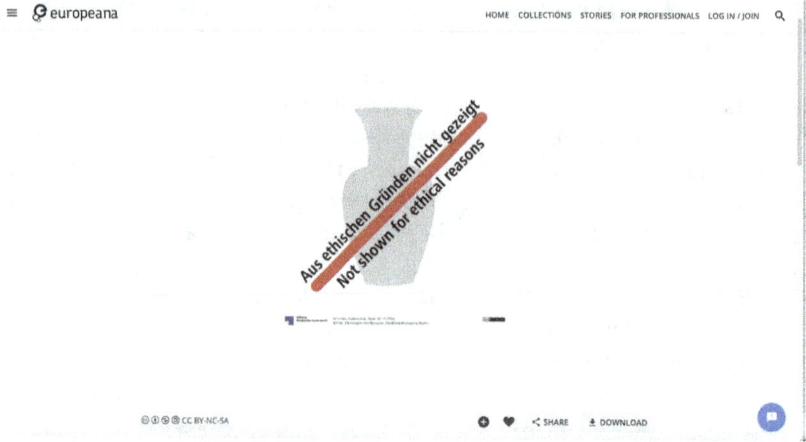

Figure 10.1: Screenshot (dated April 2023) of search result for 'mokomokai' in Europeana, showing the record of an object in the collection of the Ethnographic collection in the Staatlichen Museen zu Berlin (Berlin State Museums), and the generic message detailing the removal of the image for ethical reasons.

6.2 Tattooed skin fragments

Another substantial set of objects to emerge from our survey of the harvested data were 18 records of pieces of human skin, tattooed with various words and motifs, including French flags, flowers, human figures, and butterflies. While the descriptive texts accompanying each item describe different details, they all share the following information:

> "...purchased by one of Henry Wellcome's collecting agents. The agent was Captain Johnston-Saint, who bought it in June 1929 from Dr Villette, a Parisian surgeon. Villette worked in military hospitals and collected and preserved hundreds of samples from the autopsies of French soldiers. In the late 1800s, tattoos were often seen as markers of criminal tendencies, or 'primitiveness'. Medical men tried to interpret common images and symbols."

All of these objects are part of the Wellcome Collection in London, a museum and archive of medical artefacts, original artworks and other objects which explore the relationships and connections between medicine, health, art and society. The collection grew out of an initial bequest from Sir Henry Solomon Wellcome, an American British pharmaceutical entrepreneur, whose estate also formed the basis of the Wellcome Trust, one of the largest non-governmental funders of medical and socio-medical research in the world. As one would imagine, the Wellcome Collection contains a fairly large number of human remains, most of which have been held for them by the Science Museum in

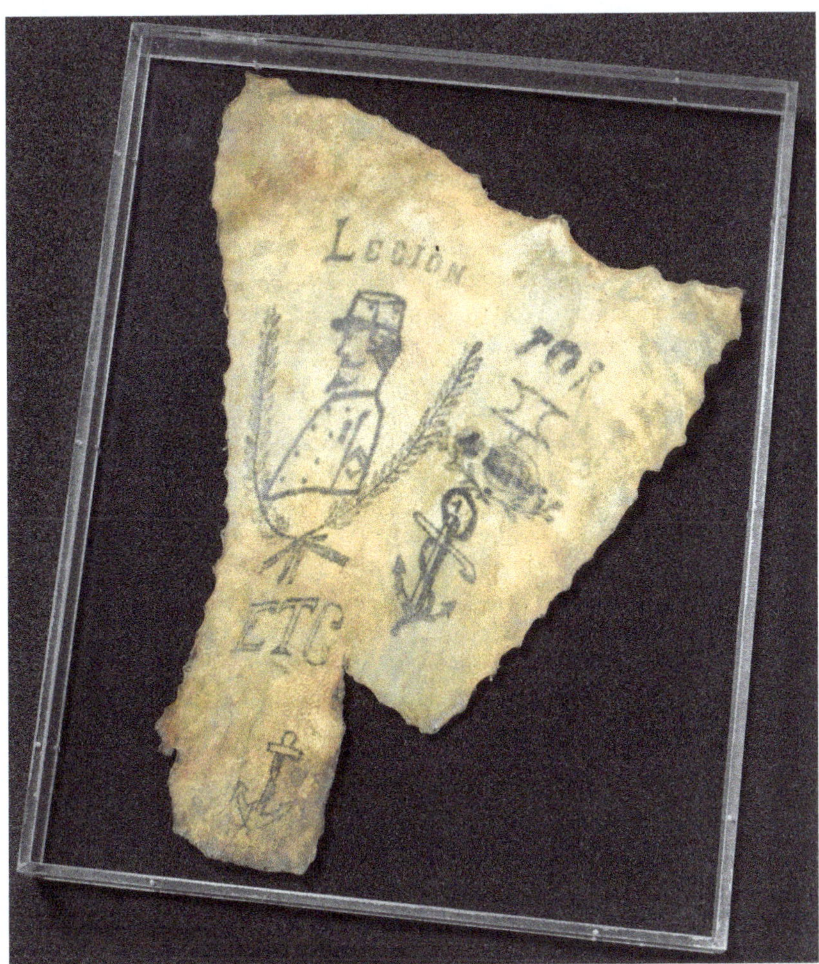

Figure 10.2: Image of human skin tattooed with a soldier, badge and anchor, France. Science Museum, London. Attribution 4.0 International (CC BY 4.0), accessed via the Wellcome Collection online catalogue, April 2023.

London since the 1970s. Helpfully, the Wellcome also provides a list of these objects,[14] which totals some 670 items. In this list, every item is recorded with an accession number, a provenance, a date made and a short description. Not all of these items are available in Europeana, which we took as evidence that only selected records were published to the portal.

---

[14] List of human remains in Sir Henry Wellcome's Museum Collection https://wellcomecollection.cdn.prismic.io/wellcomecollection%2F0e081286-9ca7-4be8-a8ad-420df58a0679_list+of+human+remains+in+sir+henry+wellcomes+museum+collection.pdf.

By cross-referencing this list with the 18 results from our Europeana harvest, we discovered that the 18 records automatically found in Europeana were, in fact, a subset of 298 examples of tattooed human skin in the Wellcome's collection, all of which seemed to share a similar provenance. Without access to the full catalogues (inaccessible via either the Wellcome Collections online, or Europeana) it is impossible to say with absolute certainty that these objects come from the same collection. However, their accession numbers run sequentially from A524 to A822, which implies that they were originally catalogued in one batch. They are all recorded as coming from France, and are dated between the late 1800s and early 1900s, information which offers strong evidence that many more items were bought from Dr Villette than are available via the Wellcome's Europeana aggregation. What we can be certain of, however, is that the images of all 18 of the pieces of human skin in the Europeana instance are from this collection, and that, if the metadata supplied is reliable, they were removed from the bodies of the soldiers after their death. Whether permission was asked or granted for this collection is not specified. In this case, the desire to collect items which fed a collector's fascination with the criminality and primitivism mentioned in the description seems to have been the driving force behind their acquisition, and the biographies of the men from whom they were collected is all but irrelevant. All 18 items are available to download, and licensed with open licences, in this case Creative Commons CC BY 4.0 licence.

6.3 Asante Skulls

The final set of objects we will look at are perhaps the most biography-less, although their stories reveal the part they played in British imperial history. Our harvest found eight records for human skulls, again from the Wellcome Collection, which were described in the title field as 'Human skull inscribed with prayers for the deceased. Collected by Robert Baden Powell's Asante (Ghana) expedition 1895'. When we checked these objects manually, using the links in the Europeana_link and edm:IsShownAt metadata fields, all eight bore the same museum accession number (A666427), although it quickly became evident that one of these objects is a complete skull, and the other is only a fragment of a cranium. After cross-referencing the museum number with the list of objects from the Wellcome stored at the Science Museum (mentioned in the previous section) we found that there were in fact two objects with different museum accession numbers: A666426 was the cranium fragment, and A666427 was the complete skull. However, somehow in the Wellcome and therefore also in Europeana, these items have become conflated.

Both objects are covered in text, which has been written or painted onto the bone in a language which appears to be Arabic—although the available metadata does not give any details of this, or provide a transcript. Whether this detail exists in the catalogue is impossible to ascertain, without access to the full record, which is not online. All we have to work with is a title, image (downloadable as a high resolution JPEG), and some technical metadata describing licensing (CC BY 4.0). But what we can deduce from their titles and combined with a bit of historical sleuthing, is that these two objects are part of a familiar narrative of British imperial violence.

The Anglo-Ashanti wars were a series of conflicts that took place in what is now modern Ghana, between 1824 and 1900 between the British Empire and the Ashanti Empire. The Ashanti were a powerful kingdom who came into conflict with the British over access and control of the coastal areas of the region. The 1895 expedition mentioned in the description was led by Lieutenant Colonel Robert Baden-Powell—who later went on to found the worldwide Boy Scout movement. In her study of the West African collections in the Manchester Museum, Emma Poulter describes how the British forces marched into the Ashanti capital of Kumasi. The Ashanti king, Prempeh, aware that his forces were outnumbered, put up little resistance, and accepted British protection, but could not pay the fine of 50,000 ounces of gold demanded by the British (Poulter 2003: 11). The British responded by arresting Prempeh and deporting him to Sierra Leone and then to the Seychelles, where he was exiled for 28 years. They also ransacked the the palace and Prempeh's other residences, which Baden Powell recorded in his diary:

> There could be no more interesting work, no more tempting work than this. To poke about in a barbarian king's palace, whose wealth has been reported very great, was enough to make it so [...] Here there was a man with an armful of gold-hilt swords, there one with a box full of gold trinkets and rings, another with a spirit case full of bottles of brandy [...] There were piles of the tawdriest and commonest stuff mixed indiscriminately with quaint, old, and valuable articles...

While it is not possible to know with absolute certainty whether the skull and fragments were taken in this particular moment, or at another point in the campaign, or how they came to the Wellcome, it is significant to place them in the context of the narrative that the British often used to describe these expeditions. They were framed as 'civilising' actions, waged in the name of the salvation of the 'pagan' and the fight against the perceived barbarity of African peoples (Poulter 2013: 12). These objects illustrate these attitudes perfectly—with no evidence of their use, origin or sacred purpose provided, or transcriptions or translations of the inscriptions they bear, we see them as the collectors did—curiosities which can be used to justify military actions on moral grounds.

7. Conclusions

It could be argued that by exposing these sensitive materials, Europeana is doing the decolonisation of museum collections a significant service, by helping to locate and expose much of this material which might, due to its relatively low volume, otherwise remain hidden in databases. However, there is another side to this argument: if Europeana's search functionality (ie: their APIs) are to be used as a source of structured data for researchers, including those looking for training data for, say, automated algorithmic tools, there is a question of ethical responsibility. If the EDM is considered too generic, and the copyright requirements too open, to ensure that museums are willing or able to share their data fully, and with deeper context, the question has to be asked whether it is appropriate for sensitive heritage materials with deep backstories to be available via the platform at all. This question also resonates when we consider the linked nature of the data accessible via Europeana. Sharing materials seamlessly over the Web has been the premise and the promise of the open semantic web, and is increasingly becoming a reality. But just because something can be shared, does not automatically mean that it should be, and in the absence of guiding principles and best practice rules for digitised human remains, and the increasing volume of materials coming online every year, the question of how to manage these collections and objects becomes ever more urgent.

8. References

Baillie, J., Andrews, T., Romanov, M., Knox, D., & Vargha, M. (2021). Modelling Historical Information with Structured Assertion Records. Paper presented at Data for History Conference 2021.

Capurro, C., & Plets, G. (2021). Europeana, EDM, and the Europeanisation of Cultural Heritage Institutions. *Digital Culture & Society, 6*(2), 163–90. DOI: https://doi.org/10.14361/dcs-2020-0209.

Dahlström, M., Hansson, J., & Kjellman, U. (2012). As We May Digitize: Institutions and Documents Reconfigured. *Liber Quarterly: The Journal of European Research Libraries, 21*(3/4), 455–74. DOI: https://doi.org/10.18352/lq.8036.

Department for Digital, Culture, Media and Sport, Government of United Kingdom. (2005). *Guidance for the Care of Human Remains. Retrieved from:* https://assets.publishing.service.gov.uk/government/uploads/system/uploads/attachment_data/file/906601/GuidanceHumanRemains11Oct.pdf. Accessed May 2020.

Europeana. (2017). Definition of the Europeana Data Model v5.2.8. Retrieved from: https://pro.europeana.eu/files/Europeana_Professional/Share_your

_data/Technical_requirements/EDM_Documentation/EDM_Definition_v5.2.8_102017.pdf. Accessed March 2022.

Förster, L., & Fründ, S. (2017). *Human Remains in Museums and Collections:* A Critical Engagement with the "Recommendations for the Care of Humans Remains in Museums and Collections" of the German Museums Association. Clio-online und Humboldt-Universität zu Berlin. DOI: https://doi.org/10.18452/19383.

German Museums Association. (2021). Guidelines Care of Human Remains in Museums and Collections. Retrieved from: https://www.museumsbund.de/wp-content/uploads/2021/07/dmb-leitfaden-umgang-menschl-ueberr-en-web-20210625.pdf. Accessed March 2022.

Gilbert, S. (2000). *Tattoo History: A Source Book : An Anthology of Historical Records of Tattooing throughout the World.* New York: Juno Books.

International Council of Museums. (2017). ICOM Code of Ethics for Museums. Retrieved from: https://icom.museum/wp-content/uploads/2018/07/ICOM-code-En-web.pdf. Accessed March 2022.

Isaac, A., & Clayphan, R. (2013). Europeana Data Model Primer. Retrieved from: https://pro.europeana.eu/files/Europeana_Professional/Shar_your_data/Technical_requirements/EDM_Documentation/EDM_Primer_130714.pdf. Accessed March 2022.

Kendall Adams, G. (2020). Pitt Rivers Museum removes shrunken heads from display after ethical review. *Museums Association Journal* 18 September 2020. Retrieved from: https://www.museumsassociation.org/museums-journal/news/2020/09/pitt-rivers-museum-removes-shrunken-heads-from-display-after-ethical-review. Accessed March 2022.

Lenk, C. (2021). Ethical Principles for Collections Containing Human Remains. In *Guidelines Care of Human Remains in Museums and Collections* (pp. 110–120). German Museums Association.

Palmer, C., & Tano, M. (2004). Mokomokai: Commercialization and Desacralization. International Institute for Indigenous Resource Management, Denver, Colorado. Retrieved from: http://nzetc.victoria.ac.nz/tm/scholarly/tei-PalMoko.html. Accessed March 2022.

Pavis, M., & Wallace, A. (2019). Response to the 2018 Sarr-Savoy Report: Statement on Intellectual Property Rights and Open Access Relevant to the Digitization and Restitution of African Cultural Heritage and Associated Materials. *Journal of Intellectual Property, Information Technology and E-Commerce Law 10*(2), 115–129. DOI: http://dx.doi.org/10.2139/ssrn.3378200.

Poulter, E. K. (2013). Silent Witness: Tracing Narratives of Empire through Objects and Archives in the West African Collections at the Manchester Museum'. *Museum History Journal* 6(1), 6–22. DOI: https://doi.org/10.1179/1936981612Z.0000000001.

Procter, A. (2020). The Whole Picture: The Colonial Story of the Art in Our Museums & Why We Need to Talk about It. London: Cassell.

Purday, J. (2009). Think Culture: Europeana.Eu from Concept to Construction. *The Electronic Library 27*(6), 919–37. DOI: https://doi.org/10.1108/02640470911004039.

Thylstrup, N. B. (2018). The Politics of Mass Digitization. Cambridge, MA: The MIT Press.

CHAPTER 11

Digital treatment of African cultural heritage: Shifting landmarks and implications for copyright exceptions for archives in Nigeria

Chijioke Okorie
University of Pretoria

Abstract

Developments in information and communication technologies have shifted the management of archival materials from paper to digital. This digital environment has created expectations and possibilities in access to and preservation of archival materials and records. Several legal initiatives have been proposed to address the emerging roles of archival materials and archival institutions. From a copyright law perspective, statutory copyright exceptions tend to be the go-to approach for addressing the copyright issues facing archival and other memory institutions.

In this environment, there are conversations around the roles of archival and other memory institutions and how the copyright law construct could design limitations and exceptions enabling those institutions to carry out their roles.

How to cite this book chapter:
Okorie, C. 2023. Digital treatment of African cultural heritage: Shifting landmarks and implications for copyright exceptions for archives in Nigeria. In: Palladino, C. and Bodard, G. (Eds.), *Can't Touch This: Digital Approaches to Materiality in Cultural Heritage*. Pp. 225–244. London: Ubiquity Press. DOI: https://doi.org/10.5334/bcv.l.

Within these conversations, there remains a general adherence to the classic landmark (i.e., guiding light) of these institutions' role being to preserve, safeguard and provide access to materials as needed. This chapter argues that from the standpoint of implementing any agenda of mass digitization before or alongside the repatriation of cultural heritage materials, this landmark of preservation and access should be challenged. This chapter proposes a complementary landmark to guide policymakers in navigating the copyright limitations and exceptions landscape for archival and other memory institutions. Agency, along with restitution and the general practice of decolonization, becomes a more appropriate landmark in this chapter's description of how at institutional level, national archival institutions and other memory institutions might want to proceed in undertaking their planning for repatriating, receiving and managing repatriated items. Furthermore, incorporating agency as a complementary landmark would ready these institutions for the forthcoming transition to specific copyright limitations and exceptions.

Nchịkọta

N'oge gara aga, n'akwụkwọ na n'ihe ndi a na-ahụ anya ka e ji a chịkọta ma na-echekwa omenala, ndụ ndị mmadụ, àgwà ndị mmadụ, na ndụ na omume nke obodo dị iche iche (Ha niile "ihe omenala"). N'oge ahụ, iwu kọpiraiti nke na-enye ndị mmadụ ihe onwunwe na ihe ha ji ụbụrụ ha na akọ na uche ha cheputa nwere ihe ndị a gbahapụrụ ka ndị ụlọ nchekwa dị iche iche nwee ike were cheekwa ihe omenala a. Ihe ndị a bu ihe a na-ele anya nwere ike ị nyere aka chekwaa ma kpokọta ihe omenala a.

Mana n'ọgbọ ọhụrụ a, a na-eji teknọlọji dijitalụ na-ekpokọta ma na-echekwa ihe omenala. Digital na-alụ ọlụ n'ikuku. N'ihi ya, ọ naghị agwụ dika akwụkwọ na ihe ndị a na-ahụ anya si agwụ. Ihe a ga-ejinwu dijitalụ mee karịrị akarị. Ima atu, a ga-ejinwu dijitalụ see imirikiti ihe omenala foto gbaa ha na mkpọ n'ikuku!

Mana dijitalụ nwere ihe so ya. Ya mere, ị na-eji otu iwu kọpiraiti ahụ nke ejiri n'oge gara aga ga-eweta nsogbu! Nsogbu nke a ka njọ na mpaghara Afrika ebe enwere omenala na asụsụ dị iche iche. Afrịka bụkwa obodo ebe ndị ọcha si na Yurop (Europe) na mba ndị ọzọ bịa mee mpụ dị iche iche ma ndị Afrika ha zuuru ihe omenaala ha ma ndị ha ji aghụghọ nara ya n'amaghị ama buru ha gaa mba Yurop (Europe). Afrịka bụkwa ebe ndị ọcha bịara kwakọọ isi na isi na obodo dị iche iche nọọrọ onwe ha mee ha ka ha bụrụ otu ka ndị ọcha nwee ike ịchị. N'ima atụ, Nigeria bụ obodo nwere mba, asụsụ na obodo narị abụọ na iri ise dị iche iche nke ndị ọcha si ebe ha si kpokoo ha ọnụ na otu obodo.

Ugbu a, ndị ọcha dị iche iche na-agba mbọ n'ụdị iche iche inyeghachi ndị Afrika ihe omenala ha ha nwerebu. Mana, ndị ọcha chọrọ na tupu ha enye ndị Afrika ihe omenala ha, ha ga-ebụ ụzọ tinye ihe omenala na dijitalụ!

Otu dijitalụ si dị, ndị isi na-ekwu ihe omenala a ga-etinye na dijitalụ nwere ike ịtịnye ma ihe ha kwesịrị ịtịnye ma ihe ha na-ekwesịghị ịtịnye. Ihe kpatara nke a bụ na ọ bụghị omenala ha nke o ji abụ ihe gbasara ndụ ha ma ọ bụ ndụ ndị obodo ha.

Alo m na-atụ ebe a bụ na ọ dịghị mma igụpu ndị ọ bụ ihe omenala ha na ndị ọ bụ ndụ ha mgbe a na-ekpebi ma a ga-etinye ihe omenala na dijitalụ ma ọ bụ na a gaghị etinye. Alo ọzọ m na-atụ bụ ka aghara ị bịakwa na ụwa dijitalụ gụpụ ndị mba nọgasi n'ime obodo Afrika dị iche iche ọzọ. Kama, o dị mkpa ka a kpọnye obodo na mba di iche iche dị n'Afrika na nkata na kpebi a na-enwe banyere itinye ihe omenala ha na dijitalụ. Ọ bụghị nani ịkpọ obodo Afrika dịka Naijiria (Nigeria) ma ọ bụ Senigalu (Senegal) ka ọ biri. A ga-akpọ ndi omenaala ha bu ihe a na-ekwu maka ya n'ime Naijiria (Nigeria). Ihe a kacha mkpa ebe a na-ekwu okwu imeghari iwu kọpiraiti nyekwuo ndị na-edobe akwụkwọ na ndị ụlọ nchekwa di iche iche ohere i tinye ihe omenala ha ji na dijitalụ. Mpụ ọzọ eme la.

1. Introduction

The landscape within which archival institutions operate has changed in recent years.[1] Developments in information and communication technologies and the emergence of the Internet have shifted record keeping and management of archival materials from paper (material media) to digital. This digital environment has created expectations and possibilities in access to and preservation of information, including archival materials and records.[2] In this regard, several legal initiatives at the international and national levels have been put forward to address the new or emerging role, which archival materials and archival institutions occupy (Sutton 2019). In particular, and from the perspective of copyright law, statutory copyright exceptions and limitations tend to be the go-to approach for addressing the copyright issues facing archives and similar collecting and preservation institutions such as libraries, museums and galleries (Dryden 2017).

In 2019, over 100 scholars and practitioners working in the fields of intellectual property law and material and digital cultural heritage at universities, heritage institutions and organisations around the world supported and signed the 'Statement on intellectual property rights and open access relevant to the digitization and restitution of African cultural heritage and associated materials,' written by Pavis and Wallace (2019). The Statement was among a

1 An early draft of this chapter was presented in 2021 at the Annual Workshop of the International Society for the History and Theory of Intellectual Property (ISHTIP) hosted by Bournemouth University under the theme, "Landmarks of Intellectual Property". The author wishes to thank the participants for their helpful comments especially the paper discussants, Peter Jaszi and Martin Fredriksson.

2 Filosa, Gad & Bodard (Chapter 3 in this volume) offers a detailed analysis of how these expectations are met in practice in relation to digital editions of ancient text-bearing objects.

number of commentaries in response to the Sarr-Savoy Report (Sarr & Savoy 2018) which recommended the blanket digitization of African cultural heritage (including archival materials and records) prior to their repatriation to the respective African countries from which they were taken during the colonial era. In condemning the omission of consideration of the intellectual property, access and control issues relating to digitization, the Statement urged the return of the material cultural heritage and the active engagement and collaboration of African communities in every facet of the decision to digitise and the actual digitization process, including decisions as to the intellectual property rights potentially generated through the digitization process (Pavis & Wallace 2019). The key issue is that digitization involves making reproductions of cultural heritage materials including archival materials and, therefore, raises the question of how their outputs may be controlled.[3] Such reproduction could involve taking new digital photographs of the cultural heritage materials and analog photographs, which may receive new copyright protections with the ownership vesting in the photographer unless there is an agreement to the contrary.[4] Texts (in print and digital editions) involving commentary on and photographs of cultural heritage materials could also enjoy copyright protection as literary works and artistic works respectively.[5] Accordingly, intellectual property law (especially copyright law) becomes directly relevant for addressing questions of ownership, incentives, control of access and any possible commercial exploitation of the results (Oruç 2020).[6]

Essentially, the Statement suggests that when cultural heritage materials are digitised, apart from the cultural heritage materials themselves, one would be dealing with a whole new 'object' (i.e., the digitised version) which may or may not enjoy copyright protection. However, beyond the question of whether those objects are eligible for copyright protection, there is still the question of control of and access to those objects. The Statement makes the point that in dealing with the material cultural heritage and in making a decision to digitise them, the repatriating jurisdiction must do so with the involvement and active participation of the countries to which material cultural heritage are to be repatriated, particularly where decolonisation is the premise or intention. This chapter takes this point further in arguing that within the receiving countries, there should be the involvement and active participation of the local communities

---

3 Kahn & Simon (Chapter 10 in this volume) highlight the need for guidelines to address the control and management issues that come with digitised collections and digitisation of cultural heritage materials, generally.

4 See section 108 Copyright Act, 2022.

5 Ibid.

6 This is quite apart from the ethical and reputational issues of such publications particularly where, as Filosa, Gad, & Bodard point out, certain scholars or editors are assigned "first-publication" rights for a body of texts on an excavation.

directly connected with the specific cultural heritage. Essentially, even or especially beyond the issue of possible copyright (and other intellectual property rights) issues, the question of control and agency remains self-evident. This chapter utilises the Statement calling for the involvement and active engagement of (and with) African communities in the repatriation and digitization process, and the manner in which it calls for the decolonization of African cultural heritage including archival materials, as a (new) lens with which to reconsider access and preservation that has represented twin landmarks of copyright law's governance of the activities of archival (and other memory) institutions. "Landmark" here is used in the dictionary sense of being both "a conspicuous object on land that marks a locality" (originally and especially as a guide to sailors in navigation) and "a structure such as a building of unusual historic and usually aesthetic interest" (Merriam-Webster Dictionary).[7]

There are conversations around the role and functions of archival institutions and other memory institutions and how the copyright law (and to some extent, other intellectual property laws) construct could and should provide limitations and exceptions enabling those institutions to carry out their role and undertake their functions. Within these conversations, there remains a wide and general adherence to the classic landmarks of these institutions' role being to preserve materials, safeguard them and provide access to those materials as needed. However, this rhetoric of preservation and access has been abused in colonial practice and has often functioned as a smokescreen for looting, theft and other objectionable processes of acquisition that has left many of the cultural glimpses of heritage and other memory materials more focused on Global North regions such as Europe and North America (Haberstock 2020; Turner 2015; Duarte & Belarde-Lewis 2015). This chapter suggests that perhaps from the standpoint of implementing the Sarr-Savoy Report and other reports or activities with a similar agenda of mass digitisation before or alongside repatriation, the landmarks of preservation and access should be challenged and questioned. This is particularly with specific reference to implementation of such reports in Nigeria. In essence, this chapter proposes a different (or at least complementary and additional) landmark to guide legislators and policymakers in navigating the copyright limitations and exceptions landscape for archival and other memory institutions. Agency, along with restitution and the general practice of decolonisation, becomes a complementary landmark in this chapter's description of how at institutional level, national archival institutions and other memory institutions might want to proceed in undertaking their planning for receiving and managing repatriated items. Furthermore, incorporating agency as a new landmark would

[7] ISHTIP applied similar language in its call for papers for its 2021 Annual Workshop. See https://www.ishtip.org/?p=1027 (accessed April 20, 2022).

ready these institutions for the forthcoming transition to specific copyright limitations and exceptions.

Copyright limitations and exceptions for libraries and archives became a separate item on the agenda of the World Intellectual Property Organisation's (WIPO) Standing Committee on Copyright and Related Rights (SCCR) in 2011 (Dryden 2017).[8] Strikingly, one of the closing proposals within this agenda was to consider limitations and exceptions for archival materials rather than archival institutions, the rationale being that an institutional approach or focus would be too restrictive since other institutions, such as libraries and museums, also handle archival materials (Sutton 2019). These limitations and exceptions were limited to preservation, conservation and access for learning (Crews 2019). By virtue of their statutory position, national archival and other cultural heritage institutions are at the forefront of receiving and subsequently managing restituted cultural heritage and engaging with digitization decisions and processes. While there is merit in considering the institutional mandates of archival and other memory institutions from the perspective of the (archival) materials they handle and the need for public access to those materials, it is also imperative to pay attention to the nature of such institutions. This is especially so, given that these institutions would be operationalizing the benefits of specific copyright limitations and exceptions as they fulfil their institutional mandates. In this environment, it is argued that agency, and specifically that of local communities, should be an alternative or at least, a complementary coequal landmark existing side-by-side with the landmarks of preservation and access. The discourse in this chapter focuses on Nigeria as one analogy for most of the countries on the African continent.

Three core arguments underpin this chapter. The first is that the decolonization of cultural heritage goes beyond repatriation and restitution to disentangling the repatriated cultural heritage from the clutches of colonial structures within the receiving countries. The second argument is that the cultural heritage decolonization process at the national level can only realise a fraction of agency and representation for previously colonised communities, which should not be mistakenly conflated with achievement of decolonization of institutional structures for cultural heritage management within African countries. The third argument is that existing and ongoing plans to establish special copyright limitations and exceptions for libraries, archives and other memory institutions should consider the nature of control that these institutions wield in determining who accesses and what materials are accessed in relation to cultural heritage. In many cases, the discourse on digitization of African cultural heritage including archival materials has mostly focused on the question of the

[8] Currently, archival institutions undertake most of their functions through general copyright limitations and exceptions applicable to all users of copyright-protected materials and to libraries when they handle archival materials.

appropriate approach for the countries making restitution, repatriating African cultural heritage, or undertaking or supporting digitization prior to or after the return of the material cultural heritage without similar focus on the (nature of the) institutions in the receiving countries. Like other African countries with a colonial past, Nigeria is a product of a colonial and heteronormative social order (Ndlovu-Gatsheni 2015). The discourse on specific copyright limitations and exceptions for archival institutions and archival materials must take place within this broad context that recognizes that the African cultural heritage decolonization process goes beyond the approach of the countries repatriating African cultural heritage, or undertaking or supporting digitization prior to or after the return of the material cultural heritage, to the role and position of the African national institutions such as national archives, national libraries and national museums, that would receive and subsequently manage the material cultural heritage and/or digitised cultural heritage.

The structure of this chapter is as follows. Part 2 outlines the access and preservation landmarks of copyright limitations and exceptions for archival and other memory institutions against the backdrop of the decolonization process represented by repatriation; Part 3 explores the character of the postcolonial archival institution—the National Archives of Nigeria (hereafter, National Archives) vis-à-vis the implementation of copyright limitations and exceptions relating to archival materials, exposing one of the myths of decolonization. The next part (4) argues for the institutional reform of the National Archives as a way to ready the institution for specific copyright limitations and exceptions which will help them discharge their functions more efficiently. In doing so, Part 4 highlights how an archival institution with vestiges of colonialism can be problematic for specific copyright limitations and exceptions and how this problem may be addressed using agency as a guiding principle. Part 5 concludes.

2. Understanding the copyright landmarks of access and preservation vis-à-vis decolonization

Copyright law grants a bundle of exclusive rights to authors of copyright-protected works such as literary, musical and artistic works, sound recordings, cinematograph films, expressions of folklore (in some jurisdictions) and broadcasts. As a result of the exclusive nature of copyright protection, any person wishing to use copyright-protected works in any manner covered by the copyright protection would require permission or licence from the author or relevant copyright owner. However, for specific activities covered by copyright limitations and exceptions, one would not require permission or licence from the author or relevant copyright owner. Under the copyright law in many jurisdictions, archival and other memory institutions are accorded copyright exceptions that permit them to reproduce copyright-protected materials without needing to procure a licence or permission. For instance, section 25 of the Nigerian Copyright Act provides an exception for archives and other memory institutions allowing them to make (i.e., reproduce) and distribute copies of works as part of their ordinary activities, including for purposes of back-up, preservation, and replacement. This is an expanded exception from the previous section 15(2) of the Copyright Act 2004 which provides that the reproduction of a copyright-protected work stored in the National Archives under the National Archives Act would not amount to copyright infringement if made in pursuance of the National Archives Act. Exceptions such as these that permit reproduction for archival and other memory institutions for purposes of preservation and conservations are also obtainable in other jurisdictions. Archival institutions under UK laws, may be permitted by copyright exceptions or statute to make a single copy at the request of a private user but require the user to be resident in the country where the institution is domiciled. Copyright exceptions can require that only unpublished archival materials may be copied or restrict the copying exception to specific kinds of works (Deazley & Stobo 2013). Digitization becomes problematic in this environment because of its ability to transcend physical borders. As such, the problems with the preservation and access landmarks persist across borders.

For archival and other memory institutions, one of the underlying rationales for according these exceptions is to preserve these works and, thereby, facilitate access to them. For material or physical cultural heritage, preservation would necessitate keeping and maintaining such materials in their original form whereas access may necessitate digitisation. In this regard, these institutions require access to the work in order to make copies (even digital copies) for preservation. However, current copyright exceptions are couched in a manner that requires these institutions to obtain a licence or permission from the copyright owners of the works which are digitised in order to distribute or make the digitised copies available to the public. Essentially, the laws conceive the purpose of digitisation in that sense to be preservation by the memory institutions and not necessarily access to the public. These are some of the copyright implications that have been distilled from the management of archival materials including their digitization (Deazley & Stobo 2013). Further, the uncertainty as to copyright subsistence and ownership status of some archival materials makes it risky to digitise without ascertaining ownership and seeking the requisite licence (Sutton 2019). By extension, there is doubt regarding the new copyright status of a digital surrogate of a public domain work i.e., a public domain work that has been digitised (Wallace 2018). These issues with the current landscape of copyright exceptions for archival and other memory institutions contributed significantly to the ongoing discourse and steps at the international level to craft specific copyright limitations and exceptions that will enable archival and other memory institutions to more effectively engage in their mission of access and preservation. But, as this chapter argues, digitisation in the context of cultural heritage is more than just making copies for purposes of preservation and protection, and increasing access to cultural heritage including archival materials.[9] As a process, digitization in relation to any given material, involves decisions as to what to leave out, what to include, how to include it, the why of inclusions and exclusions, how to explain inclusions and exclusions, the language of communication and explanation, and more. These decisions are influenced by, inter alia, the perception and wielding of statutory power. Viewed through this lens, making digitisation permissible for archival institutions such as the National Archives of Nigeria whose statutorily permitted holdings are diverse, and therefore reflective of the over 250 ethnic groups in Nigeria, requires deeper reflection on issues of agency (including autonomy) of cultural heritage communities.

The concept of "colonial difference" recognizes that there is a dichotomy between imperial values and the histories and values of ex-colonized nations and that these values (imperial and colonised) collide in the process of colonisation resulting in various responses such as adaptation, adoption, integration, etc. (Ndlovu-Gatsheni 2012a). Colonial difference, according to Ndlovu-Gatsheni is also the space where "coloniality of power" reproduces the current asymmetrical global power structure in the world—the US and the rest of the European world at the apex controlling gender and sexuality; authority and power; labour and economy; religion and rituals, as well as all other social aspects of human existence in favour of the Western world, with Africa and its peoples at the bottom. These concepts lead to questioning postcolonial discourse and realising that colonialism did not end with the transfer of juridical-political powers to African nations (Grosfoguel 2007). Instead, the character of postcolonial African states, particularly the continuing refusal to properly engage with tribal groups in the name of "national interests" reveals that apart from the transfer of juridical-political power to African states, decolonization remains a myth in so many ways.

At the heart of decolonization is the return of agency and autonomy to persons and communities to whom these were denied as part of the nature of colonialism. But, an examination of the colonial states in Africa, which were transformed at independence to the present postcolonial states, show that they are (still) rooted in colonial structures and institutions. These postcolonial states, in many cases, retained the destruction or transformation of African Indigenous civil societies such as age groups, elders' councils and the like (Ndlovu-Gatsheni 2012b). Postcolonial Nigeria for instance was shaped by colonialism into a sole political and national entity that brought under one national umbrella over 250 ethnic and tribal groups. This state of affairs extends across several legal protection frameworks including copyright and cultural heritage protection frameworks such as National Commission for Museums and Monuments (NCMM) Act 1979 (Adewunmi 2013).

---

[9] Cf. Filosa, Gad & Bodard (Chapter 3 in this volume).

The next part of this chapter engages the character of a postcolonial archival institution—the National Archives of Nigeria, its duties, functions and responsibilities regarding the control and management of archival materials and uses that to highlight and/or illustrate the challenges with providing for specific copyright exceptions to such receiving institutions without taking cognizance of the control that such institutions wield.

3. The character and power of postcolonial African archival institutions—an illustration with the National Archives of Nigeria

Agency has always been central to decolonization and cultural heritage restitution/repatriation. It is at the forefront of previous and recent attempts by former colonialist countries and well-meaning individuals and organisations to undertake the restitution and repatriation of cultural heritage to African communities (specifically, national cultural heritage institutions). One of the major related questions is how the repatriating institutions ensure complete decolonization in the manner in which the repatriation and restitution is made to the receiving national cultural heritage institutions. Related to this is also the question of the role of the receiving national cultural heritage institution in ensuring that in receiving and managing repatriated cultural heritage, they recognize and amplify the agency of the local communities directly affected by the repatriated cultural heritage materials (Geyer 2017; Sindane 2020). An examination of the relevant provisions of the National Archives Act, including in terms of its statutory holdings (i.e. the archival materials it holds), institutional leadership and management infrastructure, obligations for companies and individuals, shows that the National Archives of Nigeria is not presently in a position to enable or promote agency, inclusiveness and autonomy of local communities of origin in the decision-making, access to and management of their own digital cultural heritage.

The National Archives of Nigeria is a public office established under the National Archives Act of 1992 to have permanent custody, care and control of all papers, registers, printed matters, books, maps, plans, photographs, microfilms, cinematographic films, sound recordings, or other documentary material regardless of physical form or characteristics belonging to the Federal Government of Nigeria, made or received by public or State offices, or by business houses or companies, private bodies or individuals in pursuance of their legal obligations or in connection with the transaction of their proper business (National Archives Act s.1).[10] These records however do not "include library or museum material made or acquired solely for reference or exhibition purposes,

[10] This definition accords with the perception and description of materiality. See Carmen 2009.

extra copies of records kept only for convenience of reference or stocks of publications" (National Archives Act s.52). Such reference materials would include atlases, bibliographies, indexes, and other sources of background information and these usually within the ambit of libraries.

The Director of the National Archives has the responsibility under the Act to carry out the institutional mandate of the National Archives. In this regard, the Director would provide advice to government, private bodies and individuals on all matters relating to their records and archives, appraise, select, repair, prepare, publish and preserve any and all archival materials (National Archives Act, s.2(2)(a-f). The Director is also responsible for promoting the advancement of knowledge of the contents of the Nigerian archives through establishing and maintaining a research library, controlling access thereto by archival institutions and persons; organising seminars, visits and the likes (National Archives Act, s.2(2)(g). They are also responsible for conducting research into the contents of the archives, reproducing and duplicating archives and records; and lending archival materials to exhibitions and other displays (National Archives Act s.2(2)(h)-(m). By virtue of Section 23, the Director shall take necessary steps to acquire and have returned to Nigeria any public records or records of historical value to Nigeria which may have been exported from Nigeria prior to 1992.

The Director is also required to inspect records and historical documents of private bodies and advise on their safe custody, preservation and care (National Archives Act s.34). Further, the Director is required to keep a register of such records and documents and upon entry in the register, such records assume the status of private archives (National Archives Act s.35(1) and (5). Such a status requires the owner to preserve the contents of the archives and work with the Director of the National Archives to open the archives for public use, make arrangements for the publication of the contents of the archives, etc. (National Archives Act s.36). Disposal of such private archives is only permitted with the written consent of the Director and no sales or transfer of the private archives may be made without the knowledge of the Director (National Archives Act s.37). Further, private archives are prohibited from being exported out of Nigeria (National Archives Act s.38). The Director may also compulsorily transfer private archives that are in his opinion, in danger of loss, dispersal, deterioration or destruction (National Archives Act s.41). Such transfer requires the approval of the Minister charged with responsibility for National Archives and is subject to the payment of compensation to the owner or holder of such private archives. Once transferred, the archives assume the status of public archives (National Archives Act s.41(2).

Twenty-five years is the period prescribed for companies to mandatorily operate an archives division for the preservation and proper documentation of their organisation, functions, policies, procedures and transactions (National Archives Act s.45). State governments may establish State archives and may assign the preservation of its archives (National Archives Act s.33(1). Where a state government assigns the preservation of its archives to another organisation, such archives would be regarded and managed as part of the archives of the Federal Government and subject to the provisions of the National Archives Act (National Archives Act s.33(3).

The Director of the National Archives is a civil servant and their appointment is only required to be in accordance with the provisions of the law relating to the appointment of officers in the civil service of the Federation of Nigeria. There is no requirement that necessitates the consideration or representation of cultural heritage communities. Further, the Director is a member of an advisory council, again constituting members who are not appointed for their community membership or participation. This means that for instance, a director who is from one ethnic group may take decisions regarding collection and preservation of archival materials from another ethnic group without recourse whatsoever to that ethnic group. Contrast this scenario with the provisions of South Africa's Intellectual Property Laws Amendment Act 2013 (IPLAA). The IPLAA recognizes the significance of the cultural diversity of the South African nation and defines "indigenous communities" as a "recognizable community of people" originated or historically settled in a geographic location with social, cultural and economic conditions distinct from those of the national community who *"identify themselves" and "are recognised by other groups as a distinct collective"*.[11] Under this statute, these indigenous communities require a community protocol, which they must develop to describe their structure and claims to cultural heritage. This approach is a common one in South Africa's protection models for matters involving indigenous communities given South Africa's recognition of customary laws. Legal rules allow communities autonomy in identifying their structure and claims to cultural heritage. Indigenous communities must identify themselves and must be recognised by other groups as a distinct collective in order to effectively participate in the cultural heritage space (Nwauche 2015).

In identifying the South African example, there is recognition of the dilemma of how to negotiate the governance framework for digitisation of material cultural heritage, especially the interaction between recognition of customary law and cultural heritage communities and the traditional/conventional intellectual property (copyright) framework. The South African example is not a static situation. Instead, it is one that is dynamic and changing as the country's governance frameworks interact and grapple with how local communities deal with the recognition of their agency. In essence, the debate in South Africa, unlike the situation in Nigeria described in this chapter, is not dwelling on the

---

[11] There are problems identified with this definition still particularly because of its premise on geographical locations. Civilization and urbanisation result in migration of individuals and groups who should otherwise qualify as part of an indigenous community. See Sidane 2020.

question of whether local communities are involved or whether their agency is recognised. There is statutory recognition of their agency as far as matters of cultural heritage are concerned in South Africa. The conversation in South Africa has shifted to how those communities deal with each other, and also within themselves as organisations composed of individuals who are at different levels of creative and productive processes and capacities. By contrast, the situation in Nigeria presently requires deciphering how to kickstart the dialogue that the national government must have with cultural heritage communities including how to make the dialogue take place. The situation also requires ensuring that the outcomes of such dialogues and the recognition of the agency of cultural heritage communities are evident in the institutional design and processes of archival (and other memory) institutions that deal with cultural heritage material in any form. When the agency of cultural heritage communities is recognised, Nigeria would then move to where South Africa is currently in exploring how cultural heritage communities interact within themselves and with other communities, so that such inter-community interactions do not end up becoming a barrier to surmount in addressing the relationship between national governments and cultural heritage communities.

By extension, the issue of the agency landmark would affect the National Archives' implementation of the benefits of copyright limitations and exceptions. Archival institutions require copyright limitations in order to preserve archival materials in their care; reproduce materials for study and research; provide access to its archival materials for consultation with other institutions within and outside national territories; etc. (Dryden 2017). In order to undertake such preservation, archival institutions need to make copies of the relevant material.

For the reproduction and publication of archival materials in the National Archives presently, the public is permitted to make copies of or extracts from any public archives which have been made available to them. However, publication can only be made with the written permission of the Director in the case of public archives and written consent of the depositor, in the case of archives voluntarily deposited by private bodies or individuals (National Archives Act s.29(1) and (2)). Nevertheless, both reproduction and publication are subject to copyright laws (National Archives Act s.29(4)). Without copyright exceptions, such copying would likely infringe copyright protection (where the material is subject to copyright protection). This is also the case with reproducing archival materials for members of the public who may need it for further study or for research. Within the Act, free access to the public archives is neither automatic nor guaranteed. Instead, free access is only available where such public archives enjoyed free access when they were in the custody of the public office from which they had been transferred, where the public archives is 25 years or more, or in the case of archives relating to the private life of individuals, with the written permission of such individuals or their heirs, if known (National Archives

Act s.27). Public access to the National Archives and the archival materials under its control is subject to regulations as the Minister charged with responsibility for National Archives may make (National Archives Act s.49(a)).

In these circumstances, providing for specific copyright exceptions for such institutions even with the intent of preservation and access risks inadvertently denying agency to indigenous communities where they are the source or origin of these materials. This is even more so when the materials are digitised or to be digitised.

4. Readying archival institutions for specific copyright exceptions

Between 2017 and 2019, the WIPO commissioned various studies aimed at exploring whether the current state of copyright exceptions and limitations in copyright law are fitted so as to enable specific institutions—libraries, archives and museums to carry out their mandates. For archives, as with libraries and museums, there is consensus that the manner in which copyright protection and copyright limitations and exceptions are currently structured impede the work of these institutions in conserving, safeguarding, providing access to, using and enabling the use of various materials in their custody. To address these issues, it was concluded that there was a need to not only strengthen the international understanding of the need to have adequate limitations but more significantly, to move towards international agreement regarding specific exceptions or limitations.

For archival institutions and archival materials particularly, the WIPO's Standing Committee on Copyright and Related Rights (WIPO-SCCR) has devoted much attention to this matter including the changes that are necessary. These reforms would expectedly trickle down to African states as they ratify and domesticate them into national laws. In the face of the impending repatriation of African cultural heritage and ongoing digitization plans for Africa's cultural heritage, particularly Nigerian cultural heritage, national cultural heritage institutions need to evolve in order to be ready to support the decolonisation process in their management of material and digitised cultural heritage. Focusing solely on using copyright limitations and exceptions to empower these institutions to carry on the work of preservation of and access to cultural heritage materials loses sight of the power and control that these institutions wield.

In this regard, undertaking copyright limitations and exceptions and cultural heritage protection across national lines and by regulatory institutions reminiscent of colonial and global 'grouping', and one which obliterates or severely limits the participation of tribal (and indigenous) communities in the protection framework is extremely problematic (Eichler 2020; Nwauche 2017; Beardslee

2016).[12] Within this environment, the repatriation of African cultural heritage to Africa including the active engagement of African nations in the decision to digitise and the digitization process does not complete the decolonization process given that the African institutions involved are products of the colonial era. This is also the case where the statutory mandate of such institutions does not envisage the involvement and participation of the tribal and indigenous communities who are the direct sources and "originators" of cultural heritage. More specifically for copyright law purposes, the landmarks of access and preservation are insufficient to guide the design of specific copyright exceptions.

Therefore, it is imperative to look beyond the perspective of the repatriating institution or State and for purposes of crafting specific statutory copyright limitations and exceptions, to look beyond access and preservation rationales to the nature and character of the institutions that would implement such exceptions. This shift requires fundamentally that the institutions managing such archival materials need to pursue, establish and preserve the agency and autonomy of the local communities who are the actual source of cultural heritage including related archival materials.

One of the key questions arising from the above description of the way forward is that related to the fate of the current landmarks of preservation and access. Put differently, in proposing agency and autonomy as complementary landmarks to guide, is the existing landmark of access and preservation to be obliterated? From the foregoing paragraphs of this chapter, there is an obvious or at least potential tension between the guiding principles of decolonization and the promotion of agency which spills over to the discussion regarding institutions that handle or would handle both material and digitised cultural heritage materials. This relates particularly to the extent to which the often abused but still widely referenced 'enlightenment' idea inherent in the landmark of preservation and access remains in the picture.

It is argued that the proposed agency and autonomy landmarks should stand as a separate but coequal landmark with the current preservation and access landmarks to guide the institutional processes of archival (and other memory) institutions, as well as the establishment of specific copyright limitations and exceptions for those institutions. Think about these two real-life illustrations. In 2013, several member states of WIPO adopted the Marrakesh Treaty to facilitate access to published works for persons who are blind, visually impaired or otherwise print disabled ("Marrakesh Treaty"). The main goal of the Marrakesh Treaty is to establish a set of mandatory copyright limitations and exceptions for the benefit of the blind, visually impaired or otherwise print disabled persons.

12 This is even more challenging where the present region of origin for some objects cannot be established with certainty due to the ceding and recalibration of territories. For example, Ethiopia and Eritrea (as pointed out to me by Daria Elagina); Nigeria and the Bakassi Peninsula of Cameroun.

One of the relevant key provisions of the Marrakesh Treaty is its establishment of so-called 'authorised entity' defined in Article 2(c) as an entity "authorised or recognized by the government to provide education, instructional training, adaptive reading or information access to beneficiary persons on a non-profit basis" including "a government institution or non-profit organisation that provides the same services to beneficiary persons as one of its primary activities or institutional obligations". Within the Marrakesh Treaty, only print disabled persons and entities qualifying as authorised entities are permitted to: enforce the copyright limitations and exceptions through making an accessible format copy of a work; supply those copies to the beneficiaries of the Treaty by any means (Article 4); distribute accessible format copies in cross-border exchanges (Article 5); import an accessible format copy for the benefit of the beneficiaries of the Treaty (Article 6); etc. In essence, these entities (i.e., authorised entities) are considered co-custodians of the specially created limitations and exceptions because of the authorization or recognition of government. While entities need not fulfil any formalities to be recognized as an authorised entity, they need to fulfil specified conditions regarding their use of copyright-protected materials. For instance, authorised entities are required to take steps to ensure that only the beneficiaries of the Treaty will enjoy access to accessible format copies (Article 4(2)(a)(iii) and to undertake the conversion to accessible format copies and its distribution on a non-profit basis (Article 4(2)(a)(iv). More importantly, the beneficiaries of the Treaty (or someone acting on their behalf) have coequal power and authority (at least in terms of active participation) with these authorised entities to undertake any changes necessary to make copyright-protected materials in an accessible format for persons with print disabilities (Article 4(2)(b).[13] Access is still a landmark—a guiding principle and the goal of the Marrakesh Treaty but access coexists with the objective of active participation of visually impaired or otherwise print-disabled persons in cultural and social life (Ikeda, Ribeiro, and Teixeira 2021; Beyene, Mekonnen, and Giannoumis 2020).

The second real-life example relates to a mountain fire that erupted in Cape Town, South Africa in early 2021. This fire spread to part of the University of Cape Town resulting in the destruction of a large section of the university's Jagger Library which housed several material cultural heritage of South Africa (Wroughton 2021).[14] In the aftermath of the fire, there were several comments

[13] Beneficiaries of the Treaty are also permitted to distribute accessible format copies in cross-border exchanges (Article 5), and import an accessible format copy (Article 6).

[14] According to reports, the Jagger Library had "printed and audiovisual materials on African studies; 1,300 sub-collections of unique manuscripts and personal papers; and more than 85,000 books and pamphlets on African studies, including up-to-date materials and works on Africa and South Africa printed before 1925".

on what would have been the national (and international) mood had the materials in the Jagger Library been digitised so that despite the fire, the public could still have access to the materials albeit in intangible form. It is argued here that juxtaposed with the preservation and access premise or landmark for digitization is the question of the material cultural heritage themselves and the value in those materials "as is" as opposed to the digitised materials and who makes the decision on how and what to digitise. Essentially, digitisation is not preservation in and of itself—digital materials must (also) be preserved so they can remain accessible by future generations under future technologies and formats. It should therefore follow that the tension between the preservation and access landmarks and the (cultural heritage communities') agency and control landmarks should encourage their coequal existence and consideration in archival institutional processes and in proposing specific copyright limitation and exceptions.

5. Conclusion

For the purposes of this chapter, the proposed digitisation of material cultural heritage and open licensing mechanisms as indicated in the Sarr-Savoy report is used as a take-off point to highlight the shift in and the implications of the shift in the guiding landmarks of specific copyright limitations and exceptions for archival and other memory institutions. However, there are several other lenses through which the landmarks of specific copyright limitations and exceptions for archival and other memory institutions may be viewed. Kahn and Simon's exploration of the implications of the absence of guidelines for handling digital surrogates of human remains in museums in this volume and the analysis by Filosa, Gad and Bodard of the need to record both context and text in digitisation processes for ancient text bearing objects are good examples.[15]

In highlighting the agency of cultural heritage communities as new landmarks for specific copyright limitations and exceptions for archival and other memory institutions, this chapter does not refute the significant benefits of digitization. As Filosa, Gad and Bodard amply demonstrate in this volume, digitization makes information more explicit and allows multiple uses of material in ways that are not feasible with physical objects (including printed materials). With digitization, translations of texts in diverse languages and in a manner that serves diverse audiences become more feasible. Instead, the chapter argues that when ensuring control by an agency for indigenous communities is a goal, (not necessarily *the* goal), policymakers would be better positioned to factor these into crafting specific limitations and exceptions. In this regard, specific copyright exceptions could come with guidelines and standards whether in the form of hard law or soft law that require repatriating and digitising entities

[15] See Filosa, Gad & Bodard (Chapter 3 in this volume) and Kahn & Simon (Chapter 10). See also Pavis & Wallace 2020.

to collaborate with and involve cultural heritage communities to contribute to more accessible, more inclusive and more transparent digitization outcomes. The pre-repatriation digitization 'project' remains enmeshed in coloniality of power and colonial power structures. By extension, the cultural heritage institutions such as the National Archives who are the implementing institutions for copyright limitations and exceptions designed to control and manage digitization outcomes are equally entrapped. The Statement written by Pavis and Wallace and supported by over 100 scholars offer an opportunity to consider a coequal landmark to guide both the repatriation and digitization project and the consideration of copyright limitations and exceptions for archival (and other memory) institutions.

The purpose underlying cultural heritage repatriation and digitization means that every element of how archival institutions such as the National Archives manage and control records and archival materials need to adapt and shift. Their current statutorily-enabled practices, principles and institutional organisation undermine the benefits of repatriation in Africa, particularly in Nigeria. In this context, the National Archives of Nigeria and every other archival institution across Africa and beyond, must radically reimagine their practice to meet the agenda of returning agency and autonomy to cultural heritage communities. To do this, a starting point is to reform the ways in which archival materials are acquired, managed, preserved and controlled.

6. References

Adewumi, A. (2013). A critique of the Nigerian legal framework for the protection of cultural goods from exportation abuse. *Journal of International and Comparative Law, 1*, 85–101.

Adewumi, A. A. (2018). Cultural heritage protection and disaster risk management in Nigeria: Legal framework for promoting coherence and efficiency. *Art, Antiquity & Law, 23*(1).

Bak, G., Bradford, T., Loyer, J., & Walker, E. (2017). Four views on archival decolonization inspired by the TRC's calls to action. *Fonds d'Archives*, (1).

Beardslee, T. (2016). Whom does heritage empower, and whom does it silence? Intangible cultural heritage at the Jemaa el Fnaa, Marrakech. *International Journal of Heritage Studies, 22*(2), pp. 89–101

Beyene, W. M., Mekonnen, A. T., & Giannoumis, G. A. (2020). Inclusion, access, and accessibility of educational resources in higher education institutions: exploring the Ethiopian context. *International Journal of Inclusive Education*, 1–17.

Carman, J. (2009). Where the value lies: The importance of materiality to the immaterial aspects of heritage. *Taking archaeology out of heritage*, pp. 192–208.

Crews, K. (2019). Copyright Limitations and Exceptions for Libraries: Typology Analysis. Retrieved from: https://www.wipo.int/meetings/en/doc_details.jsp?doc_id=432051.

Deazley, R., & Stobo, V. (2013). Archives and copyright: Risk and reform. *CREATe Working Paper*. Retrieved from: https://www.create.ac.uk/wp-content/uploads/2013/04/CREATe-Working-Paper-No-3-v1-1.pdf.

Dryden, J. (2017). Copyright exceptions: an archivist's perspective. *WIPO Magazine*, (4/2017). Retrieved from: https://www.wipo.int/wipo_magazine/en/2017/04/article_0003.html.

Duarte, M. E., & Belarde-Lewis, M. (2015). Imagining: Creating spaces for indigenous ontologies. *Cataloging & Classification Quarterly, 53*(5–6), pp. 677–702.

Eichler, J. (2020). *Intangible Cultural Heritage under Pressure? Examining Vulnerabilities in ICH Regimes-Minorities, Indigenous Peoples and Refugees* (p.140). DEU.

Fitzpatrick, S. (2014). Setting its sights on the Marrakesh Treaty: The US role in alleviating the book famine for persons with print disabilities. *BC Int'l & Comp. L. Rev., 37*, p.139.

Geyer, S. (2017). Copyright in traditional works: Unravelling the Intellectual Property Laws Amendment Act of 2013. *South African Mercantile Law Journal, 29*(1), pp. 43–64.

Grafton, E., & Peristerakis, J. (2016). 15 Decolonizing Museological Practices at the Canadian Museum for Human Rights. *Indigenous Notions of Ownership and Libraries, Archives and Museums, 166*, p.229.

Grosfoguel, R. (2007). 'The epistemic decolonial turn: beyond political-economy paradigms', Cultural Studies, 21 (2–3), p.219.

Haberstock, L. (2020). Participatory description: decolonizing descriptive methodologies in archives. *Archival Science, 20*(2), pp. 125–138.

Helfer, L. R., Land, M. K., Okediji, R. L., & Reichman, J. H. (2017). *The World Blind Union guide to the Marrakesh Treaty: facilitating access to books for print-disabled individuals*. Oxford University Press.

Ikeda, W. L., Ribeiro, D. M. G., & Teixeira, R. V. G. (2021). Marrakesh treaty as a possibility of ethical and legal care of the other from Emmanuel Levinas. *REVISTA QUAESTIO IURIS, 14*(04), 2031–2050.

Li, J. (2014). Copyright Exemptions to Facilitate Access to Published Works for the Print Disabled–The Gap Between National Laws and the Standards Required by the Marrakesh Treaty. *IIC-International Review of Intellectual Property and Competition Law, 45*(7), pp. 740–767.

Logan, T. E. (2014). Memory, erasure, and national myth. *Colonial Genocide in Indigenous North America*, pp. 149–165.

Marrakesh Treaty to facilitate access to published works for persons who are blind, visually impaired or otherwise print disabled (2013).

Muiu, M., & Martin, G. (2009). *A New Paradigm of the African State: Fundi wa Afrika*. Springer.

Muiu, M. W. (2002). Fundi Wa Afrika: Toward a new paradigm of the African state. *Journal of Third World Studies, 19*(2), pp. 23–42.

Ndlovu-Gatsheni, S. J. (2012a). Coloniality of power in development studies and the impact of global imperial designs on Africa. *Australasian Review of African Studies, The, 33*(2), pp. 48–73.

Ndlovu-Gatsheni, S. J. (2012b). Fiftieth Anniversary of Decolonisation in Africa: A moment of celebration or critical reflection?. *Third World Quarterly, 33*(1), pp. 71–89.

Ndlovu-Gatsheni, S. J. (2015). Genealogies of coloniality and implications for Africa's development. *Africa Development, 40*(3), pp. 13–40.

Nwauche, E. (2017). Heritage Protection and Traditional Cultural Expressions in Africa. In *The Protection of Traditional Cultural Expressions in Africa* (pp. 79–95). Springer, Cham.

Nwauche, E. S. (2015). The protection of indigenous terms and expressions by the Merchandise Marks Act in South Africa. *Queen Mary Journal of Intellectual Property, 5*(2), pp. 214–225.

Pavis, M., & Wallace, A. (2019). Response to the 2018 Sarr-Savoy Report. *J. Intell. Prop. Info. Tech. & Elec. Com. L., 10*, p.115.

Pavis, M., & Wallace, A. (2020). SCuLE Response for the EMRIP Report on repatriation of ceremonial objects and human remains under the UN Declaration on the Rights of Indigenous Peoples. DOI: https://doi.org/10.5281/zenodo.3760293.

Sarr, F., & Savoy, B. (2018). *The Restitution of African Cultural Heritage. Toward a New Relational Ethics.* [online] pp. 1–89. Available at: http://restitutionreport2018.com/sarr_savoy_en.pdf [Accessed 13 January 2022].

Shiraiwa, S. (2021), February. Museological Myths of Decolonization and Neutrality. In *The 44th ICOFOM Symposium: The Decolonisation of Museology: Museums, Mixing, and Myths of Origin.*

Sindane, N. (2020). Morena Mohlomi le Badimo: reading decolonial articulations into the intellectual property law curriculum. *Journal of Decolonising Disciplines, 2*(1), pp. 1–23.

Stobo, V., Deazley, R., & Anderson, I. G. (2013). Copyright & risk: Scoping the wellcome digital library project. Retrieved from: https://www.create.ac.uk/wp-content/uploads/2013/12/CREATe-Working-Paper-No.10.pdf.

Sutton, D. (2019). *Background Paper on Archives and Copyright.* [online] Available at: https://www.wipo.int/edocs/mdocs/copyright/en/sccr_38/sccr_38_7.pdf.

Tong, L. A. (2017). Aligning the South African intellectual property system with traditional knowledge protection. *Journal of Intellectual Property Law & Practice, 12*(3), pp. 179–190.

Turner, H. (2015). Decolonizing ethnographic documentation: A critical history of the early museum catalogs at the Smithsonian's National Museum of Natural History. *Cataloging & Classification Quarterly, 53*(5–6), pp. 658–676.

Wallace, A. (2018). *Surrogate IP rights in the cultural sector* (Doctoral dissertation, University of Glasgow).

Wroughton, L. (2021). *South Africa wildfire that burned University of Cape Town, library of African antiquities is under control.* [online] The Washington Post. Retrieved from: https://www.washingtonpost.com/world/2021/04/18/south-africa-fire-university-cape-town/ [Accessed 23 April 2022].

www.ingramcontent.com/pod-product-compliance
Lightning Source LLC
LaVergne TN
LVHW020054110826
845155LV00022B/80

* 9 7 8 1 9 1 4 4 8 1 3 2 1 *